NANCY MITFORD

SELINA HASTINGS

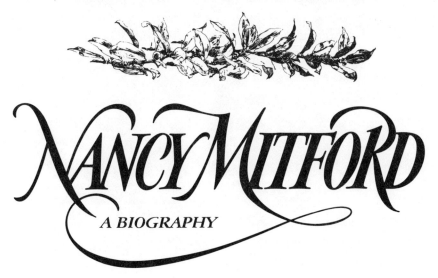

NANCY MITFORD

A BIOGRAPHY

A William Abrahams Book

E. P. DUTTON   NEW YORK

A William Abrahams Book

First published in the United States in 1986 by
E. P. Dutton, a division of New American Library,
2 Park Avenue, New York, N.Y. 10016.

Library of Congress Catalog Number: 85-73648

ISBN: 0-525-24401-8

USA

10 9 8 7 6 5 4 3 2 1

First American Edition

TO PAMELA

AND TO THE MEMORY OF DAVID

Contents

Illustrations

Acknowledgements

I would like to thank first and above all the Hon. Lady Mosley and the Duchess of Devonshire for their kind help, unfailing patience and generous hospitality; and to the Duchess of Devonshire thanks for her permission to quote from the letters and published works of Nancy Mitford. I would also like to thank the Hon. Mrs Derek Jackson for her invaluable recollections; and the Hon. Mrs Robert Treuhaft for allowing me access to her sister's letters. I owe, too, an inestimable debt to the kindness and co-operation of the late M. Gaston Palewski.

Among the many people who have given me help during the writing of this book I would in particular like to acknowledge my gratitude to the following: Sir Harold Acton; Mrs Ralph Arnold; Comte Jean de Baglion; Mrs Rosemary Bailey; Mrs Rosemary Baldwin; Mr Frith Banbury; Dr Andrew Barlow; the Marquess of Bath; the late Prince de Beauvau-Craon and the Princesse de Beauvau-Craon; the Duchess of Beaufort; Lady Beit; Mr Alan Bell; Mme Bettine Bergery; the executors of the estate of the late Sir John Betjeman; Mrs Lesley Blanch; the Keeper of Western Manuscripts, the Bodleian Library; Dr Mary Brazier; Lady Brinckman; M. Jacques Brousse; Mr Gavin Bryars; Mrs Handasyde Buchanan; Mrs Rohan Butler; Contessa Anna-Maria Cicogna; Brigadier Archer Clive; Miss R. E. Colvile; Lady Diana Cooper; Helen, Lady Dashwood; Mr Peter Day; Lady Denham; the Duke of Devonshire; Mr Maldwin Drummond; Mme Denise Duchon; Lord Dulverton; Lady Mary Dunn; Viscountess Eccles; Mr Peter Elwes; the Hon. David St Clair Erskine; Prince Jean-Louis de Faucigny-Lucinge; the Hon. Mrs Daphne Fielding; the Hon. Mrs Mark Fleming; Mr Alastair Forbes; the Hon.

Mrs Derek Gascoigne; Mme Jean Gaudin; the late Mr Geoffrey
Gilmour; Dr Henry Gillespie; Lady Gladwyn; Mme Gabrielle
Guimont; the Hon. Jonathan Guinness; Mr John Hadfield; Prof.
Robert Halsband; Mr Hamish Hamilton; Mr Christopher Ham-
mersley; Mr Charles Harding; Lady Harrod; Mr Derek Hart; Sir
Rupert Hart-Davis; Comtesse Gérard d'Hauteville; Miss
Alethea Hayter; Sir William & Lady Hayter; Mr Robert Heber-
Percy; the late Mr Peter Hesketh; Mr Roger Hesketh; Mr Derek
Hill; Mr Heywood & Lady Anne Hill; Mr Bevis Hillier; Mr
Anthony Hobson; Mme Paulette Howard-Johnston; the late Mrs
Richard Hughes; the Librarian of the Humanities Research
Center, University of Texas; the late Prof. Derek Jackson; Violet,
Lady Jackson; the late Mr Julian Jebb; Miss Rosemary Kerr; Sir
Osbert Lancaster; Miss Margaret Lane; Mrs Joy Law; Mr
Valentine Lawford; Mr & Mrs James Lees-Milne; Mr Patrick
Leigh Fermor; Mrs Peter Levi; Mrs Joseph Links; Prince &
Princess von Loewenstein; the late Mr Roger Machell; Mr
Lachlan Maclean; Mr Anthony Mann; the Dowager Viscountess
Mersey; Mrs Lewis Motley; Mr Robert Morley; Miss Lucy
Norton; Viscount Norwich; Mrs Frances Partridge; Mr Brian
Pearce; Mr Michael Pearman; Mr John Phillips; the late Mr
Peter de Polnay; Mr Anthony Powell; Mr Stuart Preston; Mr
Peter Quennell; Lord Rennell; the executors of the estate of the
late Lord Rennell; the late Hon. Mrs Gustav Rodd; Mme Jeanne
Rödel; Mrs Joan Rodzianko; Mr Ned Rorem; Mr Richard
Shone; Mr Julian Slade; Sir Hugh Smiley; Miss Madeau
Stewart; Lady Marjorie Stirling; the late Mr John Sutro &
Mrs Sutro; Mr Christopher Sykes; Lord Thomas; Mr Patrick
Trevor-Roper; Mr Hugo Vickers; Mr Auberon Waugh; Miss
Patchy Wheatley; Mr Sam White; Mr A. N. Wilson.

Finally I would like to give especial thanks to Mr Stanley Olson
for his help and encouragement.

CHAPTER ONE

The Beginnings

When Linda, penniless, sinks down on her suitcase in the Gare du Nord and bursts into tears, she knows that nothing so dreadful has ever happened to her before, and that her predicament is hopeless. Then, through her weeping, she becomes aware of somebody standing beside her: a short, stocky Frenchman in a black Homburg hat. And so begins the great love affair of Linda's life, a love which transforms her existence, breaking her free from the dark and dreary confines of her English past to release her into perfect happiness in Paris, the most beautiful city on earth.

This is how Nancy Mitford tells the story in *The Pursuit of Love*. A novelist who always wrote with a strong element of autobiography, nowhere does she come closer to the truths of her own life. As it was for Linda, her life, too, was transformed by a short, stocky Frenchman in a black Homburg hat, whom she met not in the Gare du Nord, but in the garden of the Allies' Club in Park Lane. Like Linda, she found in beautiful Paris happiness and freedom of spirit; a freedom, too, from a failed marriage, following years of frustration passed under the iron régime of a tyrannical father.

Both Nancy's parents were the children of remarkable men, and in both cases the remarkable qualities of their fathers passed them entirely by, to reappear again, at full strength and in a number of strange permutations, in the succeeding generation. Nancy's father, David Mitford, second Baron Redesdale, was descended from a long line of landed gentlemen, locally distinguished but of small importance in the history of the nation, whose fortunes were founded in the fourteenth century by one Sir John Mitford of Mitford in Northumberland. To him were granted the lands and tenements of Molesdon in that county, from which was derived the three little moles on the Mitford family crest. David Mitford's great-great-grandfather was the historian William Mitford, author of *The History of Greece*, a monumental work now forgotten although much admired in its day. David's father, Bertram Mitford, born in 1837 and created Baron Redesdale in 1902,[1] was the son of Henry Reveley Mitford, of Exbury in Hampshire, and Lady Georgina Ashburnham, daughter of the Earl of Ashburnham, who, after bearing her husband three sons, ran off with the secretary to the British Legation in Frankfurt.

Bertie (pronounced 'Barty'), eight at the time of his mother's defection, was sent to Eton at the age of nine, and from there to Oxford. Before going briefly into politics, he went first into the Diplomatic Service, making a distinguished career for himself in St Petersburg and then in the Far East, in China and Japan. He was one of the first two foreigners to be presented to the Mikado, who awarded him the Grand Cordon of the Rising Sun for his translation of a collection of Japanese legends, and in recognition of his knowledge and love of the country. At thirty-seven Bertie married Lady Clementine Ogilvy, daughter of the Earl of Airlie. The Airlies, a grand and old-established Scottish family, were not pleased with the match as Bertie had the reputation of being something of a rake (a reputation not improved by his close friendship with the Prince of Wales), and to the day of her death Lady Airlie addressed her daughter's letters to 'Lady Clementine Ogilvy'. When his father died, Bertie inherited land and a large Georgian house, Batsford, in Gloucestershire, where he and Clementine brought up their nine children, and where Bertie established a wild and exotic garden on the bleak Cotswold hillside that rose in front of the house.

It was at Batsford that Nancy's parents, David and Sydney, first met, their two fathers, Bertie Mitford and Thomas Gibson

---

[1] The Barony of Redesdale, created originally in 1802, became extinct in 1886, to be recreated for Bertram in 1902.

Bowles, having become friends when they were both returned as Conservative Members of Parliament in the General Election of 1892. Bowles, or 'Tap' as he was always inexplicably known, was every bit as clever as Bertie, and in old age the two men looked rather similar, two handsome old walruses with brilliant blue eyes and thick white moustaches. Tap was born in 1843, the illegitimate son of Thomas Milner-Gibson, a Liberal Member of Parliament, and of Susan Bowles, daughter of a brush-maker from Southwark, who was in service in the Milner-Gibsons' household. He was sent to school in France, a country he loved, insisting for the rest of his life on keeping French hours, which meant a full déjeuner at 11.30 in the morning and nothing else until dinner. At nineteen, he was set to work by his father as a junior clerk in the Legacy and Succession Duty Office at Somerset House, a job which he hated, abandoning it after six years for a career in journalism. He covered the Siege of Paris in 1870 for *The Morning Post*, and at twenty-six, with two colleagues, founded the satirical magazine, *Vanity Fair*, and some years later *The Lady*, a journal for women still published today.

In 1876 Tap married Jessica, the daughter of Major-General Charles Evans-Gordon. They had four children, two boys followed by two girls, before Jessica died at the age of thirty-five. As soon as they were old enough the boys, Geoffrey and George, were sent away to school, but their sisters, Sydney and Dorothy (Weenie), were brought up at home, very much under the eccentric influence of their father. In many ways Tap was a modern father, believing in fresh air and exercise, plain food and natural remedies, unconventional theories for an age in which four large meals a day was the custom, with often a little carriage exercise the only aid to digestion. Even more unconventional, Tap liked to have his daughters with him; cumbersomely dressed in stiff serge sailor-suits made specially at Gieves, Sydney and Weenie accompanied their father wherever he went: shooting in Scotland; on his long and dangerous sea-voyages (sailing was a passion he had inherited from his father); on his yacht during the summer season at Deauville with his artist friends, Boldini,

Tissot and Helleu; and back in London, paying calls on the fashionable ladies of Pont Street and Belgrave Square, who were not always entirely delighted to have to receive into their drawing-rooms two quaintly-dressed and silent little girls. From the age of fourteen it was Sydney who ran the household, a responsibility she enjoyed, being good at adding up and keeping accounts, although she hated having to deal with the men servants who were often insolent and drunk.

It was in the winter of 1894 that Bertie Mitford asked Tap if he would come and speak for him at a political meeting, stay at Batsford, and of course bring the children. The Bowleses went down by train, were met at the station by a waggonette and pair and driven to the house, where they were shown into the library, Tap going first, the two girls in their hated sailor-suits trailing behind. Bertie and Lady Clementine were standing before a blazing fire; and there, with his back to the fire and one foot on the fender, dressed in a shabby velveteen jacket such as gamekeepers wore, was David Mitford. At seventeen, he was already startlingly handsome. Sydney, three years younger, fell in love with him at once.

David, the second son, was the most wayward of the nine Mitford children. Given to sudden, uncontrollable rages, he also had a habit of falling mysteriously and frighteningly ill whenever he was thwarted in what he wanted to do. His interests were entirely out of doors and it was with great difficulty that his tutor ever persuaded him to open a book. Later he was sent not to Eton with his elder brother Clem, but to Radley, which he loathed, and from where it was intended he should enter the Army. However, when the time came, he failed the examination into Sandhurst, and so was packed off instead to be a tea-planter in Ceylon, an experience which taught him two things: the destructive effects of alcohol (tea-planters were notoriously heavy drinkers), and the word 'sua', Tamil for 'pig', which, spelt 'sewer' and applied to most of the people he knew, became his favourite, and most famous, term of abuse. He was back from Ceylon at the outbreak of the Boer War, when he joined the Royal Northumberland

Fusiliers, fought gallantly in South Africa, and was invalided home in 1902 with one lung shot away. (Brought back to camp after four days in a bullock-waggon, wound swarming with maggots, was a story much loved by his children.)

David and Sydney were married at St Margaret's, Westminster, on February 6, 1904. There is no question that David was very much in love: there is no knowing what Sydney felt. Having lost her heart to David at the age of fourteen, she soon fell out of love with him, and as a young girl had had several admirers, the most serious of whom was killed in 1900 in the South African War. She once told her eldest daughter that two years after Nancy was born she had been on the point of running away with another man, but had stayed for the sake of the baby. ('Which I doubt, since we know what I looked like at that age,' said Nancy.)

They were a remarkably handsome couple. David at twenty-five was tall and lean, with a smooth, buff-coloured complexion and fierce blue eyes. Sydney's beauty had an other-worldly air about it, a vague look, a look of beautiful boredom, as though her own very private life were going on deep inside, leaving her detached from the world and its people. She seemed possessed of the sort of inner tranquillity that comes to those who have risen above the passions of daily life to enter into some personal nirvana. Nothing ruffled her, nothing outwardly disturbed that Buddha-like serenity, a serenity which, however, concealed a strong character and an absolute conviction that whatever she believed was right.

They spent their honeymoon in Paris, both speaking good French and both having inherited from their fathers a love of France. On their return to London they stayed in Tap's house in Lowndes Square while their own, No. 1 Graham Street,[1] was being prepared. Graham Street, just south of Eaton Square, was then very modest indeed, a Victorian terrace of mean little brick houses, with No. 1, by far the largest and elegantly faced in cream-coloured stucco, the only one of distinction.

[1] Now Graham Terrace.

By early summer the Mitfords had moved in, settling down contentedly to a married life that was quiet as much from choice as from necessity. Money was short. They were entirely dependent on the modest allowance Tap made his daughter, and on the income from the job he provided for his son-in-law as business manager of *The Lady*, a less congenial post than which could hardly have been imagined: David hated being indoors, knew nothing of women's magazines, and had no interest whatsoever in the printed word. (The only book he admitted to having read was Jack London's *White Fang*, which he thought so good he never had the least desire to read any other.) To make his day bearable, he bought a mongoose with which he hunted the rats on *The Lady's* Covent Garden premises.

At home in Graham Street Sydney had few demands on her time. There were five servants, all female as she refused to employ men after the unpleasant experience of her father's drunken footmen. This meant that, having seen the cook in the morning, she was free to pay calls, read, and go shopping at the Army & Navy Stores in Victoria Street. This establishment was important in the lives of both Mitfords. When living with Tap in Lowndes Square, Sydney had gone there every Tuesday to order the groceries for the week, afterwards taking the lift to the top floor where she and Weenie had tea. This was a treat; it had made her fond of the place. To David, the Stores were reliable purveyors of those sacred articles, guns, traps and fishing-rods, and to choose these he liked to be there sharp at nine o'clock, before, as he put it, he could be impeded by inconveniently shaped women.

Occasionally they dined with relations but, although Sydney quite enjoyed social life, her husband did not. There was perfectly good food to be had at home, he said, and he preferred the company of his wife to that of anyone else. His favourite way of passing the evening was with Sydney in the drawing-room with a supper of bread and milk on their laps eaten in their dressing-gowns in front of the fire. Such a picture of domestic peace is hard to reconcile with the known facts of David's temperament, with

David the small boy of violent and unpredictable rages, or, as later portrayed by Nancy, as the frightening and irascible Uncle Matthew, grinding his teeth and bellowing with anger. But in the early days of his marriage, and before the arrival of that large and troublesome family, he was too happy to be anything but calm. And there was another reason for his contentment: within a few weeks of their return from France, Sydney found that she was pregnant.

David was ecstatic. 'I never dreamt of such happiness,' he wrote to his mother. 'I had never any idea of what it would be like – Now I hardly think of anything else . . . Sydney will make just such another mother as I had so he ought to be a very happy little boy.' By the middle of November the birth was due, and at six o'clock in the evening of the 28th, after a difficult labour lasting nearly fourteen hours, the baby was born. It was not a boy: it was a girl. Her name was to be Ruby.

Sixteen years later, Mabel the parlourmaid knew at once by the grim expression on his Lordship's face[1] that the news was bad, that yet another girl, the sixth, had been born. But, in November 1904, these disappointments were all in the future. Sydney had survived, the baby was perfect, and David, although appalled at the sufferings his wife had endured, was supremely happy. Once he had seen for himself that Sydney was in no danger – 'I cannot tell you how sweet and brave she has been all through' – he was able to turn his attention to his daughter. 'The baby is splendid 9½lbs at birth and the pretiest [sic] little child you could see . . . Our happiness is very great . . . Sydney sends her love and Ruby would if she knew.' Although the birth had left her weak, Sydney was determined to nurse the baby herself in spite of the considerable discomfort this caused, making her dread the frequent intervals at which the child was brought to her. But within a week the pain had subsided and she was sitting up in bed looking pink-cheeked and pretty, and feeling well enough to have second thoughts over the choice of a name. As a boy had been so

[1] David inherited the title in 1916.

confidently expected, little time had been spent over the bread
and milk considering names for a girl. Ruby she did not care for;
she preferred, as a reminder of the sea-faring ballads of her
nautical past, that the baby should be called Nancy. And Nancy
she was christened on January 26, 1905.

To look after the baby, Sydney engaged the daughter of Tap's
old sea-captain, a nice, practical girl called Lily Kersey, or Ninny
Kudgey as she quickly became known in the nursery. Lily,
although untrained, was kind, and soon became devoted to the
baby who, with her greeny-grey eyes, fresh complexion and mop
of vigorous black curls, was an appealing little girl. 'Pore gurl,
she's ravenish,' Lily would coo, rocking the baby energetically in
her arms. As was the custom of their class, neither of the Mitfords
took much part in the life of the nursery. Sydney, an elegant
figure in her big straw hat, long skirts and tightly cinched waist,
would sometimes wheel the pram to the park, but for the most
part Nancy on the top floor saw little of her parents. As soon as
she could walk, she would stagger downstairs twice a day hand in
hand with Ninny, once in the morning to see her mother and
father reading *The Times* over breakfast in their pretty white-
papered dining-room, and then again at tea-time when she was
buttoned into her best frock and taken down to the drawing-room
to be left for an hour with her mother, after which Ninny would
come and collect her for bed.

Like her father, Sydney had some unusual ideas about health.
When she and Weenie were children, Tap had hung on their
nursery wall a set of rules, rules which he expected to be
unquestioningly obeyed. They were not, of course, but that was
beside the point.

1) The window is to be open day and night six inches at the top
   (revolutionary then, when most people believed that 'night
   air' was harmful).
2) The children are not to eat between meals.
3) The children are to be rinsed in clean water before getting
   out of their bath.
4) The children are to have no medicine of any sort.

Sydney, too, believed that the Good Body would take care of itself, and that the medical profession had nothing to offer but dangerous interference. For appearance's sake she was prepared to call in a doctor for anyone seriously ill, or if an operation were necessary. When Nancy was two, she had to be operated on for a badly infected foot. The operation was performed by the doctor at home, watchfully supervised by David, the baby being anaesthetised with a handkerchief soaked in chloroform. But the usual practice was to ignore the doctor's advice and to pour away the medicine prescribed – 'Horrid stuff!' – as soon as his back was turned. Vaccination was of course out of the question – 'pumping disgusting germs into the Good Body!'

Nancy as the first-born was the subject of an unfortunate experiment in child-rearing undertaken at the instigation of David's unmarried sister Frances, Aunt Pussy, who held that no child under the age of five should ever be corrected or hear a word spoken in anger. It was better, she believed, to administer a bromide than a slap to put an end to a fit of temper. The result was a very spoiled little girl given, like her father, to uncontrollable tantrums. Nancy's progress through the first few years of her life was characterised by roaring, red-faced rages: Nancy bellowing in her pram all the way to the park; Nancy on a pony screaming to be put down. Sydney was quite unable to control these fits of temper, the causes of which were often as mysterious to her as their sudden cessation. 'The houses are smiling at me,' Nancy would say, suddenly beaming up at her mother from her pram, having screamed with fury all the way from Graham Street to Belgrave Square.

This state of affairs continued for three years until on November 25, 1907, only three days before her third birthday, Nancy's life changed suddenly and very much for the worse. A sister, Pamela, was born. This meant that not only was Nancy toppled from her position of adored only child, but faithless Ninny Kudgey instantly transferred her affections from the old baby to the new. Nancy's pathetic wails in the nursery could be heard all over the house – 'Oh, Ninny, I WISH you could love me! WHY

don't you love me any more?' – becoming so pitiful that eventually
Sydney could bear it no longer and Ninny was dismissed. But the
damage was done. Nancy had been abandoned in favour of Pam,
and it was many years before she forgave her. From the day of
Pam's birth, Nancy set out to punish her sister and make her life
miserable. When Nancy was around, Pam could usually be found
in tears; if something could be spoiled, Nancy spoiled it for her.
Throughout their childhood and well beyond, she teased and
tormented her with an ingenuity against which poor Pam, a good,
rather stolid child, lacking her older sister's wit and the cutting
edge of her tongue, was quite unable to defend herself.

Lily Kersey was succeeded by a tyrant remembered only as the
Unkind Nanny, who established a rule of terror which lasted for
three years, during which the only boy, Tom, was born, and
Diana, the one flawless beauty in that beautiful family. A couple
of months after Diana's birth, Unkind Nanny was discovered
punishing Nancy by banging her head against a wooden bed-
post. Sydney, unable to face the encounter, retired to bed, and
David himself had to come up to the top floor to dismiss her.

Then came Laura Dicks, who stayed until the last of the seven
children had left the nursery. When she arrived at Graham Street
for her interview, Sydney's immediate impression was that Miss
Dicks with her pale face and slender build was at thirty-nine too
old and too frail to look after four children, even with the help of a
nursery-maid. Nanny Dicks herself admitted to quailing at the
prospect of pushing that enormous pram to the park and back
twice a day. But then she was shown the new baby, Diana, aged
three months. '*OH*, what a lovely baby!' she exclaimed – and that
was that.

Nanny Dicks was a success from the start: all the children
adored her. Even Nancy, aged nearly six, whom Nanny found on
her first day in the nursery with her head buried in *Ivanhoe*
refusing to look up, was won over, although, having already
started school, she was inclined to consider herself too grown-up
to be counted as one of the babies. Nanny Dicks's rule in the
nursery was kind but firm. She never showed favouritism, never

boasted of the paragons she had looked after previously, and later always maintained the authority of the many governesses who held brief but turbulent sway in the schoolroom. She didn't agree with all of Sydney's eccentric theories of health and diet, but loyally carried them out in so far as seemed practical, never betraying her feelings by anything more than a sniff and a shrug. With the children, her strongest expression of disapproval was 'Hm' – sniff – 'very *silly*, darling.' Although she always accompanied them to church on Sundays, she herself was 'Chapel', and on her day off joined the local Congregationalists, after which the nursery would ring with 'Shall we gather at the river?' and 'There were ninety and nine who safely lay in the shelter of the fold'. She encouraged the children to collect farthings for the poor lepers, and silver paper which she moulded into a ball and sent off when it weighed a pound. They had to be careful that the paper was not smeared with chocolate; chocolatey paper was no good to lepers. She had a strong puritan streak which led her to distrust pleasure on principle: 'Don't expect ME to be sorry for you' – sniff, shrug – was what she always said when anyone came to her ill with the effects of over-indulgence. None of her charges suffered from vanity if Nanny had anything to do with it. A little girl dressing for a party, found staring miserably into the glass *knowing* that everything was wrong, would be consoled with, 'Don't worry, darling, nobody's going to be looking at *you*.' (When the beautiful Diana at eighteen married Bryan Guinness at the society wedding of the year, in a frenzy of nervous despair at an ill-fitting veil, she turned to Nanny. 'Never mind, darling,' said Nanny soothingly. 'Nobody's going to be looking at *you*.')

The Easter before Nanny Dicks's arrival, Nancy aged five and a half began as a pupil at the Francis Holland School, a Church of England foundation whose tall, dark-red building stood so conveniently at the other end of Graham Street, on the same side as No. 1 and immediately opposite the Pine Apple public house. Assembly was at a quarter to nine in the high gas-lit hall with its stained-glass windows depicting the female virtues. The Headmistress, Miss Morison, took prayers, accompanied by the Head

Girl on the organ, whose playing was not infrequently interrupted by the hissing and explosions from the commercial laundry at the back of the building. The girls were taught all the usual subjects – English, History, Scripture, French and Mathematics – and as well as singing lessons and dancing classes there was Swedish Drill with Miss Carlsen for the whole school every day. Games took place on playing-fields at Richmond, with a Sports Day in the summer term; while Prize Giving was in the spring, an occasion rather dreaded by the younger girls who, in their best white dresses, found it difficult to sit still on forms covered only with green baize, while Princess Marie Louise, the school's patron, was fulsomely welcomed, and the Bishop of Southwark gave his customary jovial address.

Later that year, 1910, the house in Graham Street was sold, and the Mitfords moved to 49 Victoria Road, a much larger house in a pretty tree-lined street just off Kensington (Kensy, Nanny called it) High Street. The household now consisted of David and Sydney (known to the children as Farve and Muv); Nancy (nicknamed 'Koko' after the character in Gilbert and Sullivan's operetta *The Mikado*, whom it was thought at birth she rather resembled with her dark hair and that oriental look common to many young babies), Pam, Tom and Diana, with Nanny and Ada the nursery-maid to look after them; cook, housemaid, two house-parlourmaids, and Willie Dawkins the hound-boy in charge of the animals. By now there was quite a menagerie, with Farve's mongoose, two bloodhounds, a dachshund, a varying population of mice and birds, and, until the move, a tiny pony called Brownie. Farve, on his way to work one morning, had caught sight of the diminutive Brownie being led under Blackfriars Bridge with a child on his back. This had tickled Farve's fancy and he made an offer for him there and then, bringing him home that same evening in a hansom cab, to the intense delight of the children. There was a small box-room on the first floor which nobody used, and here Brownie was installed, with hay and straw conveniently provided by the mews abutting the back of the house.

Until the outbreak of war in 1914, life on the top floor at Victoria Road went on very much as before. 'Dear Muv,' wrote Nancy one day in October 1913, 'It is a horrid afternoon, it is raining, this morning it was foggy. The little ones have been singing, but I have been reading Little Folks. Pam is creaking the rocking-horse.' The two eldest girls shared a bedroom, Nancy as usual taking every opportunity to score off the unsuspecting Pam. She offered her a penny a month if she would get out of bed first every morning and draw the curtains. Just before the first month was up, Muv got to hear of the scheme and put a stop to it: Pam wasn't being paid nearly enough, she said, for the work involved. Nancy tried to renege – 'unfair' was the word used – arguing that, as Pam had not completed the month, she hadn't earned the penny. But Muv stood firm, and Pam got her money.

The nursery day revolved around the two daily outings to the park. As soon as breakfast was over, out they would all go, with Nanny in her shiny black bonnet and streamers pushing the big black pram with the baby in it up Victoria Road, across Kensy High Street, past the old balloon woman at the gate and into Kensington Gardens. As they went, Nancy kept Pam and Tom fascinated with long complicated sagas about witches and goblins and fairy princesses. When they got home it would be time for lunch, usually some kind of stew followed by a milk pudding which none of them would eat. In the afternoon there was another walk or an excursion to one of the South Kensington museums – the Science Museum, the Victoria and Albert, or their favourite, the Natural History Museum, where the children were happy to spend hours gazing at the stuffed elephant and the unbelievable skeleton of the dinosaur. The day ended with tea in the drawing-room with Muv; and at bedtime, when Farve came home from the office, there were rough, noisy romps and games of ogres up and down the stairs. Sometimes they played with the Norman children, Hugh, Mark, Dick and the high-spirited Sibell, nephews and nieces of Montagu Norman, future Governor of the Bank of England, whose house was opposite No. 49, so near that the children were able to construct between their nurseries a 'telephone' made out of string and a couple of empty cocoa tins.

At Christmas the children were always taken to the theatre, to Gilbert and Sullivan, which they loathed, to Bertram Mills's circus at Olympia, and to *Peter Pan*, which they rather despised, making a point, when the question was put from the stage, of loudly denying a belief in the existence of fairies. Best of all was Maskelyne and Devant's Magic Show. Farve and Uncle George Bowles, keen amateur conjurors and members of the Magic Circle, would go every week during the Christmas season in the hope of improving their technique and enlarging their repertoire. They were always the first to volunteer when members of the audience were invited to come up on stage, particularly for the Vanishing Lady: there they would stand holding tightly on to her hands; but they never discovered how the trick was done – a little tug and she was gone.

Once every two or three years Farve and Muv sailed to Canada, following in the footsteps of the millionaire adventurer Harry Oakes who, during a period of near insolvency, had decided to try his luck prospecting for gold. Farve knew Oakes and, always attracted by a hare-brained scheme, went out to join him, staking his claim on a patch of rough bush country near the small mining town of Swastika, Ontario. Oakes's mine became the second richest in the western hemisphere, but needless to say on the Mitford patch no gold was ever found. Nonetheless the prospector's life was an attractive one, and living rough in a wooden shack miles from nowhere made an agreeable change from office routine at *The Lady*. They were there in 1913, when Nancy wrote dutifully to her parents, 'Dear Muve and farve, is the shack nice?', while nursing the secret hope that they, like the ill-fated passengers of the *Titanic*, on which the Redesdales originally had booked passages and which had gone down the year before, would be lost at sea, thus leaving the reins of the household in her small but capable hands, an unparalleled opportunity to boss the others. Every morning she scanned Nanny's *Daily News* for a report of the wreck. Toiling up Victoria Road after Nanny and the pram holding Pam and Diana, she would ask, 'How big is the

Titanic?' 'As big as from here to Kensy High Street,' Nanny would reply, leaving in the child's mind an impression that would remain for life of the *Titanic* as Victoria Road, houses, trees and all, steaming through the icebergs.

In the hot summer of 1911, the first since leaving Graham Street, the new house was let, and the whole family moved to a small cottage which Muv had rented in High Wycombe in Buckinghamshire. The move was something of an upheaval, with parents, four children, Nanny and nursemaid, immense piles of luggage, and all the animals including three dogs and Brownie. The guard refused to have the pony with him in the van so Farve, without wasting time in argument, changed their first-class tickets for third, and they all, including Brownie, got into the same compartment, with Pam in the luggage rack to make room.

The children loved the Old Mill Cottage and its pretty orchard and garden. Originally it had been two cottages, now joined into one. The mill was at the back and the miller used to show the children round the ancient machinery, which half thrilled, half terrified them – the darkness and the thick soft cobwebs, and the rushing sound of the mill-race below. Muv drove them about in a pony-cart with thin metal wheels, and they went for walks along the lush Thames valley to the hoop and spade factory where they always stopped to watch the electric saws at work. Nancy, aged six, was enchanted by country life. She was given a bantam hen called Specky whose egg-laying she recorded with care, and when her mother was away kept her up to date with what was growing in the garden: 'My dear Muv . . . my sweat-pease are so nice, and there is a beatiful popy and our runner is running up the stik . . . give my lothe to farve and a great many kises Koko.'

Part of the summer Muv and the children spent with the grandparents – with the Redesdales at Batsford, and with Tap at Bournehill, a small eighteenth-century *cottage orné* overlooking the Solent, belonging to the Drummond banking family. The Mitfords with their cousins Dick and Dooley Bailey[1] and the

[1] Richard and Anthony, eldest of the four children of Sydney's sister Weenie (Dorothy) Bailey.

Marconi children, who spent their holidays at Eaglehurst, the next house along the shore, raced along the shingle beach and in and out of the vast coverts of rhododendrons; they sat around under the pine trees, and, perched on the end of the wooden jetty, paddled their feet in the water. In striped bathing costumes, shrieking and splashing, they dared each other into the cold sea, and jumped out again with their teeth chattering, to be rubbed dry on a coarse towel by Nanny and given a petit beurre biscuit to take off the chill. Every day after tea they watched with interest as Caddick the butler walked grandly down to the water's edge for his swim, his hair in a rubber cap to keep it dry.

One August night in 1915 there was a fire. The house was full – Muv, the children, the Baileys and their nannies and nursery-maids. Pam and Ada the nursery-maid were sharing a bedroom over the boiler-room, and when they were being put to bed Pam said she smelt burning. 'Don't be silly,' said Ada, and took no notice. Some hours later Nancy, who had been put to sleep on her own, woke with a start to find the room full of smoke. She ran in to Nanny, sleeping in the next room with the baby; she in turn woke Muv, and within minutes all the children were safely out on the lawn, huddled in blankets and with jerseys over their nightgowns. They watched enthralled as Tap hurled anything he could lay hands on – clothes, blankets, papers, furniture – out of the window, while Caddick dashed to and fro, his arms full of silver. The remainder of the night was spent at Eaglehurst, and the next day the family returned to London. Farve, home that morning on leave, was greeted by the cook with the news that Bournehill Cottage had been burnt down, and that there was no sign of any survivors. At that moment a taxi drew up, bursting with children and animals, buckets and spades. 'Yes, everyone is safe,' drawled Muv, drifting in through the hall, 'and the dogs, such luck. It was Nancy and Pam who woke up, their room was full of smoke . . .'

Staying with the Redesdale grandparents at Batsford was usually less eventful. Grandfather, now an old man and almost stone-deaf, passed his days quietly, playing patience, reading Nietzsche and cultivating his garden, his deafness acting as an impenetrable barrier between himself and the rest of the world. To Nancy he was a very distant figure, although he did have the agreeable habit of tipping when it occurred to him, and once gave her half a crown to remember 1453, the fall of Constantinople, the most important date in the history of Christendom. Grandmother was much more approachable. Always dressed head to foot in voluminous and silky black, she, like her husband, had fine blue eyes and white hair, but her face was round and pink. Like so many of her generation, she had become immensely stout in old age, moving, when she had to, with tiny little steps, so that, like the ladies of Versailles, she looked as though she ran on wheels.

The children loved Batsford. The house, with its smell of wood fires and beeswax, was full of fascinating objects from the East. There was also the farm, and that immense garden with its ornamental dairy like a doll's thatched cottage, and an oriental rest-house entrancingly decorated with dolphins sporting on a tiled and curving roof. Nancy felt sorry for her father, confined to his office in London, and was diligent in keeping him in touch with what she was doing. 'Sweet Toad,' she wrote, 'I do dare call you a Toad . . . We went for a drive and saw a hawk, we saw the young swallows peeping out on the stable roof.'

All this changed with the outbreak of war in 1914. The children had come up to London at the end of July to say goodbye to their father, who was on the point of leaving for Canada to do a little prospecting. As Muv, expecting her fifth child, was lying in at Victoria Road, Tom and the three girls were sent to stay at the Redesdales' town house, just round the corner in Kensington High Street. London was already excitingly different: there were anti-aircraft guns in Hyde Park, regimental brass bands and a military camp in Kensington Gardens, and armoured vehicles driving up and down the Broad Walk among the nursemaids and perambulators. The four children sat on Grandfather's balcony overlooking the High Street, watching the troops march past en route for France, all of them, even Tom, busy with their knitting, turning out scratchy purple mufflers for the soldiers, khaki not yet being available. Soon Belgian refugees began to filter over, and could be seen sitting in the park, easily recognisable by their shabby clothes and strange guttural accents. The war came even closer the night Nanny got them all out of bed in the small hours to see the Zeppelin come down in flames over Potter's Bar. Next day there were gypsies in the street selling brooches made, they said, from fragments of the wrecked dirigible. It was asking too much of the children that they should pray for peace. Nancy prayed as hard as she could for war, looking forward to the invasion, when, like Robin Hood, she could take to the green-wood and ambush bands of marauding Germans.

On August 8, four days after the declaration of war, Muv gave birth to her fifth child, a daughter ('This is a boy for certain,' said the doctor. But it wasn't.) who was christened Unity, after Unity Moore, an actress Muv admired, and Valkyrie, at the suggestion of Grandfather Redesdale, a lover of Wagner. Farve had gone to join his regiment in Newcastle, and here, as soon as she was strong enough, Muv joined him, in quarters so cramped that the baby had to be laid to sleep in a drawer.

The following month Farve left for the Front, but was soon invalided home again, returning in April 1915 for the second Battle of Ypres. As transport officer, his job was to keep his Battalion supplied with ammunition. Twice every night for a month, he led his convoy of loaded wagons – an easy target for enemy snipers – at full gallop through the centre of the town and out by the Menin Gate. Not once did he fail to get through; but the strain of it nearly killed him. He reached the point where he was no longer physically strong enough to sit his horse, and had to be sent back to England in 1917, suffering from extreme exhaustion.

The children wrote faithfully to their father, and treasured his often brief replies. 'Dearest Koko,' ran one to Nancy. 'Many thanks for your last letter. Much love Farv.' Sometimes he enclosed a box of sweets or a little envelope of dried flowers, and the children in turn sent whatever they could to cheer up his rations. 'Dearest Koko,' he wrote from Belgium a week before the second Battle of Ypres,

Thank you so much for the nice things you sent me in a parcel with some from Muv. It was most amiable of you, and I think very few daughters would give up David Coperfield [sic] in order to purchase delicacies for their brutal father. The Germans went over Bailleul last night and dropped bombs from a Zepellin [sic] – they killed an old woman and a boy – so they were not very successful as of course what they wanted to do was to kill a few soldiers.

Give my love to all the others. I hope you are all being good, and not giving Muv any trouble – I am sure you try –

Much love to little missy blobnose
from Farv.'

Sometimes Nancy wrote to her father in French to demonstrate her progress, and her father's facetious commentaries delighted her:

Il y a un nid de rouge-gorge dans un arbre
J'ai écouté le coucou ce matin.
Votre chien est très sage il est dans la maison
J'aime les lapins de ma tante
De la part de votre affectionée   Nancy   (blob).

To this Farve wrote in reply:

'A robin in a tree has built!
The cuckoo has not changed its lilt!
And I have no desire to quench
My child's desire for learning French.'

At home meanwhile, it was becoming harder to make ends meet. Army pay was small, and Tap, owing he said to increased taxation, had decided to economise by reducing Sydney's allowance. Victoria Road and the cottage at High Wycombe, which Muv had now bought, were let, and the entire family moved into Malcolm House, a square Georgian house belonging to Grandfather in Batsford village.

On August 17, 1916, Bertie Redesdale died. He was suc-

ceeded by David, his second son, the eldest, Clem, having been
killed in France the year before. Grandfather was buried in the
churchyard at Batsford, and soon after the funeral Grandmother
went to live in a cottage belonging to the family at Redesdale in
Northumberland. Muv, the new Lady Redesdale, found herself
in possession of the big house, most of which was shut up and the
furniture covered in dust-sheets as it was far too expensive to
heat. The children, of course, were overjoyed to have such a
marvellous playground, and, free of the daunting presence of
their grandparents, with Farve safely across the Channel, and
with Muv and the other grown-ups too busy to pay much
attention, found themselves free to do very much as they pleased.

The following year Farve came back to England for good. He
was appointed Assistant Provost Marshal, in charge of training
the Special Reserve Battalion in Oxford, and given rooms in
Christ Church, where he installed a Pianola, put trout in the
college fountain, and generally made himself at home. From time
to time he brought a party of fellow Reservists to Batsford for
luncheon, when Muv and the cook had to stretch their ingenuity
to its limits, as food, even in the country, was desperately short.
The stand-by for luncheon parties was a chicken pie constructed
largely out of potato, the morsels of chicken being as rare and as
highly prized as sixpences in a Christmas pudding. In spite of the
difficulties in feeding her family, Muv was sensible about food.
She didn't believe in forcing the children to eat what they didn't
like, so that during the war they lived mainly on eggs, potatoes
and milk, none of them caring for the stringy beef and over-
cooked liver that was a feature of that period; nor, except for
chocolate, were they interested in puddings. Bread, which they
all craved, was heavily rationed and there was never enough of it,
the cook making do as best she could with potato-cakes and dry
little scones made out of maize. Muv kept bees and poultry, but
even so there was never quite enough to go round: as well as the
immediate family, there were numerous relations who had to be
kept supplied with honeycomb, and eggs in boxes home-made out
of wattle and felt were posted off almost daily.

All the girls kept animals: Diana and Pam had hens, the sale of whose eggs was an important source of revenue (Muv eventually did so well out of her chickens that she was able to pay the governess – £120 a year – out of the egg money), and Nancy had goats whose milk she sold to the farm. 'I don't want to make butter, as it is not profitable enough,' she explained to her mother. 'Please tell Farve that he owes me 2½d for the milk that the pigs had.' There was also Nancy's terrier Jock, Brownie the pony, who often came along for walks like a dog, and a varying collection of toads, frogs and grass-snakes kept and lovingly tended in the outhouses, while families of mice were reared in pungent little cages in the schoolroom. Pam and Nancy shared an elaborate mouse-house made by the estate carpenter, with several rooms and a staircase, but when Nancy's mouse, starved and neglected, was found to have eaten Pam's, the mouse-house was quietly abandoned.

Every weekday morning from nine till luncheon the girls, and Tom before he went away to school, had lessons in the schoolroom. Miss Mirams came to Batsford in January 1917. 'She seemed very nice – only she wears specs – and can't play chess, which is a pity,' Nancy wrote in her diary. First in a long line of governesses, some of whom were to stay no more than a few weeks, she had a difficult job teaching her class of four, with nearly six years between oldest and youngest. Tom, to prepare him for school, had to be given a grounding in Latin and mathematics, subjects which were not considered necessary for the girls; Pam had difficulty with reading and was therefore slow to learn; while Nancy was often impatient at having to listen to the simple material found suitable for Diana. But Miss Mirams was a good teacher and got on well with her pupils, although she told Muv that the Mitford way of talking was impossibly affected. Tom, she said, would be teased when he went to school if he talked like that. 'Why, what mustn't he say?' asked Muv, puzzled. 'Well, for instance, "How *amusing*!" Boys never say, "How *amusing*!"' In the holidays Miss Mirams' place was taken by a French governess, a clever, elegant young woman called Zella, to whom they were all devoted. She gave them an hour's French reading and grammar in the morning, while Farve and Muv, both of whom spoke French well, made it a rule that during the time that Zella was with them, French was to be spoken at meals – with the result that during Zella's visits meals were unusually silent.

On Sundays there were no lessons. On Sundays there was church with Nanny. '14 January Went to church,' Nancy wrote in her diary. 'Pam, Tom and Diana quarrelled the whole time. Nanny said she'd never spent such a miserable Sunday.'

For the New Year of 1917, they all went to stay with their Farrer[1] cousins in Buckinghamshire, and Farve organised a paperchase, precursor of that thrilling variation which the children loved so much when the 'hares' were hunted with a real bloodhound. For Tom's birthday on January 2 there was a fancy-dress party. 'I was a bacchanti,' Nancy recorded, 'and won the prize for the best dress. It was a lovely party'.

In 1918 when the war ended, Farve decided to put Batsford up for sale. Even with six children (Jessica, always known as Decca, had been born in 1917), it was far bigger than they needed and costly to run. When he succeeded to the title, Farve inherited 36,000 acres of farmland in Gloucestershire and Oxfordshire, and a large estate at Redesdale in Northumberland, but he was by no means a rich man. The land itself was nothing like as valuable as modern farming methods have made it today, rents were low, and the tenants' cottages were constantly in need of repair. It also has to be said that Farve was not sensible about money: he did not understand how to make it work for him and, although a man of inexpensive tastes, he indulged in one ruinous extravagance. Like his father, he had a passion for building, on which, like his father, he spent most of his income and a large part of his capital. Grandfather Redesdale had pulled down the Georgian villa at Batsford, and built in its place a vast modern mansion, the cost of which virtually ruined him. Farve sold Batsford just after the end of the war, when nobody had any money, and bought the next

---

[1] Children of Farve's sister, Joan Farrer.

house, Asthall, in which to put the family while he was rebuilding the third house, Swinbrook, at the height of a boom period when labour was expensive. Nancy used to tease 'Builder Redesdale', as she called him, with their descent in the world, from Batsford PARK to Asthall MANOR to Swinbrook HOUSE. Financial crises were an integral part of Nancy's childhood, the grown-ups spending hours closeted in Farve's business-room, after which some wholly inadequate economy would be imposed on the household – Bronco instead of Bromo in the lavatory, and the disappearance of napkins at meals. (This last measure caught the attention of the press: 'Peeress Saves Ha'pence' ran the story in the *Daily Express*.) But somehow ruin was always averted and life went on exactly as it always had. 'The family are in a terrible financial crisis,' Nancy wrote to her brother on one of these occasions when bankruptcy was looming. 'However we continue as before to eat (however humbly) drink and drive about in large Daimlers. Mitfords are like that.'

That last summer at Batsford Nancy was thirteen, a slender girl who already managed to look elegant, with her thick black hair tied back in a great brush behind her neck and her enviable height, even in the cut-down, worn-out clothes that had had to last the war. Her colouring was quite different from that of the rest of the family: the other children had blonde hair and blue eyes whereas Nancy's hair was black and her eyes a greenish grey. At thirteen she had already grown out of the childish world of chickens and goats and pet mice in cages, preferring instead to read, to read voraciously and for hours on end, sunk deep into one of the sofas in Grandfather's well-stocked library. Reading was not an occupation her parents encouraged. Reading in bed was forbidden, novels were not allowed before luncheon, and library books were to be read only in the library. 'If you've got nothing to do,' Farve would say, finding his daughter absorbed in a book, 'run down to the village and tell Hooper . . .' But Nancy became adept at reading in secret and avoiding her father's eye. In the library at Batsford were laid the foundations of her intellectual life. Here she read most of the English classics, as well as French and English biography, history and belles lettres. Tolstoy was her great passion, *Anna Karenina* inspiring in her a longing to visit the opera, the very word signifying the grown-up world in all its wickedness and glamour. Eventually Muv was prevailed upon, and Nancy, accompanied by Nanny Dicks, went into Oxford for a matinée of *Faust*. It was not at all as Tolstoy had led her to believe.

Batsford was bought by Sir Gilbert Wills of the tobacco family, one of the few men Farve quite liked; he even went back to stay with the Willses afterwards for the shooting. Sold also (Farve enjoyed selling almost as much as he enjoyed building) were many of the pictures, a great deal of furniture and, to Nancy's eternal regret, a large portion of Grandfather's remarkable library.

CHAPTER TWO

Childhood

Asthall is an Elizabethan manor house, grey stone and gabled, overlooking a quiet churchyard comfortably populated by the solid and lichenous tombs of prosperous wool-merchants. The house lies deep in the heart of the Cotswolds, one of the most beautiful parts of the English countryside, a region characterised by its patchwork of small fields with their clumps of beech and elm and great solitary chestnuts; by pretty, golden-stone villages; by hidden valleys and sudden, steep hills, so green and luxuriant in summer, in winter bleak and cold, with only the fragile tracery of Old Man's Beard to soften the black and thorny hedgerows.

Farve never cared for Asthall. He bought it because it was near his farms, and the River Windrush where he fished, and because the family had to have somewhere to live while the next house, in the neighbouring village of Swinbrook, was being pulled about and rebuilt. To him Asthall was never more than a temporary resting-place, which did not of course prevent him from building on. He put in panelling and a new ceiling in the main house, and added on a library, converted from an old tithe-barn and connected to the house by a covered walk known as the Cloisters. The garden was divided in half by the road running between Asthall village and Swinbrook; on one side of the road was a walled vegetable garden, on the other the garden surrounding the house. Neither of the Redesdales took much interest in gardening: the gardener looked after the garden and that was that, although every year Farve sowed a few seeds between the paving-stones outside his business-room window, so that he would have something to look at in the spring – 'my interster seeds,' he called them.

The front door opened into a long entrance-hall with a fireplace at either end. On one side there was the dining-room leading into the kitchen, pantry and servants' hall. On the other was the drawing-room in which were Grandfather Redesdale's beautiful Chinese screens and all the family portraits, including one by de Laszlo of Muv at the height of her beauty, and a terrible painting of Farve by a Belgian camouflage expert whom Farve, the least vain of men, had considered a good choice for the job. Beyond this was Farve's business-room, known as the child-proof room and fitted with a strong mortice lock. It was here that Farve did his paper-work, smoked and played his small collection of favourite records on a wind-up gramophone – 'Una voce poco fa', selections from *Iolanthe*, and that popular song, 'Fearful the death of the diver must be/Walking alone in the de-he-he-he-he-hepths of the sea'. Upstairs there were the grown-ups' bed-rooms, the children's bedrooms and nursery, and on the top floor the servants' rooms for a now quite substantial household con-sisting of governess, Nanny and nursemaid, Gladys who did all the sewing, three housemaids, two parlourmaids, a cook and two kitchenmaids.

Farve was an early riser, always up by five in the morning, prowling round the house in his Paisley dressing-gown, cigarette in hand, and drinking cups of tea out of a Thermos flask. There was little chance of sleep for the rest of the household after this hour as Farve was at his best first thing in the morning, playing his records, keeping a sharp eye on the housemaids to see that they laid the fires exactly to his specifications, or cracking stock-whips on the lawn, a technique he had learned from his pros-pecting days in Canada. Breakfast was sharp at eight for family and guests alike, and unpunctuality was not tolerated. It was in-clined to be a tense meal, as Farve could not bear to see food spilt – 'Look at that child! Spilling food on the good table-cloth!' – and his piercing blue eyes were quick to spot crumbs or any messiness with the marmalade. At luncheon and dinner, the family was always required to be in the dining-room a good five minutes before the meal was served, to 'sit in' round the table, hands warming on the empty plates in front of them, all eyes hungrily fixed on the door into the kitchen passage.

Farve took his responsibilities seriously: he was a good landlord, the tenants' cottages were always kept in repair; a pillar of the church, he attended Matins every Sunday, reading the lesson himself, choosing the hymns and taking round the bag for the collection; he sat on the local Bench, was a member of the County Council and while Parliament was in session, regularly went up to London to attend the House of Lords. He was particularly interested in, and passionately opposed to, the proposals to reform the Upper Chamber, in particular that Peeresses in their own right should be allowed to sit, according to the children because he could not bear the thought of women using the Peers' lavatory.

But although he did his duty in such matters, Farve was essentially an outdoor man. He hated paper-work and was not interested in books. Muv once tried to convert him to literature by reading aloud *Tess of the d'Urbervilles*, a story Farve found so moving that he began to weep. 'Don't be so sad,' said Muv. 'It's only a novel.' 'What! not the *truth*!' shouted Farve. 'The damned feller *invented* all that!' and he never looked at another work of fiction again – until his daughter began to write it and he found himself seduced by his own portrait. Farve disliked any form of society outside that of his immediate family and one or two tweedy neighbours who could be relied upon to hold the same philistine views as his own. What he lived for was sport. He fished, he shot, he coursed hares, before the war he had ridden regularly to hounds. Summer and winter he could be found, invariably dressed in the same costume of corduroy jacket and breeches, canvas gaiters and a moleskin waistcoat, cigarette in hand, furthering the pursuit of one of these sports. A day's shooting was what he loved most in the world, and his guns were his most sacred possessions. Although he maintained a state of constant warfare with most of the servants, Steele, the head keeper, could do no wrong, and Farve spent many of his happiest hours with Steele up on the hill above Swinbrook, leaning on his thumb-stick watching the pheasant-chicks feeding. Steele's hut, a dilapidated old railway-carriage stacked round with packing-cases full of traps from the Army & Navy Stores, was situated among the ferns and primroses of a woodland glade, as sinister a sight to the children as, in Beatrix Potter's story, Mr Tod's dreadful dwelling deep among the foxgloves. On shooting days the children knew to keep well out of the way: Farve was always at his most irritable, so anxious was he that nothing should go wrong and spoil the day's sport. As soon as breakfast was over, he would begin striding about the hall, bellowing at the dogs – 'Come here, blast you! Get off that coat!' Kick. 'Stop that noise, blast you!' – shouting for his loader, damning and blasting anyone rash enough to cross his path.

The fishing-season, on the other hand, saw Farve amiable and relaxed. He was an excellent dry-fly fisherman, and much of the year was spent happily preparing for those few weeks in summer when the trout were rising. In winter and spring, on days when it was too wet to go out, he spent hours in his business-room oiling his lines and looking through his boxes of flies. The section of the Windrush that flowed through his land was a famous trout-stream, and he was never happier than when messing about in the river in waders inventing glorious improvements for it, the small boy's dream come true. The reward for all this strenuous effort came in early June with the cry, 'The mayfly's up!' when Farve and a couple of carefully selected cronies would spend all day from dawn to dusk on the river-bank, cheerfully returning for a late dinner of asparagus, baby peas, tiny new potatoes, thick mayonnaise and trout en gêlée. In the long, light evenings, after they had been sent to bed, the children listened to the men talking and laughing on the lawn, could smell the smoke from their cigarettes, and hear the reels whirring as they pulled out their lines to dry.

The children's world revolved around their father and his varied and fascinating occupations, in which they always hoped to be included. But he was a man of chancy temper, given to sudden and terrifying rages. They never quite knew where they were with him, were never sure quite how far they dared go. They played a perpetual game of Tom Tiddler, dodging nearer and nearer their dangerous goal, ever on the alert, tensed for flight. Sometimes they got very near indeed; at other times they were pounced upon with a bellow of rage almost before they had crossed the border. This violent, unpredictable man was subject to fierce and irrational prejudice: like Uncle Matthew in *The Pursuit of Love*, he 'knew no middle course, he either loved or he hated, and generally, it must be said, he hated'. There was always one child who was the favourite, allowed every licence, while another for no visible reason was regarded by Farve as beyond the pale, and could do nothing right. Rat Week, this treatment was called, and nothing the wretched victim did could ameliorate Farve's loathing. Tom, of course, was always in favour – but Tom was a boy: the girls had to take their chance as it came. The switch from Rat Week to favourite was made with dramatic suddenness, and even after years of experience was impossible to predict.

This of course made life with Farve very exciting. To his children, their handsome and irascible parent was the epitome of English manhood. They delighted in his great charm, his dry sense of humour, in the wild, romping games, and although he frightened them with the violence of his rages which struck like sheet-lightning, they knew that at such times they were at least the focus of his undivided attention. They loved it when he allowed them to follow the shoot, or when he took them in to Oxford to skate (he was an expert skater and President of the Oxford Ice Skating Rink), and they loved those winter Sundays which Farve and Uncle Tommy spent coursing hares, the children hopping and stumbling after them across the muddy furrows while the dogs shot ahead to Farve's cry of 'Loo after it!' Greatest treat of all was the child-hunt, Farve's variation of Hare and Hounds in which he hunted the children over the countryside with his bloodhound and a mongrel terrier called Luncheon Tom. The hares never succeeded in outwitting their pursuers, and were caught usually about half a mile from home, when the dogs would be rewarded with hugs and kisses and juicy gobbets of meat.

Farve no longer hunted – the war had left him permanently weakened in stamina – but he still enjoyed riding. He had two huge horses, a bay and a grey, and on these he led the older children out for a morning's ride. If they were caught in the rain and had to shelter in the trees, he entertained them by standing up on his saddle and singing comic songs learned in the trenches: 'You could have seen the wall in China/If the weather had been finer/And it wasn't for the houses in between.' But soon after the move to Asthall, one of his horses reared up in the stable-yard and fell back on top of him, breaking his pelvis and making it impossible for him ever to sit in the saddle again. After this the children rode either with the agent, Captain Collison, or with Hooper the groom, nicknamed Choops, who suffered from shell-shock and was subject, like Farve, to uncontrollable rages. 'I'll kill yer!' he'd shout, brandishing his riding-crop at the offending child.

Muv was a very different proposition. Where David was dangerously unpredictable, Sydney was always the same – calm and remote, apparently unaware of the existence of any world outside the parochial and domestic. She was an efficient house-keeper and kept a good table; the food was of the nursery variety, plain and wholesome, but of first-class materials and perfectly cooked; she even went to the trouble of baking her own stone-ground bread, since a firm belief in the health-giving properties of wheat-germ was a basic tenet of her philosophy. Conscientiously she fulfilled her duties towards the church, the village, and the local branch of the Conservative Party, although she had no more than a mild interest in politics, and any discussion of religion she found positively distasteful.

Towards her family her manner was absent-minded and detached, perhaps something to do with the fact that her own mother had been an invalid and had died when Sydney was only seven. Muv rarely hugged or kissed her children or held them on her knee. That sort of thing was left to Nanny. She seemed to float through the day in a cloud of vagueness, apparently noticing nothing, her beautiful blue eyes hazing with boredom at the smallest provocation. But this absent-mindedness could not be entirely relied upon: it was never safe to assume that she was wholly unaware of what was going on around her. She could come to with an unexpected fit of severity, a couple of sentences of whiplash sarcasm which could be extremely cutting. In her very different way she was every bit as strict as her husband, and her brand of biting irony was just as much to be feared as his roaring, raging, whacking rampages.

As husband and wife David and Sydney suited each other remarkably well, her severity ideally complementing his explosive, emotional temperament. Like him she found domesticity satisfying, and although on occasion she enjoyed a little quiet social life, which he would happily have done without, she did not care for staying up late and was happy only in the company of people she knew well: strangers bored and fatigued her. Her husband's devotion she accepted without appearing to notice it: the way his eyes followed her as she went out of a room, the habit he had in the evenings after dinner of standing by her chair, literally falling asleep on his feet like an old horse, waiting for the moment when she was ready for bed and he could go upstairs and run her bath.

Muv took little part in the children's activities except, when necessary, to express disapproval; rarely joined in the jokes and the teasing, except to put a stop to it when it got out of hand – 'Don't be *silly*, children!' – and she remained unruffled by even the most frightful of schoolroom crises. Once Unity rushed in shrieking for help when Muv was writing letters in her sitting room. 'Muv, Muv, come quickly! Decca's climbed up on the roof and says she's going to commit suicide!' 'Oh, poor duck,' said Muv without looking up, 'I do hope she won't do anything so terrible', and went on with her writing.

Vague in manner though she may have been, Muv had firm ideas about her children's upbringing. From her father she had inherited an unorthodox attitude towards health and diet: any form of medicine, of course, was poison. And, to keep the Good Body in the best working order, strict rules of diet had to be followed. It was a favourite theory of Tap's that the Jews owed their survival to the foresight of the Mosaic Law; and Muv was determined that her children should have as good a chance of survival as the Jews. This meant that certain foods were forbidden. Pork, rabbit, hare, and shellfish were never to be eaten, nor was tinned food, the canning process not having been revealed to the wanderers in the Wilderness, which no doubt went further to explain, as Muv absolutely believed, that Jews never suffered from cancer. The pasteurisation of milk was also highly dangerous, anathema, because the process – obviously, how could it not? – removed all the Goodness from the milk. But it was the prohibition of pork that caused the children the greatest suffering. Farve, while doing nothing to contradict his wife's authority, saw no reason to apply her rules to himself. Morning after morning the children went through agonies as they smelt the bacon sizzling in the silver chafing-dish and watched their father tucking in to bacon and eggs, cold gammon, sausages or stewed pigs' brains. The first letter Tom wrote home from his private school stated simply, 'We have sossages every day' ('Oh, Muv, it's so unfair,' wailed the others when they heard this. 'If Tom can have sausage, why can't we?' 'Tom's a boy.') And Decca, when staying with a friend and allowed for once to relax the rule, wrote with mouth-watering gratitude, 'Darling Muv. Thank you so much for pemission to eat SAUSAGE. We loved them. I cut mine open and put butter and Devonshire Cream inside, and closed it, and put it in my mouth.'

The relationship between Muv and Nancy was never an easy one. Although he was too alarmingly unpredictable to get close to, Nancy adored her father, whose dry wit was the perfect foil for her sharp-tongued teasing. But with her mother she had little in common. Muv's domestic activities held small interest for her eldest daughter, whose high-spirited frivolity was, in turn, distrusted by her mother. There was no proper meeting ground, and Muv lacked the imagination to enable her to sympathise either with her daughter's intelligence, or with her strong desire to break away from the restricting Victorian world in which both her parents had been born. As a child Sydney had been obliged to grow up before her time. In charge of her father's household at fourteen, she was left with little time for the insecurity and silliness of adolescence, and in spite of her unusual upbringing, she herself was profoundly conventional. She may have had some strange ideas about health, but at heart she was a loyal member of the middle-class establishment.

Any real intimacy between Nancy and her mother had come to an end with the birth of Pam: from that time on, Nancy was on her own; she came first with nobody. The other children found companionship among themselves, but Nancy as the eldest was left out of this; for her there was no one within the family, no particular friend and ally in whom she could confide – Pam was too slow, Diana too young, Tom nearly always away. The result was that from an early age Nancy learned to conceal her emotions, to develop that highly polished veneer with which she confronted the rest of the world. Her defence – and her weapon – was the tease. Everything, however sad, painful or dispiriting, had instantly to be turned by Nancy into a joke. The only acceptable response to misfortune was to 'shriek' with laughter – 'How we shrieked!', 'Did you shriek?' – an ugly word with its underlying implication of distress. By quickly converting unhappiness or hurt into comedy, you anaesthetise the pain. The unendurable can be borne, the unpleasant made palatable or dismissed. And because you are on your own, and therefore none too secure, you must be sure to be the attacker. This way, you will be feared. This way, you win.

Nancy's sharp tongue made it impossible for her to be anybody's favourite sister. The children bored and irritated her, and she let them see it. (Years later Muv came across a home-made badge on which was written in pencil, 'Leag against Nancy, head Tom.') In her one fragment of autobiography she wrote, 'My vile behaviour to the others was partly, I suppose, the result of jealousy and partly of a longing to be grown-up and live with grown-up people.' She was jealous of the easy alliances forged, broken and re-made among the others, and she longed for the outside world and friends of her own age. She did have one or two: Constantia Fenwick, for example, who lived fifteen miles away in Stow-on-the-Wold, and sometimes rode over for the day. The two girls would organise pet shows with the village children, or would photograph each other covered in exotic draperies and 'frightfully made-up'. Sometimes, chaperoned by Zella, Nancy was invited to spend a couple of nights with Mrs Godman, a kind neighbour with a house in Moreton-in-Marsh. This was proper grown-up life – no children, late hours and six courses at dinner. 'Lord & Lady Willoughby de Broke are here,' Nancy wrote to her mother on one such visit. 'He has got a naturel wink and at first we thought he was winking at us, but it is naturel . . . Breakfast is at 9. (oh the joy of living!!) Lunch at 1.30, tea at 5 and dinner at 8. The beds here are most comfortable, & one has nothing to do but sleep or read all day, I never felt more like a boody [sic] hen in all my life . . . I will tell you what I eat at dinner

1. Soup
2. Mutton-on-toast
3. Fish
4. Souffle
5. Sardines
6. A banana.'

But most of the time Nancy was at home where, bored and restless, she amused herself by tormenting the others. Pam, the original target, was easy prey: she had none of the vivid imagination of her brother and sisters, and was further hampered by the effects of an attack of infantile paralysis when she was three, which left her physically weak and slow to learn. She was wholly without any power of retaliation or defence, easily overtired and often unwell. 'You've *got* to be kind to Pam. She's *ill*,' Nancy was always being told; and as a result was at her worst, constantly mocking Pam and spoiling any little treat that came her way. As for the others, Tom escaped much of it by being away at school, while the threat of school was a satisfying way of reducing Diana, who dreaded the idea of classrooms and dormitories and organised games, to a state of terror. 'I was talking about you to Muv and Farve,' Nancy would begin, an evil gleam in her eye. 'We were saying how good it would be for you to go away to school . . .' The three youngest girls, unpractised as yet and unsuspecting, could be made to cry about almost anything. 'Do you realise, you three,' Nancy would address herself to Unity, Jessica and Deborah (Debo), 'how awful the middle syllables of your names are – Nit, Sic and Bor?' Howls. For Debo, the most tender-hearted, easily moved to tears by the pathos of a situation often visible only to herself, Nancy devised a special instrument of torture, one which was instantly effective but which had to be used with care, as Muv was apt to get cross if she saw her youngest in tears yet again, and was quick at tracing the source of provocation. Debo was unbearably moved by a story Nancy invented about a little houseless match. 'A little, houseless match/it has no roof, no thatch/If it's alone, it makes no moan/That little houseless match.' It never failed, and eventually Nancy had only to pick up a box of matches while looking meaningfully at her sister for Debo to be reduced to floods.

Although often unkind, Nancy's teasing was very funny, and for those who were not at the receiving end it was the most gloriously enjoyable spectator sport. Best of all was when Nancy took on Farve, for with him she more than met her match. The children found it brilliantly entertaining, and loved the sparring that went on between Nancy and Farve, usually at table – on and on they would go, sniping and firing at each other to the accompaniment of gales of laughter from the others, until either Nancy, provoked beyond bearing, would burst into tears, or Farve would suddenly bellow with rage, signifying that Nancy had Gone Too Far.

Nancy's great complaint throughout her life, becoming louder as she grew older, was that she had never been allowed to go away to school. The Redesdales strongly disapproved of formal education for girls. Tom, of course, went to Eton; but Tom was a boy. A girl got nothing from going away to school except over-developed muscles and an argumentative disposition, two features unlikely to be found alluring by any marriageable young man. (Unity was the only one to go to school, and she distinguished herself by being expelled – 'Not expelled, darling,' Muv would explain, 'asked to leave' – the apocryphal reason being that, when required to recite, she had added the word 'rot' to the line, 'A garden is a lovesome thing, God wot'.) Nancy resented this deprivation for the rest of her life, and always attributed to it her lack of mental discipline. In fact, thanks to her grandfather's library, she was, even when very young, exceptionally well read, and the PNEU[1] system by which she was taught by her governesses was thorough and reliable. What she really minded was not the lack of education, but the enforced residence at home.

But in reality life at Asthall was not too much of a hardship: in many aspects it provided an ideal country childhood, and there was much that Nancy, while still a child and in spite of her longing for the world, enjoyed. In the summer there were tennis-parties, trips to Stratford-on-Avon, and visits to and from the cousins – Rosemary and Clementine Mitford[2], Dick and Dooley Bailey, Diana and Randolph Churchill[3]. In the winter there was coursing and riding and, for Nancy, upright and slender in black habit and bowler, hunting three times a fortnight on a mare called Rachel, which Farve had bought from the army at the end of the war. Nancy loved hunting, and passionately looked forward to those days, even though the wild excitement of the chase usually ended in a long, back-breaking jog home accompanied by Choops, as often as not on an exposed stretch of road and with the rain trickling down the back of her neck and into her boots. Farve never

[1] Parents' National Educational Union, a system of education by correspondence.

[2] Daughters of Farve's elder brother, Clement Mitford, who was killed in 1915.

[3] Their mother, Clementine, wife of Winston Churchill, was the daughter of Grandmother Redesdale's sister Blanche Hozier.

would allow a motor-car either to take her to the meet or to fetch her home.

On days when there was no hunting or the weather was too bad to go out, there was usually something of interest going on indoors. There was, for instance, *The Boiler*, a journal edited by Nancy, to which she herself contributed under the pseudonym W. R. Grue. 'The Horror of the Unknown Man' is a brief and cheerful murder story in the Gothic mode beginning in typically worldly vein: 'All was gaiety – laughter – the clatter of knives & forks, it was the luncheon hour at Claridges. The great Charles moved from table to table with the assured air of a made man. In a corner behind a palm tree, scarcely noticing the giddy scene around him sat a languid looking man, solitary & unperceived. Richly yet quietly dressed in a morning suit of grey tweed, a natty pearl tie-pin stuck airily into his chocolate tie the man presented a prepossessing exterior. No longer young (his age might have been anything between 30 & 40) but scarcely yet approaching senile decay, he had the air of a travelled and educated nobleman as he toyed carelessly with an hors d'oeuvre. Suddenly his appearance of noble languor vanished & he sat upright, fork in hand with all the air of one who sees his end approaching. A foreign looking individual of unprepossessing countenance & claw like hands drew near . . .'

In 1921, when Nancy was sixteen, her parents at last gave in to her pleading and sent her to school – school of a kind. Hatherop Castle, an Elizabethan manor house extensively rebuilt in the nineteenth century, was just over the border in Gloucestershire, and owned by a Mrs Cadogan who, having several daughters, had decided to educate them at home, and had invited a small number of girls from neighbouring families to join them. The girls lived very much behind the green-baize door, sleeping in the servants' quarters, two and three to a room, and looked after by the family nanny who acted as matron. Nancy rather enjoyed it, although of those spartan years after the war her chief memory was of the cold: the underfloor heating rarely worked and never penetrated the upper floors, the girls often having to break the ice in their

ewers before they could wash, with the consequence that some of
the less hardy never washed at all except on the two days a week
on which they had baths. The morning was given over to lessons –
French with Mlle Pierrat, everything else taught by an impressive
young woman, much loved by her pupils, called Essex Cholmondeley. After lunch Miss Cholmondeley read aloud to them while
they rested lying on the floor, and then, depending on the weather
and the season, there was either a walk and sketching, or netball
with Commander Cadogan, dreaded by the girls, since Duggie,
as they called him, was a great bottom-pincher. In the summer
there was swimming and tennis. Once a week Nancy had a piano
lesson, an instrument for which, unlike her brother Tom who was
very musical, she showed no aptitude whatever, yawning her way
through the hour spent in a freezing room thumping out 'The
Merry Peasant' in preparation for her lesson. Much more fun was
the Wednesday dancing-class, when Pam and Diana were driven
over from Asthall in the Morris Cowley, Turner and Nanny in
front, the two children in the dickey, like two blue-eyed little
china dolls in their dancing-frocks and sashes, arriving stiff with
cold in spite of Farve's fur-lined trench coats with which they
were covered.

When, after less than a year, Nancy left Hatherop, she brought
back with her a wonderful new tease, with which she was able to
torment her sisters for a considerable time to come. Mrs Cadogan
had instituted a troop of Girl Guides which both Nancy and her
best friend at Hatherop, Mary Milnes-Gaskell, had joined. The
high point of this was a one-day camp at Cirencester Park, an
experience which Nancy had found so inspiring that once home
she announced her intention of starting a company of her own,
with herself as Captain and Pam and Diana her patrol leaders.
The two younger girls, playing happily with their chickens and
their dogs, were appalled; neither of them believed it possible that
Muv would let Nancy get away with it. But for once Nancy had
Muv's whole-hearted support: an excellent idea, Muv thought; it
would keep Nancy occupied and be so nice for the village
children. To her sisters' dismay, indolent Nancy, usually to be

relied upon to prefer spending most of the day on the sofa with a book, became possessed of a demonic energy, ordering them about, making them tie knots, light fires and run a hundred yards in twenty seconds. She coerced them into putting on a play, took them to camp near Witney, and even up to the Wembley Exhibition where, chaperoned by the governess, they spent a miserable night in sleeping-bags on the floor of a youth hostel. Eventually, after more than a year of this persistent lack of enthusiasm, Nancy's keenness began to lose its edge, and she was at last persuaded to give it up.

In April 1922, aged seventeen, Nancy with four other girls went abroad on a cultural tour of Paris, Florence and Venice organised by Miss Spalding, headmistress of a school in Queen's Gate attended by one of Nancy's friends, Marjorie Murray. It was all very thrilling, and Nancy adored it. She wrote to her mother from their first stop, the Grand Hotel du Louvre in Paris, 'Darling Muv . . . it is so lovely here, there are telephones & hot & cold water in our bedrooms. I spend my time telephoning for baths etc. All the shops look so heavenly & the Place de la Concorde when lighted up is *too* lovely . . . Oh! such fun.' She went into raptures over the paintings in the Louvre, and reported in detail her meals. 'For lunch today we had an omelette aux fines herbes, salade de laitue (too good) & cakes. For tea café au lait & éclairs.' Without the family and in the company of girls her own age she felt quite grown-up at last. The only flaw in this scheme of perfect happiness was that Marjorie's clothes were so much smarter than hers – Nancy felt a ragbag in comparison – and that she was the only one not allowed to wear powder. This last was a recurring complaint: it was warm for the time of year, the trains were hot, her jacket and skirt much too thick, and she was uncomfortably aware of her shiny face. But on this Farve remained inflexible: he liked to see female complexions in their natural state; paint, however discreet, was not for ladies. Nancy had been allowed one concession, to wear her hair up, and that was enough.

From Paris they went to Florence, stopping on the way to see

Pisa – 'too heavenly' – the Leaning Tower and the Duomo, '*Too too too* heavenly'. In Florence she made her first serious purchase, a couple of strings of corals which reached down to her waist. Within a few days she was writing confidently to her mother, 'I am quite good at Italian already, as good as Miss S & better than any one else. I get along famously. I do all the bargaining for the others & always get things reduced. I talk as though I had been here a month & indeed I feel like it . . . As for the hotel the less said the better! I shall say nothing except that we have used Skeatings[1] freely but with little effect (I have just caught one on my neck.) . . . How you would love the blue sky here & the flowers & the oranges! We have them at every meal. NB. Please tell Chunkie [Pam] I couldn't bear to hear about chickens at present, & ask her to preserve a calm & undisturbed silence on these matters in her letters! Chickens & Florence dont mix.'

They visited the Uffizi, the Duomo and the Pitti, made a day-trip to Fiesole, and were serenaded every evening by a man with a guitar. It was *too* lovely, *too* romantic – those beautiful palaces along the Arno, the roses and wisteria, the deep blue of the sky, and, above all, the pictures. 'How I love the pictures,' she wrote. 'I had no idea I was so fond of pictures before, especially Raphael, Botticelli & Lippi . . . I find to my horror that there are lovely pictures in London, Italian ones & lots of good ones, I have only ever been to the Tate Gallery. This must be remedied! Marjorie knows the National Gallery by heart. I don't think it is too late to devellop a taste in pictures at 17 do you?'

Venice, if anything, was even more marvellous than Florence. As a rest from sight-seeing, they spent a day on the Lido, where they took off their stockings to paddle and ate oranges as they walked along the beach. Nancy bought presents for the family – bronze lizard for Pam, Leonardo print for Tom, crystals for Diana and 'Deb', corals for Bobo; and for herself a Spanish comb for her hair. 'I did a most rash thing yesterday,' she wrote to her mother, 'spent nearly all my worldly on a Spanish comb, knowing

[1] Keatings' flea powder.

full well that you won't let me wear it, altho' Marjorie says all girls do. It is so nice, not carved & looks rather like a shoe horn . . . I *do* look so nice in it (ahem!) & wore it yesterday evening for dinner. It looks most habillé. Now I am absolutely broke . . .' Nancy felt she had become very grown-up during her foreign tour, and was anxious that her mother should recognise the change. 'I hope you will let me wear that comb, it grows on me (this is not to be interpreted literally) I really look quite old in it, a femme du monde you know, especially when I wear a fur. I really am a femme du monde now.' The image of the femme du monde did occasionally slip: there was, for instance, that hilarious evening when Marigold was prevailed upon to throw her asparagus stalk over her shoulder at dinner!! And the last night in Venice saw some very unsophisticated ragging in the dorm: 'Turnip [Elsa, the Swedish girl] jumped very hard on Marigold's bed & burst her hot bottle. *Such* a mess!'

On the long train journey home Nancy felt she had nothing more to look forward to, nothing but England, cold and grey, and with all her money spent: 'It is a dreadful feeling only have 1/3 & an English shilling in the world.'

But in fact there was something to look forward to. In November Nancy would be eighteen, and the Redesdales planned a dance. 'The difficulty', as Muv so rightly said, 'seemed immense.' The library would serve beautifully as a ballroom; but whom to ask? With the exception of one or two boys from local families, like Togo Watney and Michael Mason, Nancy knew no young men. Tom was only thirteen, so his friends were no use, and Farve's unwelcoming manner ensured that few members of the opposite sex ever stepped inside the front-door. The situation was horribly similar to that 'horrible situation' described in *The Pursuit of Love* when for Linda's first dance Uncle Matthew had to go to London to round up aged partners in the House of Lords: 'Ten females, four mothers and six girls, were advancing from various parts of England, to arrive at a household consisting of four more females . . . and only two males, one of whom was not yet in tails.

'The telephone now became red-hot, telegrams flew in every direction. Aunt Sadie abandoned all pride, all pretence that things were as they should be, that people were asked for themselves alone, and launched a series of desperate appeals . . .

'Elderly cousins, and uncles who had been for many years forgotten as ghosts, were recalled from oblivion and urged to materialize . . .

'At last Uncle Matthew saw that the situation would have to be taken in hand. . .'

The occasion was not perhaps as glamorous as Nancy had hoped, but her parents had done their best: partners, even if middle-aged and married, had been produced; there was champagne, a band, and the house filled with flowers; and Farve had been persuaded to get in twenty coke braziers to place along the Cloisters so that, although the guests choked with the smoke as they ran between the house and the library-ballroom, at least they were warm. Nancy, her dark hair in a bun, and wearing a silver dress with a beaded belt, must have found this, her long-awaited entry into the world, about as disillusioning as Linda found hers – the dowdy clothes and red, shiny faces of her parents' friends, the smell from the stoves, the stilted conversation and the stumbling dance-steps: 'It is not at all like floating away into a delicious cloud, pressed by a manly arm to a manly bosom, but stumble, stumble, kick, kick. They balance, like King Stork, on one leg, while, with the other, they come down, like King Log, onto one's toes. As for witty conversation, it is wonderful if any conversation, even of the most banal and jerky description, lasts through a whole dance and the sitting out.'

The dance at Asthall, not a conspicuously successful occasion in itself, did, however, mark the beginning of a distinct change for the better, a definite improvement in the quality of life, underlined the following summer by Nancy's presentation at Court (chiefly remembered for the long wait in the Mall in a queue of cars on a chilly June day, dressed up in white satin and feathers, and no more sophisticated arrangement offered at Buckingham Palace than a chamber-pot behind a screen). After this she was officially 'out'. Parental authority was still strictly maintained – no make-up, a chaperon when in mixed company – but there were several important concessions that were now hers by right: she could go to as many balls and parties as she had invitations, she could stay in London during the Season (the Redesdales rented a house for the summer months), and she could entertain men as well as women friends at home in the country.

Nancy's first London Season, the Season of 1923, took place at a time when the behaviour of the Bright Young Things was reaching its most extreme. For the young of the upper classes, in violent reaction against the war and their parents' Edwardian attitudes, the Twenties was a period of high spirits and relentless frivolity, rocketing up and beyond all the established boundaries of manners and good taste. The young considered themselves a golden élite to whom nothing should be denied. It was a time when adults acted like children, many of them behaving as though they were still in the nursery, but in a nursery where every licence was allowed. It was an era of parties: baby parties, circus parties, Wild West parties; there were paper chases and scavenger hunts and Follow-My-Leader over the counters at Selfridge's. In spirit Nancy was very much at one with the Bright Young Things, although in fact she was never really of their world, never really penetrated beyond the sequinned fringes. While Babe Plunket Greene and Elizabeth Ponsonby were hitting the headlines with their madcap escapades, Nancy and her friends were going to the devil in a much more innocent fashion. 'I must tell you all the fun I have been having of late,' she wrote to Tom at Eton. 'On Friday the party arrived & we went to the Masons dance which was great fun but rather stiff . . . On Saturday we went out shooting & had a dance here in the evening from 9–12. I put the clock back 20 minutes which helped quite a lot! The whole of Sunday we spent in trying to think out charades to act in the evening. They didn't come off in the end because the plot wouldn't work out but we had great fun rehearsing. In the evening we made up our faces, which horrified the men especially Farve & Uncs! It did suit me so well but none of the others looked better than they do ordinarily. On Monday we went to the cinema in Oxford which was great fun only we made so much noise we were nearly turned out & then we went to tea at the Trout where we again made hay. Then we went home & shortly after left for Oxford this time to go to the ball in the town hall. It was a marvellous ball. We went & sat out in the court of Justice & found a book with the names of people who were going to be summoned so we wrote remarks such as "marvellous man" under their names until a policeman came & sent us away with a flea in our ear & removed ye booke. We also spilt a lot of ink & poured ink into the judge's glass of water. It was fun.'

In London the parties were rather more sophisticated; but even here Nancy's social life was on the whole conducted along modest lines: not for her Paris gowns and balls in the great houses of Park Lane and Belgrave Square; but two or three long frocks cleverly run up at home by Gladys, and small dances in Pont Street, Queen's Gate and Cadogan Place, escorted by one or other of her parents in full evening dress and struggling to keep awake on a hired gold chair. The day after a dance, Nancy was allowed to sleep late, getting up in time to dress in hat and gloves for a girls' luncheon, where the unremarkable events of the night before were discussed over lamb cutlets followed by pink jelly served in little glasses with a blob of cream.

Back at Asthall life was much livelier than it had been before. During the Christmas and Easter holidays there were dances at the houses of local families: the Watneys, Mrs Godman and the Masons at Eynsham Park. It was at the Masons' dance that she met a young man who was to become one of her closest friends and confidants, Mark Ogilvie-Grant. He was charming, amusing and silly, with an appetite for playing the fool equal to Nancy's own. He had a pleasant voice, and could accompany himself on the piano for hours, his repertoire full of the sort of romantic Victorian songs that Nancy loved: 'The Last Rose of Summer', 'I Dreamt that I Dwelt in Marble Halls', and, in imitation of Dame Clara Butt, 'Land of Hope and Glory'. 'Mark Ogilvie-Grant is the most amusing creature I have met for ages,' she wrote to her brother, 'fearfully vulgar & talks with a comic drawl. He has got the most cherubic face & whats known as a disarming smile. He & Johnny Drury-Lowe don't dare show their faces in Eton on account of certain episodes which I can't write but will recount when I see you!' She had met Johnny Drury-Lowe through Henry Weymouth[1], one of the few presentable young men to come to her dance, and it was Henry Weymouth who introduced her to his Oxford friends: Billy Bathurst, Michael Rosse, David Herbert and Brian Howard[2]. Oxford was easily reached from Asthall, and these new friends made a great difference to Nancy's life at home. At weekends during the term, she often asked three or four over for lunch. 'We have 4 Oxford people to lunch at Asthall on Sunday, Mary [Milnes-Gaskell] was there too, we had an uproarious lunch table in the Cloisters while Muv & Co had lunch in the dining room which was just as well! Afterwards we played tennis & bathed & they didn't go till 7. It was marvellous fun. I'm going to the House [Christ Church] ball on the 22nd. They are going to have a floor all over Peck, it will be too divine as I know thousands of people at Oxford & love them all dearly.'

Sometimes Nancy went away for the weekend. In June 1925, she was staying at Oare with the Frys, sister and brother-in-law of one of her girl-friends, Evelyn Gardner. 'It is being great fun here, the house belongs to Evelyn Gardner's brother in law & the party consists of Lady Burghclere Pansy Pakenham Evelyn & me & four v. nice men, 3 of them secretaries to Stanley B. . . . There is a lovely bathing pool in which the water yesterday was 78. Last night we motored in a Bentley & a Rolls to Savernack forest where we wandered for about an hour getting home at 11. It was the most beautiful place I have ever been in, & a marvellous sunset was going on, all most romantic. On the other side of the house there are rolling downs full of the ancient dead & terribly haunted. I hope we shall go there tonight after dinner.'

---

[1] Viscount Weymouth, heir to the Marquess of Bath.
[2] Poet and one of the most extravagant of the aesthete-homosexual circle at Oxford.

This new-found freedom was immensely enjoyable, and no one loved a good time more than Nancy; but the restrictions imposed by her parents chafed her. Before she came out, there was no question, and she knew there was no question, of any but the most circumscribed form of existence. Now, however, she had glimpsed freedom, and she longed to be off, off with her new friends having fun. Instead she was kept on a very short rein indeed. That she never had enough money could not be helped: Farve had seven children and was not a rich man; but on an income of £125 a year, which had to cover clothes, laundry-bills, travel and tips to other people's servants, she had little to spare for extravagance. 'I have got masses of shopping to do & as usual no money to do it with,' she complained to Tom. 'I keep asking everyone for money all to no effect. Bobo [Unity] gave Iain Hay a birthday & Xmas list beginning Two Pounds, a guinea etc. Don't tell Muv as she would be furious.' Even more frustrating were the rules governing her behaviour. Nancy was not allowed to powder her nose or shingle her hair; there were certain streets in London where it was not proper for her to walk (Sloane Street was proper; Pont Street was proper; Jermyn Street was improper); and, most resented of all, the rule that, except when with the family, she had to be chaperoned at all times in mixed company, a rule that was, of course, broken at every possible opportunity. Whenever they thought they could get away with it, Nancy and Mary Milnes-Gaskell, under pretext, say, of visiting Tom at Eton, would make a rendezvous to have tea with a couple of young men. 'I was sorry not to see you the other day when I left strawberries on you,' wrote Nancy to Tom on one such occasion, 'but Mary & I were meeting two Oxford chaps in Rowlands at 4.30 & then had to come straight back! Don't tell anyone, I mean about us meeting them as although I don't think it matters much for tea, least said soonest mended as the old saw hath it.' But it did matter; and inevitably one day they were caught.

What happened was this: Nancy and Mary had announced that they would be coming down from London on an evening train. In fact they went to Oxford in the morning, lunched in college with

Johnny Drury-Lowe, went to the cinema, and were spotted on their way to tea with Brian Howard by Mrs Cadogan. This responsible person wrote immediately to Muv, and the next day Nancy heard the words most instantly guaranteed to bring her heart into her mouth: 'Farve wants you in the business-room.' Farve was very angry indeed. 'Do you realise,' he roared at his terrified daughter, 'that if you were a married woman this would have given your husband grounds for divorce!' He and Muv then went up to London and interviewed Mary in her parents' house, Lady Constance, Mary's mother, making it clear that she held Nancy as the elder responsible for most of the blame. Oxford was declared out of bounds. 'There has been a hell of a row,' Nancy wrote to Tom. Muv and Farve were 'absolutely horrified, they thought it was the *most* awful thing to have done etc! . . . We have both had to promise never to do it again which is sad as it was such fun, & Farve is furious with the chaps, most unfair as it really wasn't their fault. I'm not allowed to go & stay with Johnny now for his balls which is *too* maddening.'

Gated and in disgrace, Nancy had time on her hands, much of which she spent in writing letters to her brother. Nancy was a compulsive letter-writer: writing letters was the most important occupation of her life. As a child she had kept a diary, but had given it up because a diary was unresponsive. Nancy needed a correspondent, whom she could tease and entertain, and whose existence would give a purpose to the highly selective, often fantastically exaggerated version of whatever she chose to re-count. At this period, Tom was the ideal recipient: although four years younger than she, he was clever and precocious, in many ways more grown-up than his sister; he spent most of the year away from home, and yet was familiar with all the dramatis personae; and most important of all, until Nancy was eighteen, Tom and his Eton friends were the only ambassadors from beyond the family enclosure, the only contact she had with the masculine world outside. His own letters are dull, convey nothing of his dry, sardonic humour, but hers are full of wit and fantasy. 'My dear Fatty,' she would teasingly address him. 'My dear great fat brother . . . If you keep my letters posterity will think you fairly bulged, & won't probably realise that I refer to fatty degeneration of the old brain.' When the events of the day were too dreary to describe, she made up for it with her own inventions, one of which was an imaginary language, Checkan, its origin a nursery game inspired by the names of the new countries – Jugoslavia, Czechoslovakia – formed from the old Balkan Kingdoms after the end of the war. 'Most Magic Yea I have just come across the most charming poems composed by a Checkan deaf mute employed in a stay making factory. The poor girl died not long ago (she was run over by a steam roller) & left the poems to me in her will. They are most delightful, realistic & yet never heavy. Take for example And puisache tie/ Affa ogc iens/ Imp outo ne/ Fillie fie pines/ Juir liga fro 'All day I sit/ Wasting my youth/ Making stays/ For fat old women/ Who overeat.'

When her source of ancient Checkan manuscripts dried up, she told Tom about the country where he and she would spend the rest of their lives. Kr was somewhere on the Mediterranean coast, its only inhabitant apart from Tom and Nancy was Ux, an Ethiopian mute with a mechanical crane (the crane of all work), to lift heavy weights and to bring on shore the few carefully vetted visitors. 'Nothing ugly will ever enter into our lives at all except when we leave Kr . . . All the intelligentsia from every land will flock to climb the 7000 steps or, if we know them & like them, to leap lightly into the c.o.a.w. with their luggage. When guests come we will go to greet them & say a few polite words & then they will be removed by Ux & thoroughly washed that no impurities many enter Kr.'

In 1926, Asthall was sold. The plan was for the female members of the family to spend the last three months of that year in Paris, while Farve saw to the preparation of the new house, Swinbrook, and completed the purchase of a house in town: with four out of the six daughters still to come out, and possibly six weddings to follow, it made sense to buy a London house rather than be obliged to rent one every season.

In October, Muv and the girls settled in to a modest hotel in the

Avenue Victor Hugo, chosen for its proximity to the Helleus, with whom, since the days of Tap and the yacht and summers at Deauville, there had been a warm friendship. His younger daughter Paulette got on well with the Mitford girls: and Helleu himself, whose violent and tyrannical temperament made Farve seem a model of tolerance and calm, was always strongly influenced by his visual sense, and greatly admired this handsome English family. With the beautiful Diana, aged sixteen, he was half in love, drawing her classical features again and again. 'Voici la Grèce!' he would proclaim as he led her into the room, a flattering change from Nanny and 'Nobody's going to be looking at *you*, darling.'

The two eldest girls did not, like the younger ones, have to do lessons. Nancy took art classes – oils in the morning, drawing in the afternoon – and spent the rest of her time sightseeing and shopping ('I bought myself a dress today in which I look exactly like one of Napoleon's young officers – too divine'). She and Pam enjoyed a rather more glamorous social life than they were used to at home. One of Nancy's girlfriends, Middy O'Neill, was in Paris staying with her grandfather, Lord Crewe, the British Ambassador, so there were invitations for the Mitfords to luncheons and dinners at the British Embassy, as well as music parties, dancing at the Florida, and grand soirées at the Robert de Rothschilds'. At weekends the two girls went several times to stay with a French family with a château just outside Paris where, Nancy boasted to Tom, 'I completely got off with a young Frenchman who is said to be le jeune homme le plus séductif du pays'.

In short, Paris was a success. Nancy loved the social life and the comparative liberty; she loved meeting new people and had revelled in her own conquests, her 'getting off', as she so elegantly described it. But more importantly these three months marked the beginning of a life-long love affair with France. From this time onwards France, and Paris in particular, represented to Nancy everything that she loved, and England, increasingly, everything that she did not love. France was freedom, elegance and sophistication; it was delicious food, sparkling conversation, prettiness and warmth. The French were frivolous and fun, and pleasure to them was a reason for living, rather than something to be treated with disapproval and distrust. 'Have you noticed the country round Paris,' she wrote to Tom on his first visit there a year later. '. . . & have you been to the Avenue Henri-Martin? Don't go on purpose but if you are there tell me if you don't think it more perfect & melancholy than any place you've ever seen. I don't know why but I waited for a bus there once & when the bus came I was in tears. At Versailles I always cry buckets its really most embarrassing to go there with me as I sob most of the time. I hope you walk about the streets of Paris waving a large & wet pocket handkerchief. And then one can be more cheerful there than anywhere in the world & I have often danced all down the Champs Elysées & no one notices they are so used to that sort of thing . . . Oh, I'm so excited, I think all day La Muette, Place de la Concorde, Place de L'Etoile, Avenue Hoch, Avenue du Bois, Place des Vosges, Palais Royal, Rue de Rivoli . . . Oh how divine.'

CHAPTER THREE

Growing Up

By Christmas the family were back in England and settled into
their new town house, 26 Rutland Gate, an imposing, cream-
coloured Victorian residence in a tree-shaded-square facing
Hyde Park. Muv had been responsible for the decoration, and
with her Frenchified taste had made it into a house of which even
the critical Nancy approved. It was a large house of six storeys,
with a ballroom on the first floor and a spacious drawing-room in
which Muv had put her French furniture from Asthall. Downstairs on the ground floor was the dining-room, and Farve's
study, for which he had chosen the curtain material himself,
a dark tapestry of dingy foliage which the children hated,
but through which he imagined he saw birds and squirrels
peeping.

For Nancy the return to England was marked by some important concessions. She was now twenty-two; her début was
four years ago, and several of her contemporaries were already
married. Childish she may have been, but she was no longer a
child; and, as a sign of her adult status and in the face of
stony-faced opposition from Muv, she had, greatly daring, gone
to a coiffeur in Paris and had her hair shingled. She was thrilled
with the result but, as the time drew near for her to go home and
face Farve, she wrote nervously to Tom: 'Tom, when you see my
shingled hair you *are* to say – in front of the Birds[1] – how you
simply adore it etc even if you think its too beastly . . . Muv said
the other day "well anyhow no one would look at you twice now."
As a matter of fact I've been much more admired since I cut it off

[1] Muv and Farve.

& everyone else says they like it much better! So lovey your role in this matter has now been indicated.'

With the confrontation over her hair behind her, Nancy then went on to wrest from Farve, after a couple of stupendous rows and much shouting and banging of doors, his agreement that she should enrol for a course at the Slade, and not only that (extraordinary in itself, given Farve's derisive opinion of modern art), but also permission to live away from home in a furnished bed-sitting room during the week. This last tremendous achievement was, however, completely wasted. Nancy abandoned her liberty – a small room in a boarding-house in Queen's Gate – after only four weeks, explaining to her sisters (who had been beside themselves with envy and correspondingly shocked by her failure) that it was no good: too squalid, the room knee-deep in underclothes, because, you see, no one to put them away.

The Slade was then under the directorship of the great Professor Tonks, a tall, thin, hawk-eyed cynic with little patience for the untalented, among whom, it has to be said, Nancy must unfortunately be counted. The two masters, nicknamed by Nancy the Bullies, were so awful to her, she wailed to Tom: 'They come up & say What a *very* depressing drawing I wonder how you manage to draw so foully, have you never had a pencil in your hand before . . . I now burst into loud sobs the moment one comes into the room, hoping to soften them.' She didn't stick it for long: the lack of encouragement was too depressing, and there was little time for fun as she had to leave Rutland Gate soon after nine and did not return home till the late afternoon. At lunchtime she usually managed to persuade Middy, or a loyal sister with time on her hands, to join her for a snack in Heal's or a sixpenny plate of what they contemptuously referred to as 'decaying vegetation' at Shearn's vegetarian restaurant. Every evening she went out, boasting to Diana dying of boredom in the country, 'I'm having a wonderful time, dances nearly every night especially before Lent, one week I danced five nights running & a play the 6th night & again Monday Tuesday Wednesday of the next week.' When nothing better was offered she went to the cinema with Middy, and those two (in their own eyes) sophisticated young women would reduce each other to fits of laughter by loudly pretending to be Germans. 'Every time someone came in we said Der ess Franz or Gert or Wilhelm & waved at them with our hankies We also quarrelled in guttural tones about whether we hated England or France most, & ate chocolates noisily. At last John Child, who was with us, was so shamed that he went. It really was fun & we laughed quite a lot.'

When at weekends Nancy came home, it was to the new house, Swinbrook. Farve had promised great things of Swinbrook. Originally a Georgian farmhouse, it had been extensively rebuilt to his exacting specifications. There was to be a squash court and tennis court, and each daughter for the first time was to have a room of her own. But, until the actual move, no one had seen it. The family had been in Paris, then Muv on her return had been too busy supervising the move into Rutland Gate to spare the time to look at what was going on – an oversight for which she now deeply blamed herself. For Swinbrook was a disaster. The situation, it is true, was beautiful, up on the hill a mile outside the village and overlooking the green and gentle Windrush valley. But the house itself was hideous, a great, grim stone barracks entirely without grace or charm, in appearance closer to an institution than a family home. Inside the look was crudely rustic with rough-hewn stone fireplaces, heavy oak beams and doors made of unseasoned elm which warped and let through the draughts. It was a cold house and coldest of all were the children's bedrooms on the top floor where fires were not allowed; in the winter the girls often woke to find their sponges solid with ice. The younger ones spent many winter afternoons giggling and whispering in the linen cupboard, a warm, cosy little room with a window, lined with hot-water pipes[1]. There was no privacy, no quiet library where Tom could play the piano and Nancy lie curled up on the sofa reading. Tom never played now as the piano

[1] The Swinbrook linen-cupboard was, in *The Pursuit of Love*, transformed into the Hons' cupboard, meeting-place of the Radlett children's secret society.

was in the drawing-room, a busy communal centre where people
were always dashing in and out and banging the door; and the
books had been put in Farve's business-room where visitors were
not encouraged. 'Deep depression has the Mitford family in its
clutches,' Nancy wrote to Tom soon after they moved in. 'The
birds never speak save to curse or groan & the rest of us are
overcome with gloom Really this house is too hideous for words &
its rather pathetic attempt at aesthetic purity makes it in my
opinion worse. I mean I would rather it were frankly hideous
Victorian because then it would at least have atmosphere whereas
at present it is like a barn rather badly converted into a temporary
dwelling place & filled with extremely beautiful & quite in-
appropriate furniture . . .

'However we have much to be thankful for having a roof over
our head I always have said.'

Farve was hurt by the family's lack of appreciation, and roared
as though in pain at Nancy's barbed remarks about 'The Buildings' or 'Swine Brook', as she called the house. (Her letters to her
father were now addressed to Builder Redesdale, The Buildings,
South Lawn – the original name of the house.) He gave up his
beloved fishing altogether and was away from home much more
often, in winter in London, taking refuge in the House of Lords
and in his club, and in summer going up to Scotland to shoot.

Once the season was over at the end of July, Nancy herself went
north for a round of house-parties. It was something to do,
although she had little in common with the hearty, sporting
couples, all tweeds and twin-sets, who spent August north of the
Border, the husbands damning and blasting their way across the
grouse-moors while their wives spent the day embroidering
chair-covers and discussing the servant-problem. The servant-
problem was of small interest to Nancy, nor did she much care for
following the guns and having to sit in the butts for hours at a time
in total silence and frozen to the marrow. As she did when at
home, she read and read (Byron, Edith Sitwell, Oscar Wilde) and
wrote long letters to her brother. 'I'm going to write a stirring
poem against hearties. Aren't they too loathesome. Most of them.

Lets have an anti-sport league. Lets go quite soon to Kr [their imaginary country] . . . Let's go abroad for *two* years together, we could buy a small palace in Venice by way of a pied-à-terre & a very tiny but luxurious flat in Paris. Then we could take the Rolls & go all over the place, in fact I can't see why we should ever return to England at all, unless to attend to the publication of our poems & even that we could easily do by letter, Byron did. Then we can search all Europe for a suitable site for Kr & then while its being built we'll go to Ethiopia to get a good cheap Ethiopian & after that we shall be quite rangé.'

But meanwhile she was in Scotland, staying at Aden, the Milnes-Gaskells' house, where she was saved from complete despair by the presence of Archer Clive, a handsome young Grenadier Guards officer from Herefordshire, who with his sister Mary were allies in the war between aesthete and hearty. Both were lively and agreeable, occasionally read books, and Archer's half-flirtatious banter Nancy found immensely exhilarating. 'Archer is being too beastly,' she wrote delightedly to Tom. 'He never spoke to me yesterday except to say he'd like to bang my head on the floor & the day before he said among other acid remarks that if it weren't for my extraordinary ideas and my men friends I should be quite nice. Is this behaving like an officer & gentleman?' Unfortunately, after a few days the Clives left, to be replaced by 'Two perfectly dire people . . . by name of Meynell . . . The boy is nul – they both are. Most objectionable I call them. Mary & I are going to try & shock them by pretending we drug. Margaret Leicester Warren (whom I can't *stand*) is also here & I am miserable because the Clives (who I adore really) have gone . . . If Mary weren't here I'd commit suicide. I think perhaps Margaret L W is the worst because she's by way of being intellectual & wrote a brochure on Reynolds!!!!!!!! I sigh for Archer because he is at any rate a very *alive* person with extremely sound if unoriginal ideas & I like arguing with him. All these people are like half dead flies. Blast them. However Mary says they are very frightened of me which cheers me enormously.'

Farve joined her at Aden and they went on to stay with

Great-Aunt Mabell Airlie[1] at Airlie Castle. Aunt Mabell,
although formidable in appearance with her stately deportment
and high pompadour of white hair – she was Lady of the
Bedchamber to Queen Mary whom in style she rather resembled
– was fond of young people and easy to get on with, full of jokes
and pleasant pastimes ('Aunt Mabel told our fortunes last night &
Farve is going to prison for 7 years!!!!'). Here Nancy found a life
of Byron, for whom she had developed a romantic passion. 'I have
to read it in private though because I'm sure Aunt M wouldn't
think it pure – it isn't at all. The wardrobe in my room belonged to
Melbourne's sister Lady Cowper so I like to think that the lovely
Caroline Lamb probably gazed at herself in the mirror of it . . .
Darling angel Byron theres no one alas like that now. What a dull
age we do live in to be sure, imagine living in 1812 sort of date
with Napoleon Byron Shelley Keats Lady Hamilton Caroline
Lamb & all sorts of other fascinating people alive. Of course Mrs.
Hemans lived then too which is rather a come down & we *have* got
the Sitwells & Brian [Howard]!!!!!' Archer was still very much on
her mind. His sister Mary had been writing to Nancy encouraging
her to read Kipling, but Nancy couldn't take to Kipling's 'awful
poems': it was Mary's brother she wanted to hear about, not her
taste in poetry. 'Sometimes do lets invent a code, there is
something I want to say now but Muv's awful theory that one
should never write down anything that couldn't be read in court
puts me off somewhat . . . I shall probably marry quite soon &
then I shall be so taken up with having babies & things that you'll
never see me & certainly never hear from me from years end to
years end. Boo what a truly pleasing prospect. If only I had any
real talent I would so much rather remain single like Edith
Sitwell. No I think it would probably be nicer to be married really
or shall I become a celebrated demi mondaine one of the really
snappy ones. I'm afraid my face is too round you need a long &
somewhat haggard one for that.'

---

[1] Mabell, Lady Airlie, was the widow of the 6th Earl of Airlie, brother of
Grandmother Redesdale.

After leaving Airlie, she and Farve parted company, Nancy to go on to Cullen to stay with a new friend, Nina Seafield, a cousin of Mark Ogilvie-Grant. Nina was a peeress in her own right, having inherited her title, Countess of Seafield, at the age of nine. At the age of nine, she inherited, too, vast estates in Scotland and an immense fortune. That such a young girl – two years younger than Nancy – should be in possession of such enormous wealth seemed to Muv not at all a Good Thing: she was afraid that Nina would be wild and have a bad influence on Nancy. For this reason she did what she could, without actually forbidding it, to discourage the friendship. 'I had a terrific fight with Muv about staying with Nina & she said at last go if you like but I'd rather you didn't which is always so unsatisfactory so I said I'd go . . . I think at 22 one is old enough to choose ones own friends dont you, especially as I'm to pay for it myself.' But Nina wasn't really wild: Muv need not have worried. A merry, dumpy little thing with red hair, white skin and an unmistakable resemblance to Queen Victoria, Nina was rather shy. The company she most enjoyed was that of her cousin Mark and his aesthete friends, such as Harold Acton, Oliver Messel and Brian Howard, the sort of young man in fact with whom Nancy was happiest. But on this occasion there was no party at Cullen. 'All those young men have gone off to Mount Athos to stay in the monastery there doesn't it sound divine.' Nancy revelled in the luxury of Cullen, a great, gaunt, baronial pile like a Victorian setting for *Hamlet*. She could lie in bed as late as she pleased, read all the latest books and magazines, gossip and giggle with Nina, and like a naughty schoolgirl experiment with drink. 'I am *very* drunk on one of Nina's cocktails,' she wrote to Tom. 'Gosh I am feeling funny all dizzy do you know. Nina's cocktails are pure gin & vermouth as far as I can make out & one drinks 'em out of enormous wine glasses. I really must give up this pernicious habit or my young health will be ruined & I shall rush round at Swinbrook having d.t.s. a dreadful fate for so young a virgin & so shaming for my family. *There* its dinner time I must sway downstairs with a hiccough so will finish later.'

In October Nancy was back in London. As the house in Rutland Gate was let, it was arranged that she should board with Middy O'Neill who was living with her grandmother in Queen's Gate. Lady O'Neill was even more of a disciplinarian than Farve and the two girls were constantly in trouble, their most innocent pastimes construed as 'wanton depravity'. The worst row was the consequence of an afternoon party for which Nancy, in a dashing attempt to emulate the 'theme parties' of the Bright Young Things, hired a Punch and Judy show from Harrods. She and Middy invited about twenty friends, including her Uncles Rupert and Jack, and the fun had, it is true, got a little out of hand – '[It] was a huge success & everyone got so worked up & rowdy that finally Pat [Cameron] was rolled up in a dust sheet & carried to the bath room where the more fervent spirits were with difficulty dissuaded from plunging him in the bath!' This was more than enough for Lady O'Neill: the girls were accused of holding an orgy and Nancy was sent home in disgrace.

Although Nancy never came to like Swinbrook, 'the horror of the Buildings is greatly mitigated for me as I have been given a room for studio,' she wrote to Tom. 'I literally live in it all the time, just seeing the birds at meal times. I am writing in it now. You can imagine what a difference this makes, living in that communal room surrounded by shrieking babies was no joke.' She filled in the time by learning to drive, learning to ride astride, taking a course in Burford on the Romantic poets ('Tom how *can* you read philosophical meaning into Keat's [sic] odes?'), and guitar lessons from a truly sweet little man in Oxford. 'My piece is called Rock Waltze & I play about a note a minute & Middy said in rather a tired voice as I played the same bar for the 50th time "we shall all be dancing to it soon" . . .'

All this was perfectly agreeable and came well within the definitions of suitable behaviour for an unmarried daughter. What was not considered suitable, however, were the friends she chose to invite to the house. To Nancy's girl-friends Farve had no objection, indeed often went out of his way to be charming; but her men friends he could not abide. Muv, too, disapproved of them – 'What a set!' she would exclaim in disgust – but at least while they were in the house she kept her feelings to herself. Farve, on the other hand, could be frighteningly rude. He despised and disliked these effeminate young men who didn't know one end of a gun from the other, and he made no effort to conceal his dislike. 'Sewer' was his favourite epithet when referring to them: 'Damned sewers!' One young man was thrown out of the house when Farve caught sight of a comb peeping out of his breast-pocket; another was threatened with a horse-whipping for putting his feet on the sofa; the shy and diffident Peter Watson was referred to, in his hearing, as 'that hog Watson'; and Jim Lees-Milne, a quiet boy who had been at Eton with Tom, provoked a terrifying explosion at dinner by venturing the opinion that it was long enough after the end of the war for anti-German propaganda to stop. 'You damned young puppy!' Farve shouted, white with rage, and, getting up from the table, stalked out of the room. It was behaviour which left Nancy very nearly as angry as her father. 'I sometimes think that parties here are more *misery* than *pleasure* . . . I haven't been in such a ghastly temper for years & for once wasn't at all put about by Farve's furious shouting & would gladly have been *very* rude to him . . . Really parties here are *impossible* The truth is that the poor old man having no building left to do is in a *very bad* temper.'

Intolerable though this was, it must be said in Farve's defence that Nancy's young men might have been expressly designed to annoy him. Frivolous and effeminate, they lolled about the drawing-room shrieking with laughter and repeating outrageous stories about each other, retailed in the exaggerated idiom of the period – 'utterly divine!', 'too too sick-making!' The sight of them in their Charvet ties, polo-necked sweaters and Oxford bags drove Farve, of the canvas gaiters and sensible moleskin waistcoat, into a frenzy. Just occasionally he would inexplicably take a liking to one of them. Mark, for instance, became a great favourite, a position almost as difficult to endure as that of sewer, for Farve liked the company of his favourites, particularly at meals. Mark was expected to be down for breakfast punctually at

eight to be greeted by Farve's roar of welcome as he lifted the lid
of the silver chafing-dish, 'Brains for breakfast, Mark!' The two
youngest girls, Decca and Debo, made up a tiresome ditty with
which they dogged Mark's every appearance: 'Brains for breakfast, Mark! Brains for breakfast, Mark! Oh, the damn sewer! Oh,
the damn sewer!'

Another exception was Robert Byron. Like Nina, he bore an
uncanny resemblance to Queen Victoria, a quality which, late at
night and after too much to drink, he was given to exploiting,
pulling down his eyes and placing a napkin on his head. At Oxford
he was one of the first to start the cult for Victoriana, filling his
rooms at Merton with Berlin-work pictures and shell flowers
under glass domes. He specialised in professing unconventional
opinions which he defended with passion, at the same time
pouring scorn on the more traditional tastes of his friends. Trash!
Muck! Rubbish! he would shout when the conversation turned to
the works of Shakespeare or the sculpture of classical Greece.
Nancy found him entrancing. 'Isn't Robert simply killing,' she
wrote to Tom. 'I love it when he talks about poetry & books, he
seems to hate everything which ordinary people like!' Greatly
daring, she invited him to Swinbrook. But, 'Would you believe it,
the family really liked Robert! We had a perfectly wild weekend
. . . Honestly I've never laughed so much. We got up a terrible
hate for Princess Elizabeth . . . We are spreading the rumour that
she has webbed feet . . . Altogether I've never enjoyed a party in
this house so much before.'

There were moments when Nancy half understood that there
was something missing from her life. She told Tom that she
worried about being 'two-dimensional'. 'How is one to find the
perfect young man, either they seem to be half-witted or half
baked or absolute sinks of iniquity or else actively dirty like John
Strachey. All very difficult!' There had been a couple of nearly
perfect men, the very handsome Archer Clive and the very
handsome Henry Weymouth; but Weymouth was in love with
another girl, whom he shortly afterwards married, and Archer
had been kept at a distance by the sharpness of Nancy's tongue.

What she failed to realise was how wounding her mockery could be. But, with her pretty young men, she was on terms of equality: they were the ideal companions for all the silliness of her long-delayed childhood; and they in turn found her teasing and high spirits delightful. She was never moody, and there was no danger of any emotional or sexual entanglement. It was all very harmless, very childish, and the greatest possible fun.

Then, in the early summer of 1928, Nancy fell in love with the most shimmering and narcissistic of all the beautiful butterflies of that homosexual coterie. Hamish St Clair Erskine was the second son of the Earl of Rosslyn. His father was a womaniser and compulsive gambler, the original of 'The Man Who Broke the Bank at Monte Carlo', a man of great character and charm, almost wholly lacking in a sense of familial responsibility. His son Hamish was small, dark and slender, with delicate features and studiedly winning ways. He had been awarded a scholarship to Eton which his father wouldn't allow him to accept as he thought it common to be a 'Tug', and while there was taken up by the actress, Tallulah Bankhead, whom he had met through Freda Dudley Ward, a close friend of his mother's. It was she who introduced him to that theatrical, night-club world of high camp and heavy drinking which Hamish found to be his element. He was amusing, he was silly and above all he was vain. He lived to be admired; and Nancy thought he was wonderful. She got to know him when he was in his first year at New College. In May he was invited to Swinbrook for a weekend, which was predictably disastrous. Nancy wrote excitedly to Tom, 'Mark says Hamish is an absolute sink of iniquity and even knows about things Mark had never heard of!' In August, she and Hamish and Mark went up to Scotland to stay with Nina, where the four of them giggled and shrieked and behaved in a manner they were happily convinced was perfectly outrageous.

'Last night we had a midnight party in Nina's sitting room, it was so awful because Nina & Mark went downstairs to get some drink leaving H & me alone & who should come in but Sparkie [Nina's mother] Hamish just had time to get under the divan & I was left looking fearfully stupid while *awful* snorts & upheavals came from under the divan.

'Tonight we're going to have a *real* midnight feast in a temple near the sea . . . We spent all day to-day bathing & sun bathing on the beach, Mark made an awful figure in the sand with jelly fish breasts, you can't simply imagine what it looked like Very lewd. Hamish & I have invented a new word, troll for a male trollop isn't it fearfully good we invented it during an awful lunch party here today with old neighbours who kept on asking Hamish when he left Eton and who's house he was at. It was fearfully funny.'

The nursery behaviour continued.

Dearest Old Bottom [Tom] . . . My dear this visit is being a perfect orgy, if only you were here you don't know what you've missed We haven't once been to bed before 2, pyjama parties every night in Nina's sitting room which is like a gala night at the Florida. Last night we had a dress up dinner. Hamish & I draped our middles in calf-skin chiffon & wore vine leaves I had a wreath of red roses & I curled Hamishes hair with tongs, he looked more than lovely. Mark just came in a bathing dress & a wreath & Nina was a lady at the court of Herod. You should have seen the Troll [Hamish] & me standing in a bath together staining our bods with coffee!!! In the afternoon we all olive-oiled each other & lay in the sun in a minimum of bathing dresses in a pretty scene, I'm literally black now!

Hamish is going to ask his mother if I can go & stay with them in Mull for a few days which I should awfully enjoy. He is such an angel isn't he . . .

Hamish Nina & I wrote the gossip for the next Vogue & put in lovely things about ourselves of course. I pray it will be published. I was "that vivid creature Miss Nancy M. She is a strikingly beautiful & witty girl" & Hamish was a brilliant conversationalist & exceptionally good shot. Oh the fun of it!

Well so long pig-face be good N

Back in London Nancy moved in to Rutland Gate, where she was able to entertain her friends without the risk of a savaging by

Farve as soon as they walked in at the door. 'It is nice to have this really lovely house to ask people to, such a change from old Swin where I really feel ashamed to have any guests and one simply couldn't have anybody artistic to stay there lest they sicked in the front hall.' She gave luncheon and small dinner parties, including one for her friend Evelyn Gardner, who had recently become engaged 'to a man called Evelyn Waugh who writes, I believe very well, he wasn't able to come'. She went to dances at the Savoy and suppers at the Ritz, and, one of the highlights of the Season, a fancy-dress pageant. 'Nina & I & Patrick Balfour[1] went to the Pageant of Hyde Park through the ages on Tuesday . . . Mark looked lovely in a white wig & knee breeches & Oliver Messel was *too* wonderful as Byron, I nearly fainted away when he came limping on to the stage, this proves that I must have been Caroline Lamb in a former incarnation He built up his face with putty & looked the living image of Byron. Stephen Tennant[2] as Shelley was very beautiful Lord Furneaux was a modern "young-man-about-town" & Frank Packenham [sic] in a sailor suit rode on one of those enormous bicycles.' The letter continues, 'Yesterday I went to a cocktail party in Oliver's studio which was *greatest* fun. He just had Nina Mark Johnny & me so we had a very amusing gossip over the fire. He's got a lovely studio & oh Boysie he *can* paint . . . Did I tell you I met Harold Acton the other day, he's *fascinating* I think.'

But, although London undeniably had its attractions, during the University term Nancy for once in her life preferred to be at Swinbrook, in reach of Oxford and of Hamish. Being in love with Hamish was not easy. Both fathers, Rosslyn and Redesdale, disapproved of the association, and Hamish himself was an elusive figure – spoilt, volatile, difficult to pin down. 'My life is dark & gloomy, full of reverses & set backs of every kind,' Nancy wrote to Tom in October 1928. 'This morning Hamish rang up &

[1] Society columnist and author, succeeded as third Baron Kinross in 1939.
[2] Painter, eccentric and flamboyant homosexual, brother of the second Baron Glenconner.

I arranged to lunch with him on Monday, no sooner done than Farve announces that he will be at the County Council on Mon & will give me lunch. Double hell. Triple damn. Buckets of blood. A virgins way is set about with sharp thorns & the eyes of the curious . . . I was quite cheered up at the idea of seeing Hamish who never fails to amuse, in fact he is the most amusing character I know, such a mass of affectation but au fond so very sweet. I think he is most amusing when he is posing as "I am such a darling little child do stroke my hair & tell me a story or shall we play at ogres" He is amusing, but less so, when he is being a very grown up man of about 40 who has been the greatest rake in every court in Europe. He's simply killing when he's being just an ordinary snob. In short I was looking forward to some entertainment on Monday & now piff-pouff oh la-la. So I hope you sympathise quite enormously. Also Mary & Middy are coming tomorrow & if theres one thing I *don't* feel the need of at present it is girl-friends. I have just read Byrons Vision of Judgement it is stupendous. I think I shall die young. I think I shall burst into floods of tears, I think I had better stop depressing you so farewell bee in my bonnet bat in my belfry, beetle in my bloomers really I think its time I stopped Adieu N.'

Four days later Tom was informed, 'I did lunch with Hamish after all yesterday, I had the bright idea of asking him if Diana & Bryan [Guinness] could come too & telling the nesting ones [Farve and Muv, 'the Birds'] that we were going to lunch in a cafe so all was well, & after lunch Hamish & I went off in one direction & the other two in another & it was all great fun H. seems to be having a riotous time as you would expect knowing the child but says there's *no* one worth talking to in Oxford. He's got a very nice room indeed I suggested he ought to have one or two aspidistras to which he replied with dignity "this room is going to be made nice, not funny" . . . Hamish wasn't a sweet little baby once yesterday its *too* disappointing I'm sure Oxford will make him stop that, but he was very sweet all the same, I *am* fond of him.'

But Tom, Nancy's most trusted confidant, now let her down.

He did not approve of the relationship, as he felt obliged to make clear. While at Eton Tom himself had had an affair with Hamish, and he knew him for what he was, a vain, shallow, silly little tart. As soon as he left school, Tom had turned with enthusiasm to women, but Hamish remained basically homosexual. In point of fact, what he responded to was admiration, and, like all good prostitutes, he was a chameleon, able to be all things to all men, or women. But one thing was clear: he was unlikely to marry. And, if Nancy believed that he was going to change in this respect, she would be made very unhappy.

But Nancy did believe it, and she strongly resented Tom's criticism. Hamish had a heart of gold, he was funny, he was clever, and she absolutely adored him. In place of Tom, she turned to Mark, a far more sympathetic recipient of her confidences. 'Hamish *was* funny yesterday I do wish you'd been there to wink at, he had 5 glasses of brandy & creme de menthe (on top of sherry etc) & then began to analyse himself He said "The best of *me* is that I can talk Homer to Maurice [Bowra] as well as Noel Coward to you, in fact I am clever enough to amuse everybody" I was faintly peeved at being put in the Nowel Coward class! I do worship that child!'

During the vacation, the two of them skipped about in London, playing the fool at parties and dashing off to nightclubs whenever either of them had a little money to spend. (Hamish was wildly extravagant, and kept very short by his father: any money Lord Rosslyn had not himself managed to gamble away, he certainly was not prepared to hand over to his son to do likewise.) 'We went to the Café de Paris . . . Well then we found (when we'd got there) that after paying the bill we had 7½d between us We were panicking rather when the sallow & disapproving countenance of old Mit [Tom] was observed. He cut Hamish but lent me £1 & we went to the Bat. As we never pay there now we are treated as poor relations & put behind the band where we can neither see nor hear & we have the buttered eggs that the Mountbattens have spat into & left. All so homey & nice dont you think. Still I feel we lend a certain *ton* to the place. Hamish has been an angel lately, not drinking a thing, I really think bar all the good old jokes which no one enjoys more than I do, that he has *literally* the nicest nature of anyone I know.'

In spite of his nice nature, it was inevitable that Hamish should cause Nancy a great deal of disquiet. He was for ever letting her down, cancelling arrangements at the last minute, telling her he didn't know whether he loved her or not. A previously unsuspected maternal instinct led Nancy to try and cherish Hamish and protect him. She loved to indulge him, and her small earnings were often spent either on paying his racing debts or on buying him presents. For his twenty-first birthday in August 1930, Nancy paid more than she could afford for a pair of gold-backed hairbrushes. She wrote to Tom, 'I'm shattered because I've got him some gold hair brushes for his birthday & he let fall yesterday that he hates gold hair brushes. Isn't it awful for me, they are so expensive too & I can't change them now as they've got initials.' Nancy worried, too, about his drinking and his gambling and the debauched life he led at Oxford, and she was intensely jealous of the pretty, smartly dressed girls in whose company Hamish delighted: Romie (Rosemary) Hope-Vere was one ('I *loathe* Romie H.V. but dont tell Hamish because he adores her & I have to pretend I do too'), Cecil Beaton's sister Nancy was 'another cross I have to bear . . . Will he ever grow out of liking all these painted dolls I wonder or will our house overflow with them always?' Bravely, Nancy tried to convince herself that basically Hamish was sound, and that once they were married (and there was no doubt that one day they *would* marry) everything would be all right. Meanwhile there was a lot to put up with. 'Oh dear *how* unhappy Hamish does make me sometimes,' she wailed to Mark. 'I'm so exactly the wrong person for him really that I simply can't imagine how it all happened. Its all most peculiar. But sometimes I really wish I were dead which is odd for me as I have a cheerful disposition by nature. Im sorry to grumble like this. I really do honestly think everything would be all right if we were married.' Marriage and children and a home of her own were what she longed for; and in Hamish she could not have picked a more unsuitable candidate to provide them for her. In his way, he was fond of her: she amused him, he liked having a partner to show off with at parties, and the fact that she thought herself in love with him was highly flattering. But he had no intention of getting married. 'I love myself so much,' he used to giggle. 'I'd marry myself if I wasn't so bad with myself in bed.'

The agonising saga continued. 'Oh Mark talk about getting to know each other or knowing ones own mind – if I had been married to Hamish for 5 painful years & born him 6 male children I couldn't know him better & the curious thing is that I'm quite certain that I shall never never be so fond of anyone again.' But everything was against her. Hamish refused to commit himself, and Farve had written yet again to Lord Rosslyn 'complaining we see each other too much. Oh my life is too difficult between trying to manage Hamish & the family.' As neither of them could meet under their parents' roofs, Nancy depended very much on the hospitality of her friends, in particular on Helen Dashwood, newly married to Sir John Dashwood, owner of a large and beautiful house in Buckinghamshire, and the once hated Romie Hope-Vere, now married to Johnny Drury-Lowe ('I like Romie now') and with a little house in Camberley where both Nancy and Hamish were invited to stay.

The most welcome asylum, however, was provided by Diana. At the end of 1928, and much against her parents' wishes, Diana had become engaged to Bryan Guinness of the brewing family, a gentle, literary young man of great good looks and an immense fortune. Both Redesdales were against it: they thought Diana at eighteen much too young and Bryan much too rich. (Muv with her instinct for thrift did not like the idea that Diana, hardly out of the schoolroom, should have at her disposal one of the biggest fortunes in England.) Diana, however, was determined. She was fond of Bryan, and she was desperate to leave home. This was her way out. 'The more I see of Bryan,' Nancy shrewdly noted, 'the more it surprises me that Diana should be in love with him, but I think he's quite amazingly nice.' Eventually her parents gave in, and Diana and Bryan were married on January 30, 1929, at the society wedding of the year. Nancy, in a huge crinoline of white tulle, was one of the ten bridesmaids.

However much, privately, she may have minded that her sister, nearly six years younger than herself, should have married first and so spectacularly well, for Nancy, Diana's translation from housebound adolescent to married lady could not have happened at a more opportune moment. Even less enchanted with family life in the country than her elder sister, longing even more passionately to escape, Diana over the previous couple of years had become an ally in the struggle against boredom at Swinbrook.

(Their hours of tedium were later echoed by Fanny and Linda in *The Pursuit of Love*:

'"What's the time, darling?"

"Guess."

"A quarter to six?"

"Better than that."

"Six?"

"Not quite so good."

"Five to?"

"Yes."')

Now she was married she could offer Nancy at her house in Buckingham Street not only a refuge from the family and a place to meet Hamish, but also a new and glamorous social life. The young Guinnesses quickly became one of the most fashionable couples in London (John Betjeman wrote a poem beginning, 'I too could be arty, I too could get on/With Sickert, the Guinnesses, Gertler, and John'). In town as well as at Biddesden, their house in Wiltshire, Nancy met many of the most interesting members of the literary and artistic intelligentsia – Lytton Strachey and Carrington, Augustus John, the Sitwells, Henry and Pansy Lamb, and the novelist Henry Yorke, as well as old friends such as Robert Byron, Mark, Brian Howard and Evelyn Waugh.

Nancy had come to know Evelyn well since his marriage to Evelyn ('She-Evelyn') Gardner. For a few months, she had lodged in the Waughs' little house in Canonbury Square. When

She-Evelyn ran off with another man Nancy's sympathies were entirely with the deserted husband. They began to meet regularly for luncheon at the Ritz when Evelyn would advise on the conduct of her affair with Hamish. He encouraged her, too, with her writing.

Nancy's first attempts at journalism took the form of anonymous paragraphs of gossip in one or other of the society magazines. She had once managed to pay for her train-fare to Scotland to stay with Nina by photographing the party for *Tatler*: 'Tom Driberg,'[1] she wrote to Tom, 'is in the same condition as us pecuniarely I mean it is such a satisfaction to think that others are isn't it. His camera is in pawn so he's going half shares with mine for the Tatler'. From this she progressed to the occasional signed article for *Vogue* – 'The Shooting Party: Some Hints for the Woman Guest. By the Hon. Nancy Mitford.' In March 1929, she told Mark, 'I'm making such a lot of money with articles – £22 since Christmas. I'm saving it up to be married but Evelyn says don't save it, dress better & catch a better man. Evelyn is always so full of sound common sense.' The following year, she was commissioned to write a weekly column for her grandfather Bowles's journal, *The Lady*, at five guineas a week. 'To celebrate this I went out today & bought myself a divine coral tiara,' she reported to Mark. 'I regard financial independence as almost the sum of human happiness don't you.' In character as 'The Lady' she attended the Chelsea Flower Show, the 4th of June at Eton, the Aldershot Tattoo and the Shakespeare birthday celebrations at Stratford-on-Avon. 'The Lady' is a rather disillusioned creature, frozen to the marrow at a point-to-point, exhausted after a Commemoration ball at Oxford and bored to death during a performance of *Rheingold* at Covent Garden ('The Lady began to be worn out with the loudness and dulness of the music. She felt stiff and tired and thought longingly of her bed'). At a coming-out dance, for Lady Fulvia Pigge and Miss Myrtle Lumpe, The Lady

---

[1] 'William Hickey' of the *Daily Express*, and later Labour Member of Parliament.

eavesdrops on the conversation of some of the guests: '"My dear, the floor! It's a sort of morass. Have you noticed? Not just ordinarily sticky, but *deep* I mean, almost reaching to the ankles."

"Yes, and full of pot-holes, too."

"Oh, the ghastliness of that band! Do let's go on somewhere else, shall we?"

"Of course, this hock-cup simply tastes like bad sweets melted in tooth water – that's *all*."

"Who are all these revolting people?"

"The entire population of Wormwood Scrubs, I should think, if you ask me."

"Do let's get out of this soon."'

With the incentive of earning money always before her, and with those days and weeks at Swinbrook when the London season was over and there was nothing to do, Nancy started work on her first novel. *Highland Fling* had its origins in the war between the generations, the war between aesthete and hearty epitomised in those holidays spent tramping the grouse-moors in Scotland, those long hours dying of cold and boredom in the butts while some red-faced old fool blazed away at the birds. Most of the action takes place in a Scottish castle, among a comically ill-matched house-party of fierce old philistines and frivolous, fashionable Bright Young Things. The love interest is provided by Jane Dacre and a camp young painter called Albert Memorial Gates, who delights in annoying his elders by his outrageous clothes and his (in those days eccentric) passion for Victoriana.

Nancy was always an intensely autobiographical writer, as she was the first to point out, and this, her first novel, written in much the same chatty style as her letters and journalism, is full of personal opinions and feelings, full of familiar faces, of private jokes and references. She herself is clearly visible in her heroine Jane (a charming, intelligent girl with a quick sense of humour, 'and except for a certain bitterness with which, for no apparent reason, she regarded her mother and father, the temperament of an angel'), while both Robert Byron and Hamish contributed to Albert's flamboyant personality. Leading the philistine forces is

General Murgatroyd, in whom, faint but discernible, can be traced the first shadowy outlines of the character, based on Farve, that fifteen years later was to appear in full and terrifying glory as Uncle Matthew: '"I heard him say that before the War the things he hated most were Roman Catholics and Negroes, but now, he said, banging on the table, now it's Germans."'

Highland Fling was published by Thornton Butterworth on March 12, 1931. It attracted little attention in the press, but Nancy earned £90, and the lending-library in Burford arranged a special display in its window with a hand-lettered sign reading, 'Nancy Mitford, Local Authoress.'

Almost as soon as her first novel was finished, Nancy started work on her second, *Christmas Pudding*, or, as she jokingly told Mark it was to be called, 'L'amour qui n'ose pas dire son nom.' 'My new book is jolly good,' she reported, 'all about Hamish at Eton . . . Betjeman is co-hero.' *Christmas Pudding* is very much in the same style as its predecessor – love and larks among the Bright Young Things. Paul, an impoverished young writer (John Betjeman's influence can be detected in Paul's air of bewildered naïvety and his love of Victorian literature), takes a job as holiday tutor to Bobby Bobbin, son of the widowed Lady Bobbin, a horrible old Master of Foxhounds, determined that her decadent son should be toughened up in preparation for a career in the army. Paul and Bobby conspire to deceive Lady Bobbin so that Paul can get on with his own work and Bobby can pursue his favourite occupations of bridge, parties and gossip. The two of them escape daily to neighbouring Mulberrie Farm rented for the winter by that one-time leader of the demi-monde, Amabelle Fortescue. As in *Highland Fling*, the plot largely depends on the clash between the fashionable young and the dowdy older generation, represented by Lady Bobbin and her friends and relations. The youthful company at Mulberrie Farm are usually to be found lying palely in front of the fire, sipping cocktails to help their hangovers after the party of the night before. Amabelle paints her eyelashes with navy-blue which interestingly matches the colour of the shadows under her eyes. They talk in up-to-the-minute slang – 'My sweetie-bo', 'What a poodle-pie' and 'I *couldn't* be more amused' – and they have no interest whatsoever in horses or dogs.

Bobby Bobbin is Hamish to the life. We meet him first at Eton where his room is described in telling detail: 'A guitar, that he could not play (lying beside a red leather gramophone that he could and did), a tasteful edition of *A la Recherche du Temps Perdu*, the complete works of Messrs. Ronald Firbank and Aldous Huxley, together with reproductions of two of Picasso's better-known aquarelles, bore testimony to the fact that young Sir Roderick [Bobby] liked to associate himself with modern culture. The possessor of keen eyes, however, observing some well used bridge markers, the masterpieces of Wallace, and a positive heap of society weekly journals, might suspect that the child was in no real danger at present of overtaxing his mind.' When Amabelle first suggests the plan of Paul coming as tutor, Hamish-as-Bobby goes into one of his most familiar routines: ' "How marvellous you are to think of it, darling. Oh, what heavenly fun it will be!" and Bobby vaulted over some fairly low railings and back, casting off for a moment his mask of elderly roué and slipping on that of a tiny-child-at-its-first-pantomime, another role greatly favoured by this unnatural boy.'

When *Christmas Pudding* was published in November 1932, Nancy was more than a little anxious about Hamish's reaction to this not entirely flattering portrait. But she need not have worried: he loved it, and took to signing his letters to her 'Bobby'.

The affair with Hamish had been continuing on its unsatisfactory course of nursery romps punctuated by quarrels (usually provoked by Hamish's heavy drinking and Nancy's desire to reform him) and a series of on-off engagements, when Hamish would play at seriously considering marriage, then feel 'trapped' and break the engagement off. At the end of the Michaelmas term of 1930, the University had finally lost patience with his dissipated ways and Hamish was sent down. Lord Rosslyn, knowing better than to let his son float loose in London, quickly dispatched him to America and a job in New York. The news of his departure

came as a frightful shock to Nancy, already in a depressed frame
of mind. She wrote to Mark, 'Hamish's family, behaving with
their usual caddery have taken him away for ever to America. I've
broken off the engagement. So there you have the situation in a
nutshell.'

She was staying at the time in the Drury-Lowes' new house in
Gloucester Place. Romie was expecting a baby, but until it arrived
had let the top floor, intended as a nursery, to Nancy. Her letter to
Mark continues:

> I tried to commit suicide by gas, it is a lovely sensation just like
> taking anaesthetic so I shan't be sorry any more for schoolmis-
> tresses who are found dead in that way, but just in the middle I
> thought that Romie who I was staying with might have a
> miscarriage which would be disappointing for her so I got back
> to bed & was sick . . . I am really very unhappy because there is
> no one to tell the funny things that happen to one & that is half
> the fun in life dont you agree . . . Im in the state in which I can't
> be alone but the moment I'm with other people I want to get
> away from them. It will be fun when my book is out [*Christmas
> Pudding*] . . . How can I possibly write a funny book in the next
> 6 months which my publisher says I *must* do. How *can* I when
> Ive got practically a pain from being miserable & cry in buses
> quite continually?
>
> Im sorry to inflict this dreary letter on you, as a matter of fact
> everyone here thinks I dont mind *at all* – rather a strain but I
> think the only attitude dont you agree.

Then Hamish, without a word to anyone, suddenly threw up
his job and returned to England. 'Hamish has come back and it is
all too frightful, we met at a party and of course it all began over
again Heaven knows what will happen in the end, he seems at
present to be busy drinking himself to death saying "my bulwarks
(thats me) have gone" We arent seeing each other at all. I suppose
it will have to be the gas oven in the end, one cant bear more than a
certain amount of unhappiness.'

In a desperate attempt to stave off despair, Nancy threw herself into a febrile social life. 'I'm having a perfectly divine time, it is certainly more fun not being engaged – I've been here [Rutland Gate] a fortnight & haven't been in any night so far . . . London is *heaven* just now, the Ritz before lunch is a party where you see everybody you've ever known & there are no deb dances because people are too poor to give them. In fact a perfect season . . . Lord Kylsant[1] going to prison, a Russian ballet of unexampled awfulness acclaimed by the highbrows as an intellectual treat, Mary Erskine [Hamish's sister] nearly killed at the Cafe de Paris by a roller skater who swung her round his head . . . Meanwhile I have broken all records (for me) by having been up really late every night for 3 weeks & here I am now, in bed with a poached egg & a long long sleep at least I hope so.' For once, she even had some money: a couple of hundred pounds from the novels, as well as '£30.30 [i.e. thirty guineas] from Harpers for a tiny short story, isn't it heaven, I'm just so rich I go 1st class everywhere & take taxis, & even refused £10 a week to write gossip for the Tatler'. She bought some new clothes and, although thin, was looking elegant and pretty. 'I was photographed by Cecil [Beaton], this afternoon,' she told Mark. 'Fantastic experience *"how do you manage to be skinny with such ruddy cheeks?"* Too easy I might have replied one has only to be crossed in love & an adept at make up.'

Except in her letters to Mark, Nancy never gave way to her misery: in company she was as high-spirited as ever, and there was no shortage of young men ready to take the place of Hamish. One of her most persistent admirers was Sir Hugh Smiley, a handsome Grenadier Guards officer with fair hair and, it was said, £5,000 a year. Sir Hugh wanted to marry her, but nice, suitable young men were of little interest to Nancy.

'Sir Hugh laid his ginger bread mansion at my feet last Monday & incapable as ever of giving a plain answer to a plain question I said I couldn't hear of it anyhow until my book is finished. So now

[1] Lord Kylsant, chairman of the Royal Mail Steam Company, was sentenced to a year's imprisonment for publishing and circulating a false prospectus.

I get letters by every post saying hurry up with the book, it is rather awful, I didn't do it from the usual feminine motives of liking rides in his car etc but believe me from sheer weakness. However its *all* right, I shall wriggle out somehow & anyway the book can't be finished for months . . . But it is awful how easily one could be entrapped into matrimony with someone like that because it *would* be nice to be rich. I'm not surprised girls do that sort of thing. Besides the old boy is really awfully nice & kind in his own way. But think of having blond & stupid children. But then one could be so *jolly well dressed* & take lovers. Romie thinks I'm mad & so do the babies [Decca and Debo] who go on at me like a pair of matchmaking mothers. But it is better to retain ones self respect in decent poverty isn't it? My life is a bore, I would so much rather be dead.'

Sir Hugh continued to propose and Nancy continued to evade him, unable to bring herself either to accept him or definitely refuse. At one point she did accept, only to change her mind again almost at once. 'Its *all* right its all *right* I've burned my boats so isn't that a relief,' she asked Mark. 'At least I never really considered it only I was so bored down here and Muv went on at me about it and said you'll die an old maid and I hadn't seen Hamish for months and months so I toyed with the idea for 5 minutes during which time I suppose I wrote to you . . . But I shall never marry anybody except Hamish really you know.'

The final offer came in April: 'I had another proposal from Sir Hugh, in great style orchids etc at the C de Paris with Hamish giggling at the next table & I gave him the final raspberry. He was very cross & said I should be left on the shelf (impertinence) so I went off with Hamish to the Slippin (new & horrible night club) which made him still crosser. Lousy young man, I don't answer any of his letters now even.'

Having successfully escaped marriage with a good, well-meaning man who loved her, Nancy turned back with relief to Hamish and playing bridge and fancy-dress parties ('Quelles frivolités! Here is the gorgeous & divine velvet of your fancy dress breeches. I send it so that you may procure white satin shoes with velvet rosettes matching this. Your tunic is of eau de nil velvet, with pink muslin ruff & cuffs'), back to suppers at the Ritz and dancing at the Bat, and anything else that was fashionable and fun. 'I was sitting at Quaglino's the other day,' she relayed to Mark, '& Harry [Lord Rosslyn] came up & said I know you keep my son & gave me £1. Don't you think that's a funny story. Hamish grabbed it too before you could say knife. Then the old boy said "If you can earn £1000 a year you may marry him" & went away, reeling among the astonished diners. So Hamish & I had a huge dinner instead of one rissole & sent him the bill.'

But however much she thought she loved him, however much fun they had together, it was impossible to pretend, even for Nancy, that the future looked promising. The engagement was broken off again, and again resumed; Hamish was to go back to America but changed his mind at the last moment, and got a job instead in a stockbroker's office in the City.

Then, in November 1932, this miserable affair was dramatically overshadowed by a family scandal: Diana had walked out on her husband, Bryan Guinness, publicly acknowledging that she was in love with another man, the prominent politician, Sir Oswald Mosley. Sir Oswald was married and there was no question of his leaving his wife; but he and Diana had committed themselves to each other. Diana knew that here was the man to whom she wanted to dedicate the rest of her life. She must leave Bryan, 'nail her colours to the mast', as she put it, and keep herself free to see Mosley whenever he could spare the time from his family and from the increasing demands of his political career.

The Redesdales were beside themselves with shock and dismay. It was unthinkable that a daughter of theirs, only twenty-two, the mother of two boys, should walk out of an apparently perfect marriage to be the mistress of a much older man, a notorious womaniser, with a wife and three children of his own. Farve, with Bryan's father, Lord Moyne, went round to see Mosley at his flat in Ebury Street to try and talk him out of it, but Mosley was inflexible. Diana, too, was deaf to argument: she had made up her mind, and the opinion of the world and of her family was a matter of indifference. Nancy, always on the side of love, was sympathetic, but at the same time tried to warn her sister of the consequences of her scandalous behaviour. 'Your social position will be *nil* if you do this. Darling I do hope you are making a right decision. You are *so* young to begin getting in wrong with the world, if thats what is going to happen. However it is all your own affair & whatever happens *I* shall always be on your side as you know & so will anybody who cares for you & perhaps the rest really dont matter.' Diana was grateful for Nancy's support but so happy that she was almost indifferent to what was going on around her. In January she moved into a little house in Eaton Square, where Muv absolutely forbade the two youngest girls to go; had she been able, she would have prevented the family having any contact with her at all. Nancy saw Diana almost daily, keeping her in touch with events in the enemy camp. 'Saw Bryan yesterday, he was pretty spiky I thought, keeps saying of course I suppose its my *duty* to take her back & balls of that sort ... I may say that the Lambs seem to have turned nasty, apparently they told B they were nearly certain you had an affair with Randolph in the spring.'

Meanwhile Nancy's own love-affair was going from bad to worse. She and Hamish were continually quarrelling – over his drinking, his gambling, over his irresponsible attitude towards their future. He had never been demonstrative, never showed her the affection she craved, but now there was cruelty in his tone. The two of them were caught in a vicious circle: the more possessive Nancy became, the more Hamish fought to get away; as she saw him eluding her, the more possessive she became. In fact Hamish was growing desperate. He knew he had to escape from Nancy, that he was trapped into a fictitious character which Nancy had invented – that of a man basically heterosexual, sowing his wild oats, but soon to settle down to marriage and a family. Then suddenly his chance came: his sister Mary announced her engagement to Philip Dunn, the son of the banker Sir James Dunn, and, the very same day, Hamish announced his engagement to Philip's sister, Kit, a wildly eccentric character in

every way the antithesis of Nancy. It was a brutal thing to do but
Hamish saw it as his only way out. His behaviour was unforgiv-
able, and it was essential that it should be: he did not want Nancy
to forgive him.

It was June 14, the day before Diana's divorce proceedings,
and Nancy, Pam and Unity had gathered at Eaton Square to
provide moral support. The butler came into the room to say that
Mr St Clair Erskine wished to speak to Mrs Guinness on the
telephone. Without any suspicion of what was to come, Nancy
said that, as she wanted to talk to Hamish, she would take the call.
She came back into the room a few minutes later, her face white.
Shortly afterwards, Hamish himself arrived and there was a
terrible scene. As soon as he left, Nancy sat down to write him a
letter.

Darling Hamish I can't sleep without writing to say I am so
sorry & miserable that I was unkind to you just now. I shan't
send this straight away, perhaps never but I must write it, for
my own sake.

Because I must explain to you that if you had told me you
were engaged to Tanis, or Sheila Berry, I could never never
have made that dreadful scene. Please believe me. I should
have been unhappy for myself certainly but happy for you & as I
love you better than myself I would have overcome my own
feelings for your sake.

But darling you come & tell me that you are going to share
your life with Kit Dunn. You, whom I have always thought so
sensible & so idealistic about marriage, you who will love your
own little babies so very very much, it is a hard thing for me to
bear that you should prefer *her* to me.

You see, I knew you weren't *in love* with me, but you are in
love so often & for such tiny spaces of time. I thought that in
your soul you loved me & that in the end we should have
children & look back on life together when we are old. I
thought our relationship was a valuable thing to you & that if
you ever broke it you would only do so in order to replace it with

another equally valuable. But that isn't so, & that is what I find intolerable.

Please understand me. Please think of me with affection always & never never blame me for what I may become without you. Don't think of me as a selfish & hysterical woman even if I appeared so tonight.

God bless you & make her be kind to you, I shall pray always for your happiness.

Nancy

After the first agonised outburst, when she, in her own words, 'made that dreadful scene', Nancy accepted that the affair was over. She had been in love with Hamish for nearly five years. Her heart was broken. And within a month she was engaged to another man.

CHAPTER FOUR

Peter

Peter Rodd, born in 1904, the same year as Nancy, was the son of Sir Rennell Rodd, one of the most distinguished diplomats of his generation. A man of many accomplishments, Sir Rennell was a brilliant linguist and classical scholar, a talented water-colourist and the author of several small volumes of verse. He had served in Cairo, Stockholm and Berlin; had been Special Envoy to the Emperor of Abyssinia, Minister Plenipotentiary to Sweden and Norway; and in 1908 was appointed British Ambassador to Rome, where his noble bearing and unfailing politeness made him much admired among the Italians: they saw in him the epitome of the English gentleman, the very flower of diplomacy.

His wife, Lilias, was quite different – nothing diplomatic about her. She was a prima donna, a woman who loved bossing other people about, a firm believer in speaking her mind. Behind her back the Embassy staff referred to her as Lady Rude, or Tiger Lil. She came from a wealthy Scottish family, the Guthries, and all her life remained typically Scotch about money, reading the *Financial Times* from cover to cover every morning and keeping a sharp eye on household accounts. She was not mean exactly, but, when it came to spending money, she had a clear idea of her order of priorities: herself first, her husband second, her children very much third. Lady Rodd, it was widely known, lived for beauty – not, it has to be said, an impression easily obtained from her personal appearance: she had no interest in clothes (her one hat was sent back to London every year to be retrimmed), and her dowdiness was almost magnificent in its indifference to fashion. She had, however, a strong aesthetic sense; she was an artist: she spent hours a day at her easel; gave a great deal of thought to the garden; and, above all, staged magnificent parties. As English Ambassadress in Rome, she was famous for her entertaining. Her guests would arrive to find the garden of the Villa Torlonia transformed into a wood near Athens or a glade on the slopes of Mount Olympus, with their hostess blazing forth to greet them gorgeously attired as Juno, or Titania, or Queen Elizabeth I, attended by her five children dressed as elves or fairies or miniature characters from classical mythology. In the accounts in the society papers of the colourful goings-on at the British Embassy ('Parmi les hôtes de l'ambassade, hier soir, ce n'a été qu'un long cri d'admiration . . .'), Lady Rodd's appearance was always described dotingly and at length – cloth of gold, peacock feathers, attendant company of nymphs and maidens – while that of the Ambassador himself seemed rather to fade into the background, a shadowy figure to be mentioned only in the final paragraph: 'Sir Rennell Rodd looked well in a costume of pearl grey satin', or 'Sir Rennell Rodd figured in a group of foreign Ambassadors of the 16th century'.

But although she loved the centre of the stage, Tiger Lil loved her husband even more, and deferred to him in all essentials. He, an Englishman typical of his class and time, inclined in domestic matters towards the quiet life and the line of least resistance: let Lil have her head, then he could be left in peace to write his poems ('Hail, ancient people of the northern sea . . .') and work on his book on the history of medieval Greece. Lady Rodd was a devoted wife and conscientious as a mother. The business of having babies bored her, but it was one's duty, one did it, and that was that. Of her five children she loved best the eldest Francis and her second son Peter, mainly because as boys they were both exceptionally beautiful, and beauty was what she lived for. The two girls, Evelyn and Gloria (Golly), coming between the brothers in age, she was not much interested in, and by the time her last child, Gustav (Taffy), was born, any enthusiasm had long since evaporated. Francis, as his father's heir, was given a conventional upbringing at Eton and Oxford, but the others, of much less importance, were subjected to their mother's highly individual educational theories: she did not approve of the public-school system, and saw no reason why the younger boys should have to endure it before they absolutely must. So Peter and Taffy, with Evelyn and Golly, were shunted about Europe, moving every term to a different country. By the time the boys were old enough for public school (Wellington, not Eton for Peter), they spoke several European languages fluently, and had almost no experience of their own country.

In spite of this fragmented education, Peter, or Prodd as his family called him, showed early signs of intellectual brilliance, together with an unusual precocity arising from his cosmopolitan background and an independence of necessity learned young. By the time he arrived at Oxford, he felt himself, with some reason, older and more sophisticated than the immature schoolboys who were his contemporaries. His moody beauty and arrogant air led his friends to compare him to the young Rimbaud, and there was current a verse about him which went: 'Mr Peter Rodd/ Is extraordinarily like God/ He has the same indefinable air/ Of savoir faire.' Prodd's belief in his own superiority did not endear him to his male companions, although his blond good looks made him from the start a success with women. Having made no effort to hide his contempt for what he considered the petty regulations of undergraduate life – regulations which he constantly and openly flouted – he was sent down from Balliol before taking his degree on the charge of entertaining women in his rooms after hours.

This was the beginning of Peter's long career in delinquency, a delinquency made almost inevitable by his upbringing. He loved and admired his father, felt under an obligation to win his respect, while at the same time recognising that this was impossible. His father represented a standard of unattainable perfection. His mother was more accessible. She and Peter used to quarrel, mainly about money, as one of Lady Rodd's favourite tenets was that it was good for her children to be kept short, but at least at those times he knew he had her attention. He knew, too, that she loved him in her way, even if her way was more concerned with his tow-headed good looks – he had made a lovely elf – than with the difficult, anarchic person behind them. But his father was an impossible act to follow: not only did he excel at everything he did, but his flawless courtier's manner meant that any real confrontation was out of the question. He was the perfect prototype of an ambassador, a stage version, a cardboard cut-out, never losing his temper, never raising his voice, theatrically handsome, immaculately dressed, always deferred to and admired. His attitude towards his second son was one of weary resignation: instead of anger he expressed disappointment. And then there was the example of Francis. Nearly ten years older than Peter, Francis was the perfect son, as good and obedient as Peter was rebellious and rude, always doing what was expected of him, always succeeding in what he did, to the end of their lives the greatest possible comfort and support to his parents. They made no secret of the fact that Francis was the favourite, and it was to Francis that they turned for help in extricating his younger brother from a long series of disastrous escapades.

In these circumstances, it is hardly surprising that Peter, in the words of Evelyn Waugh, was 'an obstreperous minority of one'. The pity was that, given his remarkable intelligence, he was not better at it. Nearly everything he did turned out badly. On leaving Oxford he was despatched to Brazil where he worked in a bank, which he hated, spending most of his spare time getting drunk – and incidentally adding Russian and Portuguese to his linguistic repertoire. He was eventually arrested for being destitute, and Sir Rennell, as usual with the help of Francis (at that time usefully placed in the Foreign Office) was obliged to use his influence to get Peter repatriated as a distressed British subject. Back in England he managed to land a job in the City, was sacked from that, went as a journalist to Germany, was again sacked, and again rescued by Francis, who took him off on a two-year expedition in the Sahara, an undertaking far better suited to Peter's buccaneering spirit than a desk in the City or a newspaper-office in Berlin.

At the time of his proposal to Nancy, he was working, with the greatest reluctance, for an American bank in Lombard Street. He and Nancy had known each other slightly for some years, having many friends in common, chief among whom was Hamish. He and Peter used to fool around together at parties, both very drunk, the game being to give false names to the photographers from *Vogue* and *Tatler*, then claim damages when the inaccurately captioned pictures appeared. It was at a party that Peter proposed: he was in the habit of proposing to pretty girls. It was meant as a joke. Nancy accepted, and the thing was done.

The speed with which Nancy and Peter changed course and turned towards each other came as a surprise to everyone. To Peter, Nancy had been no more than another lively, pretty girl he was used to seeing about; she for her part, less than a month earlier, had had her heart broken by the man whom, for a period of nearly five years, she had believed she would marry. When they came together, each represented for the other a kind of life-line. They were both approaching thirty. Peter, well aware of his reputation as a failure, saw marriage – the only resort he had not so far tried – as his last hope; and he rather liked the idea of a home and a wife and some children. For Nancy the ending of her engagement to Hamish had been painful, but it had also jolted her into a realisation of the fatuity of that relationship. It had been fun, no doubt about that, and Hamish-the-tiny-child had made a strong appeal to her maternal instincts, but emotionally it had been sterile and frustrating. She and Hamish were not interested in each other sexually – prancing about in fancy dress was a far more satisfactory pastime – but the fact remained that Nancy had longed for love, and that was something that he had never been able to give. Hamish did not love her – Hamish loved no one but 'Little Me' – and he was frequently unkind. Now here was Peter Rodd, strikingly handsome, strikingly masculine, self-confident, full of jokes and impressively well-informed. Nancy rather liked pompous men, and she had that undiscriminating respect for intellect often felt by those themselves lacking a formal education. Prodd knew a lot, and he talked a lot about what he knew. Although he had not yet become the famous bore he turned into later on, he was already given to lecturing anybody he could

Grandfather Redesdale

Grandfather Bowles

Nancy with her parents

Farve in uniform during the First World War

Tom

Out walking at Batsford. From left to right: Muv, Tom, Miss Mirams, Nancy, Aunt Daphne, Nanny Dicks with Unity in front of her, Pam and Diana

Pam, Tom, Diana and Nancy in the garden at Asthal

Nancy (on the right) with Constantia Fenwick

Nanny Dicks

Nancy on the Venice Lido   Self-portrait

Nancy photographed by Derek Jackson at Rignell

Hamish St Clair Erskine

Diana

Nina Seafield and Mark Ogilvie-Grant

Hamish with Nancy and Anne Armstrong-Jones at the Ritz

Peter and Nancy on their
wedding-day

ncy with her French
lldog Millie

ter in his role as artist,
ortrait by his sister-in-
Mary Rodd

Lord and Lady Rennell of
Rodd

Peter and Nancy on their
ill-fated holiday in
Brittany

waylay, at great length, on preferably obscure subjects. Prodd thought he knew everything – and the trouble was that he very nearly did. His friend, and Nancy's cousin, Ed Stanley, said of P. R. Odd as he called him, that 'whatever topic is under discussion, he will pose as an authority outstanding over anyone present . . . to quote him: "I know, I know, I *am* a hospital nurse/ war criminal/ displaced person/ painter/ journalist/ financier/ poet/ Italian pimp/ diplomat/ geographer".'

The engagement was announced in July in the *Daily Telegraph*. The Rennells (Sir Rennell this same year, 1933, had been raised to the peerage as Lord Rennell of Rodd) were uneasy at the news: this was the first they had heard of it. They both wrote at once to Francis. 'The whole thing has its rather inexplicable side,' Lord Rennell confided, 'and it worries me not a little'. Lil's reaction was less circumspect: 'About Peter, we hear there was an announcement in the Daily Telegraph that he was to be married in October which is probably not true. He has not written to us himself on the subject so I suppose as usual it was made up.' The Redesdales had been rather better prepared. Nancy, begging him to stay sober for the occasion, had sent Peter to have lunch with her father at Rutland Gate. She herself, unable to bear the suspense, left the house, returning two hours later to find Farve coming out into the hall reeling with boredom, having been lectured by Peter for two solid hours on the toll-gate system of England and Wales ('The Old Toll-Gater' became one of his nicknames from that moment on). But although Farve did not like Peter much – 'talks like a ferret with its mouth sewn up' – he saw no reason to refuse his consent. Almost anyone was preferable to Hamish.

To Nancy Peter was as near perfect as it was possible for a man to be. She wrote to Roy Harrod[1], 'I am absolutely happy for the first time in my life.' And to Mark, 'Well, the happiness. Oh goodness gracious I am happy. You *must* get married darling,

---

[1] The economist, at this period University Lecturer in Economics at Oxford.

everybody should this minute if they want a receipt for absolute bliss. Of course I know there aren't many Peters going about but still I s'pose everybody has *its* Peter (if only Watson) So find yours dear the sooner the better And remember TRUE LOVE CANT BE BOUGHT. If I really thought it could I'd willingly send you £3 tomorrow What I want to know is why nobody told me about Peter before – I mean if I'd known I'd have gone off to Berlin after him or anywhere else, however I've got him now which is the chief thing.' Peter, too, was in a state of high excitement, posting off love-letters from the Savile Club whenever he and Nancy were apart. 'Darling darling Pauline [Pauline was Peter's private name for Nancy] . . . My darling I am glad that all this started as a joke. I love you I love you my darling Pauline . . . I should like to see your head lying on your pillow This Peter who loves only you.' To Hamish, his old companion in debauchery, he wrote a manly letter courteously accepting the fiction that Hamish as the vanquished lover would be suffering from a broken heart. 'It is absurd for me to pretend that I am sorry for taking your Nancy from you, but I know that it is hell for you and I wish it wasn't I am so much in love with her that I can understand how you feel.' Evelyn Waugh was among those who wrote to express approval of the match. 'Well I think its top hole about you and Rodd and I foresee a very wild and vigorous life in front of you . . . I hope you have numerous piccaninnies and that Mr Erskine will now disappear from your novels. But listen, I won't have you writing books about Rodd because that would be too much for me to bear.'

The wedding, first planned for October, was postponed to November, then from November to December. At the beginning of November, the Rennells spent a weekend at Swinbrook, a situation fraught with danger which in the event passed off smoothly: Farve behaved himself and Nancy admitted to being fascinated, in a slightly horrified way, by Lil. Wedding-presents came pouring in, mainly of the disappointing cut-crystal-vase variety. Bryan Guinness gave Nancy her wedding-dress, Lord Rennell a diamond wrist-watch, Muv a diamond ring, Diana a dining-table, some chairs and a sofa. The three youngest sisters, Unity, Decca and Debo, contributed gilt fittings for the dressing-case which was the bridegroom's present to the bride. But what they both needed was money. Lady Rennell, true to form, was keeping a tight hand on the purse-strings – if Peter couldn't afford to keep Nancy, then he shouldn't marry her, was the line – and Farve, undergoing yet another financial crisis, had very little to spare. 'I note that your father refuses to tie himself up to any settlement,' Peter drily remarked. 'I hope he does his stuff about your allowance even if he sours on the marriage.'

They were married on Monday, December 4, 1933, at St John's, Smith Square. Peter, having planned his stag-night for the Saturday before, appeared sober, upright and wonderfully handsome in his tail-coat. Nancy, in a dress of white chiffon with a train, wore a wreath of white gardenias securing a long veil, and carried a bouquet of gardenias and roses. Farve gave her away, and she was attended by eleven little pages in white satin Romney suits. After the service there was a reception for over two hundred at Rutland Gate presided over by Muv in brown velvet and a feathered hat. Lady Rennell was in red. Among the guests were Hamish's parents, Lord and Lady Rosslyn, with their daughter Mary, Hugh Smiley and his wife Nancy (Cecil Beaton's sister), Mark Ogilvie-Grant and his mother, Middy and her mother, Helen Dashwood, Roy Harrod, Nina and her husband Derek Studley-Herbert, Robert Byron's two sisters, Constantia Fenwick, and the Osbert Lancasters.

They went to Rome for the honeymoon, staying in the Rennells' magnificent apartment in Palazzo Giulia. 'Why do people say they don't enjoy honeymoons?' wrote Nancy to Unity, 'I am adoring mine.' To Mark she sent a teasing postcard: 'I am having a *really dreadful* time, dragging a badly sprained ankle round major & minor basilicas & suffering hideous indigestion from eating goats cheese. However I manage to keep my spirits up somehow.'

Peter and Nancy began their married life in a tiny house overlooking the Thames at Strand on the Green, just down river from Kew Bridge. Rose Cottage was like a little dolls' house, with a walled garden back and front, a stone-flagged garden path, bow-windows, and a pink china pig and two parrots balanced on top of the porch. With help from Mark, who was good at that sort of thing, Nancy made the interior elegant and pretty. Although she had almost no money she was clever at picking up bargains in the sale-room, and had bought among other things a big sofa for £2 and a carved mantelpiece for £1. Although small, the rooms were airy and light, made more so by the pale colours of the walls and carpets. In the sitting-room was a handsome, if shabby, Aubusson carpet and Nancy's beloved desk, her *bonheur-du-jour*. Upstairs in the bedroom were the festooned curtains that throughout her life were such a distinctive mark of her Parisian taste; from this window Nancy could look over the garden, and on the other side of a quiet road, across to a tree-lined tow-path and the pleasant, wide expanse of the Thames. Once or twice she caught sight of something not so pleasant, the sodden mass of a suicide's corpse drifting on the tide: this, according to the story, was the cue for Nancy to telephone the old boatman whose job it was to fish it out, at ten shillings a time – a shilling more if he had to cross over to the far side of the river.

Nancy enjoyed her little house, she enjoyed being married – and the liberty marriage gave her. With Peter away all day at work, she had no one to please but herself. 'I am awfully busy learning to be a rather wonderful old housewife,' she wrote cheerfully to Mark. 'My marriage, contracted to the amazement of all so late in life is providing me with a variety of interests, new but not distasteful, & besides, a feeling of shelter & security hitherto untasted by me.' That her husband was the last person to be relied on to give either shelter or security was not yet apparent. For the moment she was more than happy to be away from her parents and free to play at keeping house. She had acquired a couple of French bulldogs, Millie and Lottie, on whom she doted: they were allowed to sleep, wheezing, under the eiderdown on her bed. It became a familiar sight to the neighbours, Nancy in a pair of slacks walking briskly along the tow-path with the two stout little dogs trotting after her. When the weather was fine, the garden was a great pleasure to sit and read in. 'I go less & less to London as I *love* it here so much,' she told Unity. And there was plenty of social life of the young married variety – lively entertaining done on the cheap with the emphasis on bridge, which both Rodds played well. One of these bridge-parties at the cottage was described in the *Evening Standard* as 'a gay, light-hearted affair of the cheerful kind that hasn't happened much since the days of the fabulous past when there were those Bright Young People about', a comparison hardly justified by the modest reality of furniture pushed back against the wall, cider-cup to drink and card-tables crammed into the bedroom.

But, even in these early days, the marriage had its problems. Peter's new responsibilities had not changed him, and he was once again out of a job. Concerned letters were soon flying to and fro between Francis and the rest of the family. Nancy had confided to Golly, her sister-in-law, that she was worried by Peter's lack of financial sense, and that the two of them had had some bad rows on their honeymoon over his devil-may-care extravagance. This piece of information was now being chewed over by the Rodd clan, together with the details of Peter's lack of employment. Francis's wife, Mary, an enthusiastic Moral Re-armer, wrote to her husband, 'What are we to do with Peter. You know if Peter doesn't make good over this it will be the end of him for so far marriage is the only thing he has not tried.' 'Taffy mentions in his last letter to me that Peter is not in a job,' Lady Rennell came chiming in. 'Once more his future seems in the balance. What on earth have they got to live on except the allowance he gets from us.' Her husband, more in sorrow than in anger, expressed disappointment in his son, whose failure to get the job he had assured everyone was in the bag had rather upset his father. 'What you say about Peter has rather upset me,' he complained to Francis. 'I was under the belief that he had a definite engagement with Hamburger and was to begin on £500 a year. It was on the strength of this assurance that I went into the question of settlements and discussed the whole matter with

Lord Redesdale who was equally convinced that he had a definite undertaking from H. I am now afraid that as usual the whole story was built on a mere possibility without any substance. It is always the same story with him . . . I have not said much about it but his unconcern for every one else in order to gratify his whim of the moment has made me unhappy for many years – when all the rest of the family are only joy to us.' This sort of thing had become the established pattern with Peter – never holding on to any job for long, leaving one position always with the much-vaunted promise of something better in the offing which somehow never quite materialised. Lord Rennell was perplexed by Peter's fecklessness – so different from the reliable Francis – and, being a kind man, he worried about their poverty. 'One feels a little scared about the young couple and I am wondering whether their house is healthy or whether they get enough to eat and keep warm . . . They do not tell us much, but one cannot help realising that since he gave up £600 a year on an over optimistic hope of a better job it must be rather difficult for them to get along on the remainder, unless there are other sources of revenue about which I do not know . . . I should like to be reassured that these repeated attacks of flu are not the result of inadequate resources.'

Although not, in Nancy's phrase, 'poor like poor people', certainly by the standards of their families and friends the Rodds were fairly hard-up. Between them they had an income of about £500 a year, which included allowances from both sets of parents, the little Nancy made from her journalism, and from the stocks and shares bought with the proceeds of *Highland Fling* and *Christmas Pudding*. On this they could live modestly at Rose Cottage, with one servant and later on a small car; but there was no margin for treats or extravagance, no margin for the good clothes for which Nancy longed, nor for the expensive drinking bouts at fashionable night-clubs to which Peter was quickly becoming addicted. More than once Nancy had to rely on discreet gifts from her father-in-law ('Don't tell Lil'), and more than once she was visited by the bailiffs. Nancy being Nancy, she made a good story out of this, telling how she got to know them so well that she used to ask them in to tea, which no doubt she did. Nonetheless to be in such a predicament was unnerving and this period of acute economic insecurity, after a childhood in which financial crises were a regular occurrence, was to influence her attitude to money for the rest of her life.

Nancy never really became fond of Peter's family. 'I lunched today with the Rennells,' begins a typical account. 'It was an awful lunch, most of the guests had to be carried upstairs on account of senile debility & there were 5 courses. So now I feel ill & liverish & cross.' She was grateful to her father-in-law, was touched by his kindness while remaining unimpressed by the role of perfect courtier; Lady Rennell she frankly disliked (the feeling was mutual – Lil liked none of her daughters-in-law: 'at least she's a lady,' was the most she was ever prepared to concede); and she found little in common with the brothers and sisters and their husbands and wives. Mitford frivolity did not blend well with the Rodd breed of public servant, with their salt-of-the-earth seriousness and their tendency towards Doing Good. The only member of the family, apart from Peter, whom Nancy did like was Aunt Vi, Lady Rennell's sister, a spirited old lady who lived with her husband, Edward Stuart Wortley, at Highcliffe, an immense and immensely grand Gothic castle on the Dorset coast. Aunt Vi was fond of Nancy and admired her patience in dealing with her husband. 'My word, how lucky Peter was to find a wife like that. She adores him, and is marvellously patient, for he is like an irresponsible school boy, still, and hopelessly unpractical.'

But the Rennells had their uses, one of them being a villa at Posilipo near Naples, built by Lord Rennell as a summer retreat on land presented to him by a grateful Italian government. The villa itself was hideous, but its situation could hardly have been more beautiful, on top of a cliff looking across the Bay of Naples, with Vesuvius in one direction, the island of Capri in the other. Nancy, who went there for the first time the summer after her wedding, loved the luxury and the swimming and sunbathing, though not, it must be said, the company. 'In this family everyone is either too high brow or too low brow for me,' she told Diana.

'Lord R is fearfully erudite & the others think about nothing but making money. None of them have heard of the Russian ballet for instance so one can never have a really cosy chat.' Peter himself stayed only for a few days so that Nancy was thrown very much on the company of his brother Taffy ('a miserable worm') and his wife Yvonne, who irritated her past bearing. 'That awful Yvonne is coming tomorrow which will wreck all,' she wrote to Diana. 'She made £40 in Venice sewing (a new name for it eh? & one to be remembered I feel for future use) I can't bear the idea of her face, you know the feeling.' Nancy's natural indolence and lack of curiosity about the local sights did not fit in with the Rodds' natural vigour and keenness for doing things. 'Tomorrow I am off at 9 to Paestum, so you see what a culture hog I have become. I must say oh dear oh *me* I would rather sit on my bottom here.'

Nancy returned to England at the end of August to find herself on the brink of what was to turn into a row of truly Mitford proportions. In the spring of 1934, before her holiday in Italy, she had started work on a new novel, the idea being a tease on Unity and Diana, whose recent conversion to Fascism had provided Nancy with her inspiration. The heroine was modelled on Unity, and there was to be a lot of comic business about the Führer, and about the English Leader, Captain Jack (Mosley), and his uni-formed band of Union Jackshirts (the British Union of Fascists). Unfortunately this was a tease that neither Unity nor Diana found in the least amusing.

When Diana fell in love with Mosley, she became set on a course that would stay unchanged for the rest of her life. For her (as later for Nancy), falling in love with a man meant an unswerv-ing dedication to his cause: love for the man and belief in his cause became one and the same, leading both to a rare depth of devotion and a corresponding blindness to flaws in either the man or in his ideal. Mosley had launched the British Union of Fascists in the autumn of 1932, the year he and Diana had met. His wife, Cimmie[1], died in May of the following year, which meant that he

---

[1] Cynthia, daughter of Lord Curzon.

and Diana could now plan to marry, as soon as the cumbersome process of her divorce from Bryan Guinness was complete. With Cimmie's death, Diana could more publicly 'nail her colours' to the Leader's mast, colours which to most of her friends were of a most disturbing hue. To the liberal-aesthete circle, Nancy among them, which comprised most of Diana's friends, Mosley's brand of Fascism, distinct from but sympathetic towards the German version, was abhorrent. When in the summer of 1933 Diana returned from her first visit to Germany, full of enthusiasm for what she had seen of the Nazi Party on show at the Nuremberg Parteitag, several of them tried to argue her out of her, as they saw it, disastrous illusion. It seemed inconceivable that a woman as charming and sophisticated as Diana, a lover of the arts, a passionate subscriber to all that was most civilised in their world, should be in thrall to such a dark and ugly creed. But in thrall she was, and argument was a waste of breath.

Fanatical as Diana's committal to her Leader and his cause appeared to most of her friends, Unity's seemed little short of lunatic. Having met Mosley with Diana at Eaton Square, she had succumbed at once to his mesmerising charm and the appealing simplicity of his argument. Eagerly she joined the Movement, and accompanied her sister on that decisive first visit to Germany in 1933. She and Diana drew close over their common interest. But while Diana in her first exposure to Hitler's Fascism saw, in common with many English people of that time, a marvellously efficient organisation, effectively transforming Germany from poverty and chaos into a well-ordered and prosperous nation (and could not the same be done for Britain, also in a state of economic decline and with a distressingly high rate of unemployment?), Unity at the Nuremberg Parteitag underwent nothing less than a religious conversion. Transported by the martial music and the sight of thousands of marching men, ecstatic under the spell of the Führer's hypnotic oratory, she took to Hitler and Fascism as a born-again Christian takes to God. She went home full of her new enthusiasm, and as soon as she could returned to Munich, ostensibly in order to learn German (Muv was surprised and pleased: Bobo's refusal to learn French had distressed her, and she was glad to see a sign in her recalcitrant daughter of some cultural curiosity), in fact to devote herself to following Hitler, studying details of his movements in the papers, and positioning herself outside his flat on the Prinzregentenplatz, or by the Brown House, or at a table at the Osteria Bavaria where he frequently came for lunch. Her perseverance was eventually rewarded with a personal introduction and the entrée to the inner circle of Nazi Prominenten to which Hitler made her known. He gave her a special swastika badge all of her own with his signature engraved on the back. As Hitler's guest she appeared at rallies, at the Olympic Games of 1936, at the Parteitag celebrations and much of the rest of the Nazi propaganda performance, which she described in letters home childishly adorned with swastikas and 'Heil Hitlers!'.

And in many ways Unity was still a child, emotionally and intellectually immature. Nazism appealed to her on a very simple level: she liked the marching and the songs and the good-looking young men in their uniforms; she liked the badges and the pamphlets and being able to dress up in her black shirt and gauntlets. Being with Hitler gave her for the first time in her life a sense of her own importance, and she found no difficulty in swallowing his anti-semitic propaganda, propaganda which she was only too willing to regurgitate on every possible occasion.

Nancy was fond of her eccentric younger sister, who with her statuesque proportions, expressionless face and thick fair hair did rather resemble the warrior maidens after whom she was named. Unity had charm and originality, she could be very funny and there was something endearing about her naivety. But to Nancy her obsession with Nazism, uncomprehending though it may have been, was anything but endearing. By her taunts she tried to emphasise the ridiculous aspects of Unity's behaviour, while at the same time maintaining a façade of good-natured sisterly affection. She loved her sisters, but she loathed their politics, and this love and loathing were difficult to reconcile. There was Bobo as she always had been, sitting at the lunch table with everybody else at Swinbrook, and here was this demented Valkyrie brazenly proclaiming herself in alliance with all that Nancy most abhorred.

In June 1935 Unity had gone to Hesselberg at the invitation of Julius Streicher, and had publicly declared her Fascist beliefs and her hatred for the Jews: following this up by giving an interview to the *Münchener Zeitung*, along very much the same lines, headed 'Eine Britische Faschistin erzählt'. True to character, Nancy responded to this unappealing behaviour with mockery:

> Darling Stony-heart. We were all very interested to see that you were the Queen of the May this year at Hesselberg.
>
> Call me early, Goering dear
>
> For I'm to be Queen of the May Good gracious, that interview you sent us, fantasia, fantasia.

She responded with mockery to every aspect of Unity's obsession: to Horst Wessel ('Hoarse Vessel'), to Hitler and the whole of the Nazi régime: 'By the way aren't you going abroad, to England, quite soon. Well then I shan't bother to send this to the nasty land of blood baths & that will save me 1d We were asked to stay with somebody called Himmler or something, tickets & everything paid for, but we can't go as we are going to Venice & the Adriatic for our hols . . . Actually he wanted to show us over a concentration camp now why? So that I could write a funny book about them.'

Nancy remained all her life politically immature, her opinions too frivolous and too subjective to be taken seriously – a limitation which restrained her not at all in the airing of these opinions. Her loathing of the Fascist Right coupled with a feeling for moderation and a dislike of extremes of behaviour in any direction led her towards a middle-of-the-road Socialism. She considered herself a Socialist, and as such could hardly be expected to show sympathy to the family Fascists, but, as always, her feelings were ambivalent, particularly where they concerned Diana. Bobo, bad backward Bobo, firmly entangled in the lunatic fringe, was a much easier target than Diana, closer to Nancy not only in age but in sympathy and interests. When Diana left Bryan, Nancy stuck loyally by her, but she could not bring herself either to like or to approve of Mosley. To Nancy Sir Ogre, as she referred to him behind his back, was a sinister influence. She could not help, either, being aware of the passion, the emotional intensity which almost tangibly existed between Mosley and Diana, and which was, as she subsconsciously recognised even during her brief period of happiness with Peter, something entirely lacking in her own life. In her typically equivocal manner, right hand carefully not looking at what left hand was doing, she supported her sister while simultaneously undermining her. In 1933, Nancy had attended a BUF meeting in Oxford, and had written to describe it to Diana, trying to please by expressing admiration for 'the Leader', while at the same time making clear her instinctive disgust for his methods. 'Darling Bodley,' she wrote from Swinbrook. 'TPOL's[1] meeting was fascinating, but awful for him as the hall was full of Oxfordshire Conservatives who sat in hostile & phlegmatic silence – you can imagine what they were like. I think he is a *wonderful* speaker & of course I expect he is better still with a more interesting audience.' That was all right; but, unable to leave well alone, she continued, 'There were several fascinating fights, as he brought a few Neanderthal men along with him & they fell tooth & (literally) nail on anyone who shifted his chair or coughed. One man complained afterwards that the fascist's nails had pierced his head *to the skull*.'

Then, to complicate the situation further, Nancy made a complete about-turn by moving in one effortless step from Left to Far Right, abandoning her Socialist pink ('synthetic cochineal', as Diana accurately referred to it) for the uncompromising black shirt of the British Union of Fascists. Peter, at first thrilled by Mosley's new Movement, had enthusiastically joined up; and Nancy, with no political mind of her own, had gone in with him. The two of them bought black shirts, attended the meetings, and

---

[1] The Poor Old Leader, derived from nicknames for Farve, the Poor Old Male (TPOM) and Muv, The Poor Old Female (TPOF).

Nancy even went as far as to write an article[1] (couched in that curious quasi-oratorical style that was always a sure indication that she hadn't the faintest idea what she was talking about) acclaiming Fascism as the hope for the future: 'We British Fascists [believe] . . . that our Leader, Sir Oswald Mosley, has the character, the brains, the courage and the determination to lift this country from the slough of despond in which it has for too long weltered, to an utopia . . . Soon the streets will echo beneath the feet of the black battalions, soon we will show the world that the spirit of our forefathers is yet alive within us, soon we shall be united by the sacred creed striving as one man for the Greater Britain.' And so on.

Both Peter and Nancy had been at Mosley's mass meeting at Olympia of June 1934[2], during which an open battle had broken out between the Communists and the BUF. Peter's presence there was reported to his father who sounded a warning note, writing anxiously to Nancy, 'Can you not persuade him to stick to the business in hand and not to advertise himself in these Fascist demonstrations? . . . if he becomes identified with an anti-semitic campaign in England you must see yourself what that would lead to . . . There is a good deal in the spirit behind the movement [Fascism] which I should be disposed to encourage. But things are manifestly taking a wrong direction.'

Whether or not as a result of this timely interference, the Rodds' support for Fascism came to an abrupt end, and within a few weeks they were vociferously condemning the Fascist cause they had so recently championed. Nancy returned to her satirical novel, *Wigs on the Green*, and later Peter came near to provoking a diplomatic incident when, on receipt of an invitation from the German Ambassador, Ribbentrop, he wrote his refusal in Yiddish. The invitation, it is true, had been worded in German, an offensive departure from diplomatic precedent, but it was

[1] *Vanguard*, July 1934.

[2] Years later Nancy wrote about it to Evelyn Waugh, 'Prod looked very pretty in a black shirt. But we were younger & high spirited then & didn't know about Buchenwald.'

perhaps fortunate that Peter's letter was intercepted by Nancy
before it reached the post. 'I took the letter away,' she confessed,
'because of my weak mind & not wanting to be tortured when the
G's have conquered us'.

Nancy started work on *Wigs on the Green* in the spring of 1934.
The plot concerns two young fortune-hunters, Noel Foster and
Jasper Aspect. Noel has inherited enough money to enable him to
leave his dull job in the City and keep himself in style for six
months, a period he intends to devote to landing a rich wife – and
no one more suitable, he considers, than England's wealthiest
heiress, the seventeen-year-old Eugenia Malmains. Noel and his
friend Jasper make their way to the village of Chalford where their
first sight of the heiress is of Eugenia standing on an upturned
wash-tub on the village green, haranguing the villagers on the
virtues of the Union Jack Movement. Eugenia is Unity to the life:
'Her straight hair, cut in a fringe, large, pale-blue eyes, dark skin,
well-proportioned limbs and classical features, combined with a
certain fanaticism of gesture to give her the aspect of a modern
Joan of Arc.'

Noel and Jasper listen admiringly to Eugenia's peroration
('Soon your streets will echo 'neath the tread of the Union Jack
Battalions, soon the day of jelly-breasted politicians shall be no
more, soon we shall all be living in a glorious Britian under the
wise, stern, and beneficent rule of Our Captain'), and eagerly join
up in order to ingratiate themselves with her. Returning to their
hotel, they are intrigued to find a couple of pretty young women,
newly arrived, who have signed the register as Miss Smith and
Miss Jones, who clearly they are not, an impression strengthened
by a glimpse of Miss Jones sitting in the orchard with a pair of
scissors picking ducal coronets off her underwear. Heiresses,
clearly; and Jasper decides to investigate.

Noel meanwhile entangles himself with the local beauty, Mrs
Lace. Anne-Marie Lace (born Bella Drage) was pretentious,
ambitious and beautiful. 'She had the satisfaction of knowing that
most of the women disliked her, while their husbands, loutish
boors whom she despised, thought her lovely but much too

high-brow. This was satisfactory, still more so was the whole-hearted adulation which was laid at her feet by some ten or twelve rather weedy youths who formed every summer a kind of artistic colony in thatched cottages near Rackenbridge. They supposed her to be rich, ate quantities of free meals beneath her roof, and painted incompetent little pictures of her in the most extravagant poses.'

The climax of the plot is a pageant, part Social Unionist rally organised by Eugenia and her Union Jackshirts, and part Olde Englyshe Fayre and historical pageant dominated by Mrs Lace and her artistic young men. Needless to say this ends in chaos, with a furious confrontation between the Pacifists (Mrs Lace's aesthetes) and the Jackshirts. There is a pitched battle between Jackshirts and Pacifists, who 'fell upon the defenceless comrades with life preservers, knuckle-dusters, potatoes stuffed with razor blades, bicycle bells filled with shot, and other primitive, but effective weapons'. The book ends with Eugenia being congratulated for her bravery by the Leader, Captain Jack himself, who 'as a token of gratitude, plucked, like the pelican, his own little emblem from his own bosom and pinned it, still warm, upon hers'. Jasper marries his runaway heiress, Poppy St Julien; and Noel returns thankfully to his dull job in the City.

As always the text is seeded with private jokes and references. Muv throws her shadow on Eugenia's grandmother, Lady Chalford: 'Religious fervour was, in her eyes, almost as shocking as sexual abandon, and quite likely to be associated with it.' Farve appears in the joke of the building peer (used before in a story Nancy wrote for *Harper's Bazaar* in 1931) and also in character as Mr Wilkins. When Wilkins is asked by Eugenia to join her movement he says: '"Is it against foreigners and the League of Nations, because if so I'll join with pleasure. Damned sewers." Mr Wilkins had spent several years tea planting in Ceylon where "sewer" is apparently a usual term of approbrium [sic].'[1]

---

[1] In his copy of the book, Farve wrote in pencil against the dedication 'To Peter' ('Filthy rat'), and opposite the usual disclaimer, 'This is a work of fiction,

In her portrayal of Unity as Eugenia, Nancy's ambiguous feelings about her sister emerge more clearly than she was probably aware. She had taken pains to make Eugenia lovable, but, although disguised by the comic approach, there is a detectable feeling of distaste on the author's part for the violence and fanaticism in Eugenia/Unity's obsession with her Jackshirt/Fascist movement. Her mania, though made into a joke, is not pleasant.

' "I really don't know what an Aryan is."

' "Well, it's quite easy. A non-Ayran is the missing link between man and beast." '[1]

Under pressure from Unity and Diana, Nancy removed a lot of the jokes, leaving in only brief references to Mosley/Captain Jack,[2] and only one reference to Hitler: Poppy St Julien says, ' "I don't know a thing about politics, but I'm sure Hitler must be a wonderful man. Hasn't he forbidden German women to work in offices and told them they never need worry about any-

---

and all characters in the book are drawn from the author's imagination', he had written 'Beastly lie'. He had also taken the trouble heavily to delete two jokes (told by Mr Wilkins) which he obviously found in bad taste: ' "And have you heard about the man who went into W. H. Smith?" Mr Wilkins was saying.

' "No," they cried, in chorus.

' "He said to the girl behind the counter, 'Do you keep stationery?' And she said, 'No, I always wriggle.'

'Roars of laughter greeted this story.

' "And do you know about the man who was had up by the police?"

' "No."

' "They said, 'Anything you say will be held against you.' He said, 'Anything I say will be held against me?' and they said, 'yes' and he said, 'Right Oh, then, Greta Garbo.' " '

[1] Nancy wrote to Evelyn Waugh in 1951 when her publisher wanted to reissue her early novels, '*Wigs on the Green* is a total impossibility. Too much has happened for jokes about Nazis to be regarded as funny or as anything but the worst of taste. After all, it was written in 1934, I really couldn't quite have foreseen all that came after.'

[2] Both Unity and Mosley had appeared before in similar guise in a sketch Nancy wrote in 1932, 'The Old Ladies', but this was a private joke, never intended for publication.

thing again, except arranging the flowers? How they must love him."

' "They do," said Eugenia. "Heil Hitler!" '

When Nancy began on the novel she was confident that Bobo would be both flattered and amused. 'Darling Eugenia, I can't write *to* you very often as I am so busy writing *about* you. You get more & more wonderful every day & more like yourself – in the last chapter you even make that gesture when you try to snap your fingers but no sound comes!' At first Unity rather liked the sound of this, although she was too interested in her own affairs to pay it much attention. 'Well its wonderful to be in the Deutsches Reich once more, what do you think, I saw the Führer the *very day* I arrived, if that isn't being the Luckiest Person in the World I'd like to know what is . . . How is Eugenia getting on, when you have done a bit more you must come out here & read it to me. Or you might read it over the phone . . . Heil Hitler! Love Bobo.'

Soon, however, she began to grow apprehensive. 'Now seriously, about that book. I have heard a bit about it from Muv, & I warn you you can't *possibly* publish it, so you'd better not waste any more time on it. Because if you did publish it I couldn't *possibly* ever speak to you again from the date of publication.'

By the end of the year, Nancy was beginning to realise that she might have Gone Too Far; she wrote placatingly to Diana to explain what she was up to, hoping for a sisterly shriek. 'Peter says I can't put a movement like Fascism into a work of fiction *by name* so I am calling it the Union Jack movement, the members wear Union Jackshirts & their Lead is called Colonel Jack. But I shall give it to you to edit before publication because although it is very pro-Fascism there are one or two jokes & you could tell better than I whether they would be leader-teases.' But no shriek was forthcoming. Diana disliked the book, and insisted that, if it could not be stopped, it must at least be cut and toned down. The BUF was a new movment which Mosley was working hard to establish; the last thing he wanted was his future sister-in-law publicly poking fun at it. What to Nancy were the comic aspects – the black shirts, the militaristic formations, the clockwork marching and inspiriting songs – were important elements in identifying, unifying and organising the Party. If it were mocked, if ever he were seen to condone the mockery, it might be thought that he was not serious.

Nancy refused to abandon the book, but she did agree to substantial cuts. 'Darling Stone-Heart Bone-Head,' she wrote to Unity, 'I am very glad to hear that you are returning anon. Do leave all ye rubber truncheons behind & pump some warm palpitating blood into that stony heart for the occasion. I have taken out all references to the F.[1] (not the[2] POF, the other F.) in my book, & as it cost me about 4/6 a time to do so you ought to feel quite kindly towards me now . . . Nardie[3] is off to Rome . . . just as well . . . now you won't be able to hot each other up about me Head of Bone/ Heart of Stone/ Sister Hater/ Mother-Baiter/ I will finish this poem later.' But as the publication date drew near Nancy became nervously aware that a row was unavoidable. She wrote to Diana a week before publication to explain her position.

> Darling Bodley My book comes out on the 25th inst:, & in view of our conversation at the Ritz ages ago I feel that I must make a few observations to you.
>
> When I got home that day I read it all through & found that it would be impossible to eliminate the bits that you & the Leader objected to. As you know our finances are such that I really couldn't afford to scrap the book then. I did however hold it up for about a month (thus missing the Spring list) in order to take out everything which directly related to Captain Jack amounting to nearly 3 chapters & a lot of paragraphs. There are now, I think, about 4 references to him & he never appears in the book as a character at all.
>
> In spite of this I am very much worried at the idea of publishing a book which you may object to. It completely

[1] The Führer.
[2] Poor Old Führer, ie. Mosley.
[3] Diana.

blights all the pleasure which one ordinarily feels in a forth-coming book.

And yet, consider. A book of this kind can't do your movement any harm. Honestly, if I thought it could set the leader back by so much as half an hour I would have scrapped it, or indeed never written it in the first place. The 2 or 3 thousand people who read my books, are, to begin with, just the kind of people the Leader admittedly doesn't want in his movement. Furthermore it would be absurd to suppose that anyone who was intellectually or emotionally convinced of the truths of Fascism could be influenced against the movement by such a book.

I still maintain that it is far more in favour of Fascism than otherwise Far the nicest character in the book is a Fascist, the others all become much nicer as soon as they have joined up. But I also know your point of view, that Fascism is something too serious to be dealt with in a funny book at all. Surely that is a little unreasonable? Fascism is now such a notable feature of modern life all over the world that it must be possible to consider it in any context, when attempting to give a picture of life as it is lived today.

Personally I believe that when you have read the book, if you do, you will find that all objections to it except perhaps the last, (that my particular style is an unsuitable medium) will have disappeared.

Oh darling I do hope so!

She foresaw that her careful position sitting on the fence was about to cause her to topple into the mud, and to Unity three days later she wrote:

Darling Head of Bone & Heart of Stone Oh dear oh dear the book comes out on Tuesday. Oh dear, I won't let Rodd give a party for it, or John Sutro either, who wanted to. Oh dear I wish I had never been born into such a family of fanatics. Oh dear.

Oh dear, this is probably the last letter you'll ever get from me because its no use writing to Stone-Hearts.

Miss Stony Heart/ What shall I do/ Oh how I wish I was/ Stone hearted like you *Please* don't read the book if its going to stone you up against me Anyway Eugenia is the only nice character in it except for Lady Marjorie who becomes nice after joining up with the Union Jack Shirts. *Do* remember that.

Oh dear *do* write me a kind & non-stony-heart-letter to say you don't mind it *nearly* as much as you expected, in fact you LIKE it, in fact, after I face the stars it is your favourite book even more favourite than mine comf. I wonder what Mr Wessel will think of it. Are you going yachting with him again by the way?

Oh dear, I am going to Oxford with Nardie tomorrow, our last day together I suppose before the clouds of her displeasure burst over me. She doesn't know yet that its coming out on Tuesday. Oh dear I have spent days trying to write her diplomatic letters about it. Oh dear I wish I had called it mine uncomf now because uncomf is what I feel whenever I think about it. Oh dear.

So now don't get together with Nardie & ban me forever or I shall die. Could you forgive me quite soon? Otherwise Xmas & other feasts at home will be *so* uncomf.

So now write quite soon & say you forgive me. I did take out some absolutely wonderful jokes you know & all the bits about the Captain. OH! DEAR!'

Wigs on the Green attracted little critical attention – 'Miss Mitford has simply (if I may be allowed a highly metaphorical expression) kicked up her heels on the village green':[1] – but within the family the damage had been done. Diana was seriously annoyed, and for a time the relationship between the two sisters was strained. As for Bobo, as John Betjeman rightly said after he had read the book, 'I suppose it will now be all up with Unity Valkyrie and you.'

---

[1] *News Chronicle.*

CHAPTER FIVE

Married Life

For the Mitfords, 1936 was a year of general upheaval: two sisters married – Diana to Mosley, Pam to Derek Jackson, the millionaire physicist and amateur jockey. Swinbrook was sold, Farve keeping only the Old Mill Cottage next to the Swan public-house in the village. And Nancy and Peter, enjoying a brief period of comparative prosperity, left Rose Cottage for a house in town.

12 Blomfield Road[1] was small and elegant, one in a shady, tree-lined street of early nineteenth-century houses, each with its own garden, running alongside the Grand Union Canal in Maida Vale (now the fashionable area known as Little Venice). As at Strand on the Green Nancy's outlook was one of trees and water, the wide reach of the Thames giving place to the narrow banks of a sooty urban waterway.

Turning her back on the steely, tubular modernity of the thirties Nancy indulged to the full her love of Victoriana. The house 'is exactly like a French lodging house,' she told Golly and her husband Simon Elwes. 'I see people *struggling* to say some-thing nice about it & falling back with relief on the canal (which is enchanting) I found a wallpaper for the dining room which consists of swags, roses, urn & bows & is printed on PINK MOIRÉ. So there . . . Lottie has 2 beautiful puppies which are a great help with the new carpets of course.'

With her new house and her little dogs and an unaccustomed sense of financial security, Nancy should have been happy; but she was not. Her marriage was going badly: she and Peter were

---

[1] Demolished after the war.

often barely on speaking terms, and Peter's drinking was beginning to get seriously out of control. It is true that he was holding down a job: 'Peter is getting awfully nice & rich,' she loyally relayed to the Elweses. 'I mean it wouldn't seem rich to you but I can hardly believe it. Not a bailiff now for months & every prospect of a mink coat next winter (only now I can *only* think of sable)'; but this hardly made up for the horror of the drunken arguments ('I know, I know, I *am* a journalist, a banker, a veterinary surgeon . . .'); nor for the scenes in public ('Brenners[1] to you!' he once shouted in the face of a distinguished Italian to whom he had just lost at bridge); nor for the frequent occasions when he and a couple of cronies would reel home in a taxi at four in the morning, completely intoxicated, and hammer at the door until Nancy came down in her dressing-gown to pay off the taxi and cook them all scrambled eggs. Nancy never complained, the shop-front was kept locked into place, but it was obvious to those who knew her that all was not well. She did her best to turn each incident into yet another Prodd funny story, but although that to some extent saved her face, it did not improve relations with Peter. Nor did it help that she was now on bad terms with most of his family. She was irritated by Taffy and his wife Yvonne, found Mary Rodd and her Moral Rearmament ludicrous, had quarrelled with Francis, Mary's husband, and then – 'a real sacrifice just before Xmas' – had rounded off with a steaming row with her mother-in-law. 'I am no longer Aunt Lily's pie eyed girl it is a curious change & has its point. We had a terrible quarrel about the King (not Dumbert[2] I mean the proper one) So she only gave

---

[1] The Brenner Pass was the scene of an Italian defeat during the First World War.

[2] This was the year of the Abdication and Nancy had taken against George VI, 'Dumbert the Slow', and his family: everything they did annoyed her, even, or especially, the doings of the little Princesses—'I believe somebody will have a pot shot at them if they go to church in white gloves much more often you can't imagine what a bad impression it makes.' It made an excellent tease, and it was typical of Nancy's contrariness that she should make a point of taking against the most popular members of the royal family at the height of their popularity. Thus when the entire nation was oohing and aahing over Lilibet and little

me a bath salt jar with no bath salts for Xmas & to Yvonne (to show the difference) a necklace made entirely of the insides of watches very Surréaliste.'

But worse than all this was the fact of Peter's infidelity. Peter had always boasted of himself as a womaniser, had had a number of love affairs, and now, after only eighteen months of marriage, had fallen in love again, this time with Mary Sewell, daughter of the architect Sir Edwin Lutyens and the wife of a stockbroker. She and her husband lived a few doors away from the Redesdales in Rutland Gate, and the Sewells and the Rodds used to meet regularly to play bridge. Although in theory the two women had quite a lot in common – only four years younger than Nancy, Mary too was a novelist – they never liked each other. Mary, pretty, sexy and chic, had according to Nancy 'a spoon face & dresses at Gorringes'; while Mary found Nancy sharp-tongued and sour. Their bridge evenings were characterised by Nancy and Peter sniping at each other, Peter boasting he had made a habit of proposing to every girl he met, but only Nancy had been fool enough to accept him; while Nancy harped on their poverty and the bailiffs coming to the house, with implications Peter did not care for. Peter flirted openly with Mary over dinner, and in retaliation Nancy would stage a faint, which annoyed Peter. 'She's only doing it to get attention,' he would say impatiently, as he carried her upstairs and dropped her onto the drawing-room sofa. Nancy did not like staying up late and the Sewells led very separate lives, which made it easy for Mary and Peter to spend evenings together, as well as meeting nearly every day for lunch at a little Italian restaurant in Maddox Street, in easy reach from the City.

In August 1936 the two couples had the ill-advised notion of

Margaret Rose, or Princess Elizabeth on her wedding-day (the Corgi Wedding, as Nancy referred to it), or the newly-born Prince Charles ('I say what a *beastly* little face that Prince Charles has – really frightening . . . And maquillé to the eyes to boot') for Nancy it was a matter of principle to find them ridiculous or offensive.

going on holiday to St. Briene in Brittany, together with Patrick Balfour and Decca, then aged seventeen and marking time before coming out. It was not a success. Peter, a keen sailor, arrived by yacht several days after the others, days which he had spent writing love-letters to Mary on lavatory paper, the only paper available on the boat. They all stayed at the same hotel, Peter and Mary meeting secretly on the beach before the others were up. Nancy, miserably aware of the emotional tension between her husband and Mary, sulked through the day and went to bed straight after dinner while the others drove off to a night club. Decca, cheerfully oblivious to these adult complexities, described one such outing to Debo, a visit to a nightclub 'run by an ex-follies bergère lady called Popo (or Pot-Pot) And there are notices on the walls saying things like "Popo a soixante ans, elle est garantie pour cent" And she did a dance & took off her jersey. Wasn't it extraorder. And then she waltzed with Mary Sewell. Nancy didn't come. She thinks nightclubs boring.'

Back at home, the unhappy situation continued until the beginning of the following year, 1937, when it was overshadowed by yet another colossal Mitford crisis. In January Nancy, who had been feeling depressed and unwell, had gone without Peter to stay with Aunt Vi in the Rennell appartment in Rome. (Peter wrote unconvincingly from London that he was 'not doing anything except going to bed early'.) From there she described to Decca the uneventful social life, 'as dreary as could be', that Aunt Vi went in for. It is a childish letter, deliberately so, to appeal to the second youngest member of the family, hardly out of the schoolroom and still, presumably, interested exclusively in animals.

Darling Sooze[1] Thanks oh thanks for all those delishwish long letters you keep writing me evidently you quite realise how much one likes getting letters when abroad. (This Susan is called irony & it means that the iron of yr unkindness has entered/is entering into my sishwish or soul)

[1] Nancy and Decca always addressed each other as 'Susan'.

Susan this *is* a place. Not one FR bulldog have I seen since I got here. Not a Dollie not a Millie not a Lottie & alas not the merest shadow of a creech have I set eyes on. No wonder the Italians feel so low, talk so loud & sing all those screaming songs. The low crooning of a creech at their fireside is absent from their lives. I pity them . . .

Give my love to Tiny Swine[1] & ask her why the poor thin Roman cab horses won't eat the delishwish apples I keep buying for them? Surely horses used to like apples in my young day? . . .

The verbs of this lingshwish are nearly impossible & are breaking my heart I have a lesson every day with a lade who keeps telling me that of course Hitler is a great man but M.[2] is greater because the germans only fear H while the ice creamers love M with a spiritual & mystic love. I seem to have heard this before only the other way round eh what

'Well Sooze tinkety tonk tiny tot from Susan.

But Decca had grown up more quickly than Nancy or anyone else had realised. Of all the sisters she was the one who had resented most bitterly her parents' refusal to send her to school, had suffered most from the boredom of Swinbrook. At first in childish reaction to Unity's Fascism she had declared herself a Communist. The two of them divided their shared sitting-room down the middle, Bobo's half decorated with Fascist insignia and photographs of Mosley, Hitler and Mussolini, while Decca in her half had a hammer-and-sickle flag and a small bust of Lenin. By the time she had gone through her first London Season, Decca was smouldering: she hated the world she had been born into and she could not wait to leave. It was at this precise moment that she met for the first time her cousin Esmond Romilly. At nineteen Esmond was already a committed left-winger and rebel (founder of a subversive magazine, run away from school, six weeks in a remand home), recently invalided home after fighting on the

[1] Debo.
[2] Mussolini.

Loyalist Front in the Spanish Civil War. A born anarchist, belligerent, bullying and brave, he was possessed of that useful combination of intelligence and insensitivity that meant he was adept at getting what he wanted with not very much regard to the methods employed. He could have been made for Decca, and by the time they actually met, in the house of an elderly cousin, she was more than ready to follow Esmond to the ends of the earth – or rather to Spain, where he intended as soon as possible to return. With a degree of ingenuity and brazenness that surprised even herself, Decca deceived Muv into believing she had an invitation to spend a couple of weeks with friends in Dieppe. Instead she and Esmond ran off together, making their way through France to Bilbao in the Basque Republic.

When the fortnight of the mythical holiday in Dieppe was up and it dawned on the Redesdales that Decca had disappeared, the effect was shattering. Muv sat in the drawing-room at Rutland Gate wringing her hands and being comforted in turn by Diana, Unity and Tom; Farve was beside himself with anger; Nanny Dicks was in tears; and Aunt Weenie added to the general turmoil by unhelpfully turning on Diana and accusing her of having 'set the example'. Nobody knew anything except that Decca was not and never had been in Dieppe with the Paget twins. Eventually she was traced, and Muv, realising that it would be pointless for Farve to go out to Spain – he was far too angry to be rational and, used to being obeyed, would be incapable of conducting what might be a lengthy and delicate process of negotiation – and knowing that Nancy would soon be on her way back from Italy, she turned to her eldest daughter for help.

Peter, meanwhile, confronted with an unparalleled opportunity for knowing best, had proved himself 'a *great* prop & stay', coming up with the one plan most certain to antagonise Esmond – that of making Decca a Ward in Chancery so that she could be legally extradited, sent home and placed under court supervision. Esmond, more than a match for the Bilbao Consul, rose effortlessly to the challenge and defied the order to send Decca home, agreeing only to leave Spanish soil. He and Decca then sailed to St Jean de Luz where they found Nancy waiting for them on the dockside with Peter square and stocky beside her, his hands thrust into his pockets in his usual tough-guy attitude. Pushing through the crowd of reporters and press photographers, the four of them got into a waiting taxi and went straight to the hotel where Nancy had taken rooms for the night – and the arguing began. But the harder the Rodds talked, the more obstinate the runaways became. Nancy, a former ally, had betrayed Decca by going over to the enemy and siding with the grown-ups; Peter, too, previously so much looked up to (Decca was the only one of the Mitfords not to find him a bore: she had been entranced by his bragging talk of joining the International Brigade and of starting revolutions in South America), had also shown himself a turncoat by a display of governessy behaviour of the worst kind. Nothing the Rodds could say had any effect, and the following day they returned to England alone.

From Blomfield Road, Nancy wrote to Decca, more from a sense of obligation to register her rather half-hearted disapproval than with any conviction that she could change Decca's mind. 'Susan it isn't very respectable what you are doing . . . after all one has to live in this world *as it is* & society (I don't mean duchesses) can make things pretty beastly to those who disobey its rules . . . Susan do come back. No Susan. Well Susan if anything happens don't forget there is a spare room here (£4.10. bed) Love from Sue.' Although shaken by the sight of her parents' distress, and a little shocked by Decca's brutal disregard for convention, Nancy could not help sympathising: always on the side of love, and understanding only too well the stifling quality of life under the Birds' wings, she was unable to be more severe than she felt her duty required. Esmond she frankly loathed, but he was Decca's choice, and it was up to her to lead her life as she pleased.

Decca, however, had taken offence. She was furious at what she saw as Nancy's disloyalty, furious with her letter, and with the one accompanying it from Peter in which, as one black sheep to another, he advised her seriously to consider the consequences of her behaviour. But she eventually calmed down, and on May 18,

1937, she and Esmond were married in the presence of Muv and Mrs Romilly in Bayonne, after which Nancy was able to turn back with relief to the old bantering, childish tone that with Decca she never afterwards varied. Writing to her sister in July of that year to congratulate her on the news of her pregnancy ('Susan fancy you with a scrapage'[1]), she talks to her exactly as though she were still in the nursery, telling of the hedgehog bought at Harrods ('we call it hog watson & give it bread & milk'), the sweetness of Millie who had just won 4th prize in a dog show, and the fact that Dolly (Lottie's daughter) has 'just been on heat so I covered her with Keep Away & she went round saying

> I do not like the 'Keep Away'
> Because it keeps the dogs at bay
> The dogs with whom I wish to play
> Are kept away by 'Keep Away'.

You must say not bad for 9 months I bet your scrapage won't make up lovely poems like that . . .'

In August Nancy went out to Posilipo where, she informed Decca, she was writing a play: 'It is about a Communist who is the Bowd [Unity] so I expect I shall catch it from all.' But in fact her next piece of work, started at the end of that year, was something quite different. This was an edition in two volumes,[2] of nineteenth-century family letters belonging to her cousin Ed Stanley[3]. The Stanleys were a lively, funny, querulous lot. 'Their common characteristics were a sort of downright rudeness, a passion for quarrelling, great indifference to public opinion, an unrivalled skill in finding and pointing out the weak points in other people's armour, thick legs and eyebrows, lively minds and a great literary sense.' Their letters give a vivid picture of that safe, rich Victorian upper-class life that Nancy found so attrac-

---

[1] Baby.
[2] *The Ladies of Alderley* published in 1938, *The Stanleys of Alderley* in 1939.
[3] Nancy's great-great-grandmother, Blanche Airlie, was the daughter of the second Baron Stanley of Alderley and Henrietta Maria, one of the two ladies of the first volume.

tive. The upper-classes of those days were so enviably secure, never questioning 'the fact that each individual has his allotted place in the realm and that their own allotted place was among the ruling, the leisured and the moneyed classes', sentiments with which Nancy whole-heartedly identified. Indeed for all her protestations of Socialism, her view of English history as here expressed reveals nothing more nor less than a traditional, true-blue, schoolroom Conservatism, full of nostalgia for The Past as a kind of Gilbertian golden age in which every Englishman knew his place, the lord, a sensible man of ample means and a classical education, living in perfect harmony with the commoner at his gate. 'During the whole of the nineteenth century,' Nancy explains with a courageous disregard for historical fact, 'the English and their rulers were in perfect accord, they understood and trusted the integrity of each other's aims and methods, and consequently this country was enabled to achieve a greatness, not only material, but spiritual, which has never been equalled in the history of the world.' She laments the coming of 'the terrible twentieth century', cruelly driving the lord from his God-given land, thus resulting in 'the segregation of the classes' and a loss of the trust between ruler and ruled. In those days statesmen were men of noble bearing whose 'pronouncements were elegant and exact, such words as jitterbug were not a part of their vocabulary nor were they often photographed having breakfast in bed'. They ruled England and England ruled the world. 'The proudest title we can acquire is that of "a nation of governesses". We are the only adult nation and until the others come of age we must be their governess, lecture them at all times, put iodine on their knees when they fall down and graze them; when we see them torturing a kitten we must slap them hard and take away the kitten.'

This preface was not included when the book was reissued after the war. The opinions in it nevertheless remain at the basis of Nancy's understanding of her social position. No wonder the twentieth century seemed so 'terrible', brutally destroying the order established over centuries of the divine right of the upper

classes to live in beautiful old houses set in beautiful old parks,
and waited on by perfectly sweet members of the lower orders.

Nancy found the research immensely congenial, sorting
through the mass of papers in the attics at Alderley, and bringing
to the subject her love of history as well as her novelist's shrewd
eye for character. She wrote to Robert Byron who had shown a
sympathetic interest in the project, 'It is like being under chloroform. I feel in another world while doing them . . . I do long to talk
about the letters . . . Rodd *is so* discouraging.'

It was one of the ironies in the worsening situation between
Nancy and Peter that, while neither was happy with the other,
each resented it when one went away or was otherwise absorbed.
She resented his late nights and philandering; he resented the
fact that when he was at home she was too interested in her work
to pay him any attention. Then in the summer of 1938 Nancy
found she was pregnant.

She had wanted a baby for the last three years, and when she
failed to conceive her gynaecologist recommended curettage,
after which he declared her perfectly fit, with no reason why she
should not safely have children. As she was told this just before
leaving for the ill-fated holiday in Brittany, when it seemed that
the sexual side of her marriage was finished for good, the news
did little to raise her spirits. In spite of her frequently aired views
on the disgustingness of babies (when Decca was expecting hers,
Nancy wrote encouragingly, 'One has to do such awful things to
scrapages I saw one being put to bed the other day & oh sooze the
smell first its nappy then its potty ugh –'), she had nonetheless
always looked forward to having a family of her own. Now to her
joy she was pregnant, and all seemed to be well – provided, her
doctor warned her, she spend the first few weeks in bed.

The summer of 1938 was hot, and in August Muv took Nancy
down to stay with the Dashwoods at West Wycombe, Peter being
on holiday with Ed Stanley somewhere in France. After a couple
of weeks, she went back to London, first to Rutland Gate, then at
the beginning of September to Blomfield Road, where she was
looked after by a nurse and her Norwegian maid, Sigrid. She

wrote happily to Robert Byron that all was well, she was still 'fostering the foetus', and had just broken the glad news to her mama-in-law but so far had received no reply. 'I suppose she is furious at my improvident behaviour. (Of course it is *lunatic* really I quite see that but one must never be deterred from doing what one wants for lack of money don't you agree.) Aunt Vi wrote that she hoped it would be a boy "as you know I don't like R.C.s & I should hate Rennells well earned honours to go to one" I replied that I could not wish for a boy even in order to keep Ld R's many titles from falling into the clutches of the Scarlet Woman . . . Actually if I thought for a minute it would be a boy I should go for a long bicycle ride here & now – 2 Peter Rodds in 1 house is unthinkable.' But such precautions were unnecessary: in the middle of the month the nurse left as everything seemed to be going so smoothly, and Nancy returned to Rutland Gate. There, perhaps as a result of the move, she almost immediately suffered a miscarriage.

The loss of the baby was a sadness of which Nancy never spoke. She complained of the tedium of having to stay quiet, how 'deadly' it was not to be allowed to go in a car – 'I mayn't even take a taxi & go out to lunch' – but never of her grief. Her doctor had told her that there was no reason why she should not conceive again, but at thirty-four she was not hopeful. Her husband's attention was for women other than his wife, and, a further cause of worry, Peter was yet again out of work. He had been hoping for a job in the BBC, but Francis, helpfully stepping in, had advised the Corporation against employing his irresponsible brother, a gratuitous act of interference which had made Nancy furious. 'I have put F's name in a drawer & I *hope he dies*,'[1] she told Robert Byron, begging him to use his influence to get Peter the job of Registrar at Kensington School of Art.

But the problem of a job for Peter was soon to be solved, quite unexpectedly, by a turn in international events. The Spanish Civil

[1] It was a favourite superstition of Farve's that, if you wrote somebody's name on a slip of paper and put it in a drawer, that person would die within the year.

War had broken out in 1936; by January 1939 General Franco's rebel army was moving north through Valencia and Tarragona, driving before it half a million Republicans from Catalonia who were fleeing over the Pyrenees into the Roussillon, an impoverished region of France with no resources to spare and no provision made for the feeding and sheltering of thousands of refugees. The French authorities hastily set up a few barbed-wire enclosures on the salt-marshes along the coast, into which, without food, water or medical supplies, the Spaniards were herded. There they were left, until the international charitable organisations arrived to do what they could to feed and clothe them and provide passage for those with relations in France, Mexico or Morocco.

Peter, who had felt slightly guilty at not having fought in the war in Spain, immediately volunteered to help with the refugees. He arrived in Perpignan to find over 200,000 people encamped in appalling conditions and dying at the rate of 400 a day. 'Darling Paul,' he wrote to Nancy, 'the thing that was happening is so appalling that it amounts to the cold blooded murder of thousands of chaps. It is impossible to get at the mortality figures but the dying has not even properly begun. They've got typhoid and possibly cholera as well now and it began raining today.' He threw himself into the seemingly impossible task of imposing order on this miserable chaos, distributing supplies, writing reports, and instituting a system whereby separated members of the same family could be put in touch with each other. It was in this kind of work that his talents lay; although by and large indifferent to the sufferings of any one individual, especially if that individual were his wife, to incidences of mass wretchedness he was very much alive.

Nancy, who had been doing what she could to ensure that Peter's reports were seen by the right people, went out to Perpignan in May to join him. Peter himself was far too busy to give her more than an absent-minded peck on the cheek and rush her over to his office – a large shed on the Avenue de la Gare – to introduce her to his assistants, Donald Darling and Humphrey

Hare, '2 chaps who talk the *New Statesmans* English which is always a comfort abroad I find'. Fortunately both Darling and Hare took to Nancy – her jokes cheered them up – and they went to the trouble, as Peter had not, of finding her something useful to do, a problem requiring a certain ingenuity as she spoke not a word of Spanish, knew nothing about First Aid or calories, and had not the faintest idea what to do with a newly-born baby. In the end she spent most of her time behind the wheel of a dilapidated Ford van, a straw coolie hat on her head, delivering supplies, waiting around for messages, and on one occasion driving a group of expectant mothers to Sète for embarkation on a ship bound for Mexico. 'Well we got our ship off,' she wrote to Muv.

There was a fearful hurricane and she couldn't get into Port Vendre so all the arrangements had to be altered & she was sent to Sette (150 miles from P.V.) & at an hours notice special trains had to be changed etc etc the result was Peter was up for 2 *whole* nights, never went to bed at all. However he is none the worse. I was up all yesterday night as the embarkation went on until 6AM & the people on the quay had to be fed & the babies given their bottles. There were 200 babies under 2 & 12 women are to have babies on board. One poor shell shocked man went mad & had to be given an anaesthetic & taken off, but apart from that all went smoothly if slowly. The women were on the quayside first & then the men arrived. None of them had seen each other since the retreat & I believe thought really that they wouldn't find each other then, & when they did you never saw such scenes of hugging. The boat sailed at 12 yesterday, the pathetic little band on board played first God Save the King, for us, then the Marseillaise & then the Spanish National Anthem. Then the poor things gave 3 Vivas for Espana which they will never see again. I don't think there was a single person not crying – I have never cried so much in my life. They had all learned to say Goodbye & thank you & they crowded round us so that we could hardly get off the ship. Many of them are great friends of Peter, & I know a lot of them too by now as some have

been working in our office, & it was really sad to see them go –
to what?'

The plight of the refugee families was desolate and pathetic,
and Nancy was deeply moved by the dignity with which they
accepted their dreadful situation. Peter's office was in a state of
constant siege, surrounded all day by patient men, women, and
children with their little parcels and their cardboard suitcases,
their dogs, their donkeys and their goats. Peter was in his
element, the uncrowned King of Perpignan, with even the official
English representative, General Molesworth, under his thumb.
(Molesworth was a type Nancy knew: 'When confronted with a
foreigner he breaks into fluent Hindostanee & he has already
confided in me that he is longing to get away & throw a fly over a
salmon.') Sometimes Nancy saw nothing of her husband for
several days at a time, and then he would turn up light-headed
with exhaustion, get quickly drunk, abuse everyone within ear-
shot, then still drunk, still abusive, plunge into the sea for a
swim.

At weekends, true to national habit, the British contingent shut
up shop, and with the arrival of the warmth of early summer went
picnicking in the Pyrenees or bathing at Collioure. In spite of the
misery around her, Nancy found a lot to enjoy, happy to be in
beautiful France again and enchanted by the prettiness of Perpignan with its narrow streets of rose-coloured brick, its huge,
wild-looking plane-trees, its river and broad quays. With her
sharp eye for comic detail, she was quick to notice such curiosities
as the leech in a bottle kept in the window of a chemist's shop
beside a typewritten notice: 'SI LA SANGSUE MONTE
DANS LA BOUTEILLE IL FERA BEAU TEMPS. SI LA
SANGSUE DESCEND – L'ORAGE.'

Nancy returned to England in June determined 'to enjoy my
last fling before the war ... I am leading a very gay life, &
tomorrow am dressing lamb (powdered hair, white satin, blue
bows & roses) for the ball at Osterley.' She was much taken up,
too, with her 'dear bullies', as Millie had given birth to four

puppies one of which, Agnes, was to go to Robert Byron. 'Really Agnes is such a pet I can hardly bear to let her go – couldn't to anyone but you . . . She is very anti-appeasement.'

But that unsettled summer ended with the declaration of war between Great Britain and Germany on September 3 when, for Nancy as for the rest of the country, more serious preoccupations took over. There can have been few families in England more deeply divided between right and left, Fascist and Communist, appeasement and war, than the Mitfords. The Mosleys, with Unity and Tom, Derek and Pam Jackson, made up the anti-war faction; Decca and Esmond Romilly were ranged vociferously on the opposite side – anti-German and in favour of war and of the overthrow of the established order; while Nancy and Peter stood in the middle, believing, with the majority of the British nation, that war with Germany was necessary and inevitable, largely to preserve this established order. The Redesdales themselves, for the first time in their lives, were in bitter opposition. Originally Muv had gone along with her husband's contempt for Hitler: the man was, after all, a Hun, one of the categories – on a par with Negroes, Jews and Roman Catholics – that Farve most loathed. But then they both went to Germany to visit Unity, had been present at the Nuremberg rally of 1938, and had met the Führer himself. Farve had instantly succumbed and the phrase 'that feller Hitler' turned overnight from opprobrium to a term of the highest approbation. Muv, at first, had been less impressed but was eventually won over by the sheer *niceness* of the man. She had been taken to tea with Hitler in his flat in Munich and, although neither could speak the other's language, it was a friendly occasion. 'He is very "easy" to be with,' she told Decca, '. . . & such *very* good manners.' Back in London Farve spoke in the House of Lords in favour of returning the German colonies confiscated after the First World War while Muv made her contribution with a couple of newspaper articles in defence of Nazism ('In Fascism and National Socialism there is no class war, but friendship and co-operation between all classes for the common welfare . . .'); and she gave a luncheon for a group of forty-five visiting Hitler Jugend in the ballroom at Rutland Gate[1].

When war broke out Farve, his country first and foremost, immediately recanted. 'Farve has publicly recanted like Latimer in the *Daily Mirror* & said he was mistaken all along (& how),' Nancy wrote. Muv, however, although as fiercely patriotic as her husband in wishing for victory, refused to yield in her admiration either for Hitler or for his régime. To her, war with Germany was a disaster. To Farve, as to Nancy, it was a matter of necessity.

Nancy had already had several run-ins with her mother on the subject. She had written to her from Perpignan in May: 'If you could have a look, as I have, at some of the less agreeable results of fascism in a country I think you would be less anxious for the swastika to become a flag on which the sun never sets. And, what ever may be the *good* produced by that régime that the first result is always a horde of unhappy refugees cannot be denied. Personally I would join hands with the devil himself to stop any further extension of the disease. As for encirclement, if a person goes mad he is encircled, *not out of any hatred* for the person but for the safety of his neighbours & the same applies to countries. Furthermore, I consider that if the Russian alliance does not go through we shall be at war in a fortnight, & as I have a husband of fighting age I am not particularly anxious for that eventuality. *You began this argument so don't be cross if I say what I think!*'

On the day that war was declared Nancy was on her way home, having been staying with her mother on Inch Kenneth, an island in the Hebrides Farve had bought on the spur of the moment the year before from a man at his club. Inevitably an argument started and Nancy, always one to put comfort before principle, had rather hurriedly to climb down. 'I was leaving the island & Muv was taking me to the station & I said something only fairly rude about

[1] The occasion turned out to be something of an anti-climax: 'I was much disappointed,' Muv wrote to Debo. 'Instead of the wonderful looking boys of 17 & 18 I expected to see, a party of intensely dreary looking & ugly young men of at least 30. I then realised how very sensible it is of H to put all Germans into uniforms, as they have such terrible other clothes . . .'

Hitler & she said get out of this car & walk to the station then so after that I had to be honey about Adolph. Then later I said Peter had joined up so she said I expect he'll get shot soon which I thought fairly tactless of her. Altogether she is acting *very* queer.' Two weeks later she was retailing with relish a highly selective version of Muv's opinions. Rarely able to let pass an opportunity of portraying her mother in an unflattering light, Nancy took a wicked pleasure in exaggerating the one aspect of Muv's beliefs guaranteed to shock, while choosing to ignore the rest. 'Muv has gone finally off her head She seems to regard Adolph as her favourite son in law (the kind of which people say he has been like a *son* to me) . . . she is *impossible*. Hopes we shall lose the war & makes no bones about it. Debo is having a wild time with young cannon fodders at the Ritz etc. Apparently Muv said to her "*never* discuss politics, not even for 5 minutes, with Nancy" Rather as some devout RC mama might shield her little one from a fearful atheist!'

This letter was written to Violet Hammersley, whom Muv had known from the time she and Violet were girls, as their fathers had been friends. Now a widow with three grown-up children, Mrs Hammersley had become almost part of the Mitford family, as important a figure in the lives of the children as of their parents. Her husband had died in 1913, leaving her very well off, but she lost the bulk of her fortune when the bank in which he had been a partner went into liquidation ten years later. From that time on Mrs Hammersley considered herself the most unfortunate of mortals. Always dressed in black or dark brown, swathed in shawls and veils, she looked the picture of prophetic doom, with her melancholy expression and low, hollow laugh. But she also had a strong sense of humour, was intelligent, musical, and widely read in English and French literature. (She had been born and brought up in Paris and loved France and the French.) To Nancy, she was in part a maternal figure, but cleverer and more worldly than Muv, to whom could be confided details of her life which she would never dream of revealing to her mother. Mrs Ham, as the girls called her, had an appetite for gossip nearly equal to Nancy's own, and with her fondness for, and intimate knowledge of, the Mitfords and their affairs, she became an invaluable correspondent, relied upon as an appreciative recipient of Nancy's wit, while at the same time trusted to know better than to believe the more elaborate exaggerations.

Both Nancy and Peter volunteered at once for war work. Peter, with a commission in the Welsh Guards, was filling in time before being called up working at a First Aid Post in Chelsea. Nancy did the same at St Mary's Hospital, Paddington, sitting from eleven to seven every day in a gas-proof room with little to do and a cracking headache from the lack of fresh air. 'This is my 9th day & feels like 7 years (which I am told the war will last),' she complained to Mrs Ham. 'Anyway in case I didn't I must tell you about the foreheads. Well my job is writing on the foreheads of dead & dying in indelible pencil. *What* I write I haven't yet discovered. What happens when a coloured man presents *his* forehead I also ignore. I was just about to ask all these little details when the Queen arrived to see over (in fawn) so I never found out. Isn't it awful.

'Meanwhile I sit twiddling my indelible pencil & *aching* for a forehead to write on . . . Sitting in this hateful cellar (gas & therefore air proof, electric light all day & cold as the grave) my brain has become like the inside of a bad walnut . . . I really see nobody, impossible to lunch out & in the evening I am too tired & it is too dark & frightening to go out.'

Then at the beginning of October came the news of one of the first casualties of the war: a friend of Tom's in Budapest sent word that Unity had been taken seriously ill and was in hospital in Munich. Nobody seemed to know exactly what was the matter. The next bulletin, retailed by Nancy to Mrs Hammersley with a detectable lack of sisterly sympathy, revealed that Bobo was 'in a concentration camp for Czech women which much as I deplore it has a sort of poetic justice. Peter is going to make the Aostas[1] get

---

[1] Duke of Aosta, member of the Italian royal family and a friend, of course, of Lord Rennell's.

her out in a month or two when she has had a sufficient dose to wish to go.' The truth finally came out when the story broke in the *Daily Express*: on the day war was declared Unity had shot herself. Badly but not fatally wounded, she had been taken to a clinic where it was found that the bullet had lodged at the back of her skull and would be impossible to extract. As soon as she was well enough to travel, Hitler had arranged for her to go to neutral Berne, where, at the end of December, Muv accompanied by Debo went to fetch her home. In a blaze of press publicity they arrived back at Folkestone on January 3 and the next day were at the Old Mill Cottage in High Wycombe, where Nancy was waiting for them. She described to Mrs Hammersley her sister's pathetic state: 'The whole thing is most poignant. She is like a child in many ways & has very much lost her memory (a mercy I expect) does not know why she was ill but seems to think the doctor made a hole in her head . . . She is very happy to be back, keeps on saying "I thought you all hated me but I don't remember why." She said to me You are not one of those who would be cruel to somebody are you? So I said I was very much against that.

'She saw Mr X continually the last time 2 days before she left. Don't tell this. She was unconscious for 2 months.

'I think that is all of interest, such a scribble but you do understand. They were literally hunted by the press . . . Of course M & F were *not* clever – !'

After a few days, Nancy returned to London, as Peter, looking glamorous in his Welsh Guards uniform – 'masses of gold on his hat & a *wonderful* coat lined with scarlet satin which cost £25' – had been called to join his regiment in Colchester. Nancy was left to do what she could to make ends meet at Blomfield Road. Their financial situation, always precarious, was in an even worse state than usual: Farve in a gesture of economy had cut Nancy's allowance by £50, while Peter, whose army pay barely covered his mess bills, had chosen that moment to dive deep into hot water with his parents. 'I have just received a rare stinker from Pa, clearly written at Ma's dictation', he told his wife. 'I think you will have to go and mend something there, though really I don't see that the old boy has any serious grouch. He bloody well has to pay the settlements because he signed on the dotted line and when he makes an advance he stops it out of the settlement. So that's all square anyway except that he's had the fun of making a noise.' To eke out the housekeeping money Nancy started taking occasional paying guests: Robert Byron came for a short time, and so, looking tired, did her brother Tom, now in the Rifle Brigade and stationed nearby. She also established a hen-house in the garden and started growing her own vegetables. 'Words long forgotten like creosote & bran mash are never off my tongue, not to speak of droppings board & nest box,' and, she told Mrs Hammersley, 'I am hoarding, in a very small way, shoes & olive oil . . . I have also bought . . . 12 pkts of you know what, which I'm told are already nearly unobtainable!'

But, although London was prepared for war, the war had not yet reached London. There were, however, plenty of rumours of what was in store: the Nazis were said to be employing pygmy spies 'so small they can hide in drawers. I just daren't open mine now to look for a hanky'; and '*Hitler's secret* is it seems (I sat next Prof Lindemann at dinner) a bomb which can destroy all life in a radius of 40 miles. The Prof was good enough to add that whilst the bomb can do this *on paper* practice may not make so perfect a result. We of course have the secret too but nobody can spare 40 sq miles & so nobody knows whether it will work. Delirious suspense prevails.' Over the previous year Londoners had grown accustomed to gas-masks, the black-out, barrage-balloons, men in uniform, anti-aircraft guns in Hyde Park, and the tearing up of iron railings round squares and public gardens. But it was still possible to go over to Paris for the weekend, except for petrol few goods were rationed, and already in the West End black-out regulations were beginning to be disregarded. It was the period of the Phoney War. The air-raids were yet to come. No air-raids, no casualties: and, with no casualties to inscribe with her indelible pencil, Nancy at the hospital had very little to do. She chatted with the other volunteers, sorted the nurses' laundry, got on with her knitting, wrote letters, read Macaulay's *History of England*, and, with the wireless going full blast all day, began work on a novel. It was to be called *The Secret Weapon: a Wartime Receipt*, a funny story about spies. In a letter to Mrs Hammersley she outlined the plot, supported as usual by private jokes and the personalities of her friends. 'It is about me married to Francis Rodd & Peter is my lover & Mary Rodd is Francis's mistress.' The key character was an easily recognisable version of Mark Ogilvie-Grant. 'You,' she wrote to him, 'are called Mr. Ivor King the King of Song & your wigless head horribly battered is found on the Pagoda (headless wig, favourite, on Green) so you are presumed dead & there is a Catholic because you are one mem. service at which Yvonne appears as a Fr. widow. Well as you were about to open a great world campaign of Song Propaganda for the BBC SABOTAGE is suspected –

'UNTIL

'Your *dreadful* old voice is heard in Germany doing anti-British propaganda & singing songs like Land of Dope you're Gory . . .'

The heroine is Lady Sophia Garfield, married to Luke, a rich bore, and in love with a handsome journalist Rudolph Jocelyn. The book opens with the outbreak of war imminent, a situation described in the nursery terms familiar from the introduction to the Stanley Letters. 'The belligerent countries were behaving like children in a round game, picking up sides, and until the sides had picked up the game could not start. England picked up France, Germany picked up Italy. England beckoned to Poland, Germany answered with Russia. Then Italy's Nanny said she had fallen down and grazed her knee, running, and mustn't play. England picked up Turkey, Germany picked up Spain, but Spain's Nanny said she had internal troubles, and must sit this one out. England looked towards the Oslo group, but they had never played before, except little Belgium, who had hated it, and the others felt shy. America, of course, was too much of a baby for such a grown-up game, but she was just longing to see it played. And still it would not begin.'

But then it does begin. Sophia, returning to London from a visit to the north to take up her voluntary job at a hospital first-aid post, finds that in her absence her husband Luke has installed his dreary girl-friend Florence in the house. Florence is a member of the Boston Brotherhood, a Christian sect from America to which she has recruited Luke. Sophia dislikes her, and is therefore surprised to discover that Florence is secretly keeping a pigeon in her bedroom: anyone who keeps a pigeon as a pet, Sophia innocently thinks, cannot be all bad.

The crux of the plot is the kidnapping by Florence and Heatherly her American associate of Sophia's godfather, Sir Ivor King, 'the King of Song', a figure dear to the heart of the nation for his lovable personality and for the versatility of his voice: 'It could reach higher and also lower notes than have ever been reached before by any human being . . . he was the only man ever to sing the name part in the opera *Norma*, the script of which had been re-written especially for him, and re-named *Norman*.' At first he is believed to have been murdered, his corpse (too battered to be positively identified) and favourite wig (blood-stained) having been found outside his house on Kew Green. But shortly afterwards his voice is heard broadcasting apparently from Germany a series of propaganda programmes devilishly designed to undermine the British fighting spirit. Thus a concert of subversive songs is punctuated with snippets of disquietingly accurate information, for instance that Mr Eden had been seen that afternoon entering the Home Office at 5.46. 'Now the sinister thing about all this was that Mr Eden really had entered the Home Office at 5.46 on the afternoon in question. How could they have known it in Berlin at 6.30?'

How indeed? Needless to say, Sophia becomes intricately involved – not always intentionally – in supplying the answer. There is a grand pantomime finale, with Sir Ivor discovered buried in the basement of the FAP by Rudolph in drag, Sophia in hysterics, and a policeman in a tin-hat ready to arrest the German spy. Outside the sky is dark with the slowly-descending bodies of the enemy parachutists for whom, thanks to the timely foiling of the plot, there is a well-prepared reception. 'Squads of air-raid wardens, stretcher-bearers, boy-scouts, shop assistants and black-coated workers awaited them with yards and yards of twine and when they were still a few feet from the earth, tied their dangling legs together. Trussed up like turkeys for the Christmas market, they were bundled into military lorries and hurried away to several large Adam houses which had been commandeered for the purpose. Soon all the newspapers had photographs of them smoking their pipes before a cheery log fire, with a picture of their Führer gazing down at them from the chimney-piece.'[1]

As usual the cast-list is compiled of Nancy's own acquaintance. Sophia bears a strong resemblance to her author; the pompous Luke is based on Francis Rodd; the dashing, insolent, unreliable Rudolph on Peter; Sir Ivor King, the King of Song, owes everything he has to Mark, from his love of popular music, to his interest in botany, his passion for Greece, and even his sexual preferences. ('Sophia poured out tea, and asked after his Lesbian irises. "They were not what they seemed," he said, "wretched things. I brought the roots all the way from Lesbos, as you know, and when they came up, what were they? Mere pansies."') Florence and her Boston Brotherhood are taken straight from Nancy's observation of Francis's wife, the plain and pious Mary Rodd. It was to her that Nancy owed the Moral Rearmament scene, with 'a hundred people to every meal, great jolly queues waiting outside the lavatories, public confessions in the drawing-room, and quiet times in the housemaid's cupboard'. From Mary, too, came Florence's frank voice, bright, crucified smile, and her

---

[1] There is, perhaps it should be mentioned, one serious flaw in the plot: one morning, after the disappearance of Sir Ivor King, Sophia sees faintly pencilled on her breakfast boiled egg the words, 'Agony 22.' She knows it must be a code message but cannot for the life of her puzzle it out. Even when she turns to that morning's *Times*, and sees in the Agony column under Box 22, 'Poor old gentleman suffering from malignant disease would like to correspond with pretty young lady' (Poor Old Gentleman and Pretty Young Lady were Mark's/ Sir Ivor's, Nancy's/Sophia's names for each other) she makes no connection. The reader, however, has been alerted: this must be an important clue. What can it mean? And the disgraceful answer is, nothing. Nancy abandons it, shamelessly brushing it out of sight on almost the very last page. 'Sophia asked Sir Ivor about Agony 22, but he was quite as much in the dark about the great egg mystery as Heatherly had been.'

sense of familiarity with God. It had not escaped Nancy's attention that God 'is kept awfully busy round the house in Holland Park. Mary behaves rather as though she had a new secretary,' she told the Elweses. Accordingly, Florence is made to say, 'Personally the only people I care to be very intimate with are the ones you feel would make a good third if God asked you to dinner.'

'Sophia wished that Florence would not talk about the Almighty as if his real name was Godfrey, and God was just Florence's nickname for him.'

Pigeon Pie, as it was finally called, was finished with customary speed just before Christmas 1939. Its publisher was Hamish Hamilton, who had started his own firm nearly nine years earlier. He had seen promise in Nancy's three novels, and had been impressed by her lively editing of the Stanley letters[1]. His partner, P. P. Howe, writing to congratulate Nancy on the book, told her that they would try to get it out 'at the earliest possible moment. It should be just what people are in the mood for, if we are quick'. But they were not quick enough. By the time it was ready for publication, the war had begun in earnest. It came out on May 6, 1940, a month after the invasion of Norway, only four days before the invasion of Holland and Belgium, and less than three weeks before the fall of France. It is not surprising that *Pigeon Pie* sank almost without trace, as Nancy wrote in her note to the second edition of 1951, 'an early and unimportant casualty of the real war which was then beginning'.

In answer to her apologetic letter on the book's failure some months later – 'I'm *awfully* sorry that Pigeon Pie was such a flop' – Howe replied, '*Pigeon Pie* was *not* a flop, but wasn't lucky in the moment of its publication,' courteously adding that 'both Hamilton and I . . . eagerly look forward to its successor'. This, on Howe's part, may have been more gallant than truthful. Certainly neither he nor Nancy can have foreseen just how well rewarded the firm was to be by its faith in her. *Pigeon Pie* marks the end of

[1] Published by Evelyn Waugh's firm, Chapman & Hall.

that early period, the decade 1929–1939, of those bright, brittle, essentially ephemeral novels so much a part of the fashion and idiom of the thirties. Nancy was now on the point of change, on the brink of a new maturity. At last she was to find access to her emotions and to her creative imagination – entirely as the result of the influence of a man who, in 1940, she was yet to meet.

CHAPTER SIX

The War

Disappointment over the failure of *Pigeon Pie* to attract significant notice on publication was quickly submerged in larger events. In the second week of May, Peter was warned for overseas. He had been in Cambridge for training ('Prepare to laugh. It seems he is to do German local government with a view to becoming a gauleiter when the war is over'), but was now back in Colchester in command of his own company, about to leave for France and in a heroic frame of mind. 'It is perhaps something to be destined to fight in the biggest battle since the world began,' he wrote to his wife. 'I don't pretend not to be frightened, but duty and destiny are all so clearly defined that it will be easier to take a proper part . . .'

No sooner had Peter left than the news came that Sir Oswald Mosley had been taken to Brixton Prison under arrest. Nancy's reaction to this was curious. She had seen nothing of Mosley and not much of her sister Diana since the row over *Wigs on the Green* four years earlier; but with Nancy, as with all the Mitfords, family feeling ran deep, and she was fonder of Diana than of the others. Perhaps for this reason, Diana's defection was particularly painful. 'I am thankful Sir Oswald Quisling has been jugged aren't you,' Nancy wrote to Mark, 'but think it quite useless if Lady Q is still at large.' And, to make certain that Lady Q got her just deserts, Nancy went to the trouble of going in person to the Home Office where she was interviewed by Gladwyn Jebb, then Principal Private Secretary to the Under-Secretary of State. She told him that in her opinion Diana was as dangerous as her husband, that her frequent visits to Germany[1] were sinister and suspicious,

---

[1] For the past three years, Diana's visits to Germany had been on business:

and that no time should be lost in putting her under arrest. 'Not very sisterly behaviour,' as Nancy uneasily admitted, 'but in such times I think it one's duty?' Nine days after Nancy had given her testimony Diana was indeed arrested[1] and committed to Holloway Prison, where she remained for two years on her own before Mosley was given permission to join her in married quarters. Nancy was intrigued, rather than harrowed by her sister's unpleasant predicament. 'What *can* Holloway be like?' she asked Mrs Hammersley. 'I would die of the lights out at 5.30 rule wouldn't you? I suppose she sits & thinks of Adolf.' To Diana herself, meanwhile, Nancy said nothing of this, but behaved as any affectionate sister would, writing chatty letters, visiting Diana's children, and keeping her supplied with interesting new books.

Diana may have been the chief offender, but at this period there was no single member of the family on whom Nancy looked with approval. As in childhood at Asthall, it was Nancy versus the rest. Even Debo, recently engaged to Lord Andrew Cavendish, second son of the Duke of Devonshire, 'has become simply horrid . . . a very exigeante little creature & dreadfully spoilt'. As for her parents, Nancy was in 'a spit of hate' against both: Muv, *in love* with Adolf, was being too beastly for words, and Farve was a monster of selfishness, when in London rampaging about the house and 'roaring like a bull because everything is not just as he always has it'.

Indeed the Redesdales' situation was wretchedly unhappy. Unity was in a pathetic state, confused, bad-tempered and physically incontinent. The Redesdales, cooped up together in the Old Mill Cottage, under surveillance all the time by newspaper reporters, were tense and angry, quarrelling with each

---

she and Mosley wanted to set up a light-music radio advertising-station in order to raise money for the Party. They had licences for receivers in France and Ireland, and negotiations were in progress for a third to be set up in Germany.

[1] Later it became clear that it had been the Government's intention all along to arrest Diana: Nancy's evidence was contributory, not crucial.

other over the war news they listened to every evening on the wireless. Nancy reported to Mrs Ham that things were terrible there, Muv and Farve absolutely at loggerheads. 'Muv goes so far as to say now "When the Germans have won you'll see, everything will be wonderful & they'll treat us very differently to those wretched beastly Poles." It drives poor Farve absolutely dotty & can you wonder . . . He says he can't live with her any more – I really think they hate each other now. He is more violent now against Germany than anybody I know, & against any form of peace until they are well beaten.' Eventually, to the relief of the rest of the family, they did decide to part: the quarrels were too terrible and, for a man of Farve's emotional temperament and fastidious nature, Bobo's state of near-idiocy, her damp sheets flapping on the line, were too painful to bear. So Farve went up to Scotland, to Inch Kenneth, his Hebridean fastness, where except for the occasional visit to London he remained for the rest of the war. Muv and Bobo moved to the cottage next to the Swan at Swinbrook, much less vulnerable than High Wycombe to the prying eyes of the press.

This was a particularly depressing time for Nancy: Peter, Tom and many of her closest friends were overseas – Evelyn Waugh was in Crete, Hamish and Mark were in Egypt, from where they sent off bulletins of their war. 'Darling,' wrote Hamish, 'who d'you think is my great company commander here Johnny Drury-Lowe – isn't it heaven? Though I suppose in a trivet my tiny bayonet will be whistling through those beastly German tummies and I shall see him no more;' while Mark reported from GHQ, Cairo, that 'the erstwhile songster has turned into a tired old typist, but it doesn't prevent him letting out a periodical bat-like trill as he patters away at the keys . . . How is Bobo? better I hope. Give her my love and say that not long ago, I went to the most heavenly town called Tel Aviv. Both sexes always wear crumpled shorts just long enough to cover their tails.' Then came the news that Robert Byron, on his way to Cairo by sea, had been torpedoed and drowned. He was the first of Nancy's friends to die in the war, and his death shook her badly.

And Nancy herself was far from well. In April, she had again found herself pregnant (news acknowledged by a courtly letter from her father-in-law signing himself 'Devotissimo, Rennell') and had again suffered a miscarriage. To recuperate she spent a few days on the Isle of Wight with Mrs Hammersley – full of moans about food shortages and the dangers of invasion – and then on to Aunt Vi at Highcliffe, where she stayed on for a few weeks to help with an early consignment of evacuees[1].

Back in London she took a job in White City helping to run a canteen for French soldiers temporarily interned after Dunkirk. They were a high-spirited lot, full of jokes and no nonsense about heroics. '[I] simply love the frogs more & more . . . I now give English lessons & am teaching the whole class Come into the garden Maud they like it because of the bit about woodbine which they all smoke. At first they thought it meant "venez dans le jardin maudit." They are such *kittens*, I never stop laughing all day . . . Honestly what shall I do without them life will be a blank & English soldiers or brave de Gaulle ones can never replace these nice lily-livered jokers.'

On Saturday, September 7, during a period of perfect Indian summer, the Blitz began. The first planes came over at five in the afternoon, and for nearly twelve hours 300 bombers with an escort of 600 fighter planes screeched and dived over London. Nancy at Blomfield Road was in the thick of it. Forty-eight hours after it started, she wrote to Mrs Hammersley, 'Darling the nights! Nobody who hasn't been in it can have the smallest idea of the horror one is going through. I never don't feel sick, can't eat anything & although dropping with tiredness can't sleep either. No doubt one will get used to it soon – last night I shall never

---

[1] Staying at Highcliffe, Nancy was unable to resist teasing Mrs Hammersley with the difference in the standard of living between the widow's little villa at Totland Bay and the grandeur and security of Highcliffe Castle: 'Butlers are the great problem – impossible to find & Mr Fife *has not brought a man.* Nevertheless, clattering tea on silver tripods is succeeded by 4 course dinner & how can one help but enjoy it . . . I insist on getting up for breakfast & this is well received, so the war effort goes on.'

forget as long as I live ... Ten hours is *too* long, you know of concentrated noise & terror, in a house alone. Thank heaven for Milly (dog) who is a rock. So is Gladys – really a heroine. She arrived back at 6 this morning all smiles & was ready with my breakfast punctually at 8, & when I announced rather hysterically that I intended to spend tonight in my trench in the garden she cheerfully said she would come too.'

A few days later she wrote again to Mrs Ham:

This part (Mai Vale) has got it worse than almost anywhere (except the East End of course) as they are trying for Padd. On Sunday night & again Tues: they never let up for 10 hours. Too long you know ... I find my nerves are standing up to the thing better now – I don't tremble quite all the time as I did ... NOBODY can have the slightest idea of what it is like until they've experienced it. As for the screaming bombs they simply make your flesh creep but the whole thing is so fearful that they are actually only a slight added horror. The great fires every-where, the awful din which never stops & the wave after wave after wave of aeroplanes, ambulances tearing up the street & the horrible unnatural blaze of light from search-lights etc – all has to be experienced to be understood. Then in the morning the damage – people ring up to tell one how their houses are completely non existant, & in nearly every street you can see a sinister little piece roped off with red lights round it, or roofs blown off or suddenly every window out of a house, & lorries full of rubble & broken furniture pass incessantly. Of course the number of dead is absolutely tiny but everybody now sleeps in the shelters, at about 7 one sees them queueing up with thermos flasks & blankets for the night. People are beyond praise, everyone is red eyed & exhausted but you never hear a word of complaint or downheartedness it is most reassuring.

I am trying to get some work in the East End – am temporarely rather cross with the frogs who really are behaving like spoilt children, complaining they are kept awake at night & one today started a long histoire about how he hadn't been taken to the theatre at all. Ça je trouve un peu exagéré quand même.

Oh dear there are the sirens again What a horrid life.

As Blomfield Road was such a favourite target of the Luftwaffe ('Oh the secret weapon every evening one *hopes* for about 5 minutes until the familiar whizz bang comes in with the soup'), Nancy moved to Rutland Gate, to the mews flat at the back, as the main house had been requisitioned to provide provisional living-quarters for families of Polish Jews evacuated from the East End. Nancy was fascinated by these East End families and took on the job of looking after them with enthusiasm. They were 'so hard working clean & grateful', and there was always some interesting drama going on to take her mind off the bombs. 'Oh dear a little creature here aged 16 is in the family way. I advised her, in the words of Lady Stanley, a tremendous walk a hot bath & a great dose but will this have any effect on a tough little Jewess? Or shall I be obliged to wield a knitting needle & go down to fame as Mrs Rodd the abortionist? (I might join Diana which would be rather nice) Really, talk about big families I feel like the mother of 10 here or old Mummy Hubbard.'

Rewarding though this was, the work was also extremely hard, and Nancy often felt ill with exhaustion. She was also suffering a private misery over her marriage to Peter. Although on friendly terms, they had been drifting further and further apart. On his few periods of leave in London, Peter usually preferred to stay at his club, asking the friends he ran into not to tell Nancy that they had seen him. But, whether or not Nancy knew of these visits, she did know that her marriage was in all essentials over. In a sad memorandum inside the cover of her appointment diary for 1941, she wrote, 'Love is a punchy physical affair & therefore should not be confused with any other side of life or form of affection, & while it makes an agreeable foundation from which to begin a marriage the absence of physical love, *love* in fact, should never be allowed to interfere with the continuity of marriage. Marriage is the most important thing in life & must be kept going at almost any cost, it should only be embarked upon where there is, as well as physical love, a complete conformity of outlook. Women, as well as men, ought to have a great many love affairs before they marry as the most critical moment in a marriage is the falling off of physical love, which is bound to occur sooner or later & only an experienced woman can know how to cope with this. If not properly dealt with the marriage is bound to go on the rocks.'

Peter was now in Addis Ababa, doing the kind of work he liked best – 'trying to mend and organise the broken and disrupted lives of wretched people over whom the blizzard of war has passed and left a little stunned and helpless . . .' Nancy had offered to join him but his response was not encouraging. Letters took months to arrive, and the cheques he sent home were infrequent and small. She was once again desperately hard-up. Lord Rennell had died in July, and 'my dear mother in law has stopped my allowance in order to build a ball room in memory of my pa in law. I keep saying how I wish she were religious, a nice marble X would cost far less'.

But life was not entirely black. At about this time, the Free French under the leadership of General de Gaulle were beginning to arrive in London. In a letter to Mrs Hammersley written in March 1941, Nancy had this interesting piece of news: 'A friend of mine at the War Office (MI) begs me (this is a secret) to worm my way into the Free Frog Officers Club in any capacity & try to find out something about them. They are all here under assumed names, all splashing mysteriously large sums of money about & our people can't find out a thing about them. Isn't it tricky. Seriously I don't see what I could do & it would bore me to death.' But, doubtless regarding it as a patriotic duty, Nancy overcame her fear of boredom, and was soon in a whirl, as she called it, of free froggery: 'very agreeable the way French chaps look at one, kiss ones hand etc without being rendered gaga with love first like the English ones, if you see what I mean.' Well-connected young officers with assumed names and stories of heroic escape were to be seen at the Allies' Club in Park Lane or dining with Lady Cunard in her suite at the Dorchester. Nancy with her prettiness, her chic, her high spirits and fluent French, was much in demand, to her great satisfaction as there was nothing she loved more than the frivolity and flirtatiousness of these charming and civilised young Frenchmen, so flattering and funny at the dinner-table, so desperately brave at the front.

It was not long before one Free Frog in particular swam into prominence. His nomme de guerre was André Roy[1]. He had arrived in London in October 1940 to join De Gaulle's Français Libres, and by the time Nancy met him was working as Liaison Officer in the Quartier Général. He was exactly Nancy's age, tall, slim, charming and clever. With Peter away and in the wartime atmosphere of danger and excitement, Nancy allowed herself to be temporarily swept off her feet. She was lonely, not at all happy, and the feeling of impermanence which the war brought with it made normal life seem a long way off. During the summer of 1941, Roy was the perfect companion. He knew, as most of Nancy's English men friends did not, exactly how to make love to her: he made her laugh, was not afraid to be romantic, flattered her outrageously while letting her see that underneath it all he meant every word. Although never much interested in the sexual side of a love affair – it was the banter that she enjoyed – this time she succumbed. The result was that once again she became pregnant.

In November she was staying with Roy Harrod and his wife Billa in Oxford, and while there was taken ill with severe abdominal pains. Fearing the worst but telling Billa only that it was probably an attack of appendicitis, she got herself back to London, carrying her suitcase to the bus for the station as she was determined not to let on how ill she felt. In London she went straight into University College Hospital, where it was found that the foetus was lodged in the fallopian tube, and must be immediately operated on. Nancy begged the surgeon to leave her with the chance of having children, but when she came round

---

[1] In reality Roy André Desplats-Pilter, of a Huguenot family, son of a French father and English mother.

from the anaesthetic it was to be greeted with the news that a complete hysterectomy had been unavoidable. It was a crushing blow, and brave though she was this time the keeping up of the shop-front was almost more than she could manage. Doing her best, she wrote to Diana, 'I have had a horrible time, so depressing because they had to take out both my tubes & therefore I can never now have a child . . . The Rodds have been wonderfully true to form – my mother in law was told by the surgeon I shld be in danger for 3 days, & not one of them even rang up to enquire let alone sending a bloom or anything. I long to know if they bothered to look under R in the deaths column, very much doubt it however.' Even more true to form was Muv, who when told by Nancy that both ovaries had been removed exclaimed, 'Both! But I thought one had hundreds, like caviar!' 'Then I said how I couldn't bear the idea of a great scar on my tum to which she replied "But darling who's ever going to see it?" '

Nancy left hospital in December, and at the invitation of Helen Dashwood went down to West Wycombe to convalesce. The Dashwoods' beautiful Palladian house was one of the few big private houses still run very much as it had been before the war, as Helen was allowed to keep her servants in exchange ('war-work') for filling the house with evacuees, strangely enough nearly all of them personal friends of Helen. On her arrival Nancy found an exceptionally congenial company: Jim Lees-Milne and Eardley Knollys, as part of the National Trust secretariat, her cousin Clementine with her husband Sir Alfred Beit, and at weekends frequent visits from, among others, Cecil Beaton, Sibyl Colefax and Eddy Sackville-West[1]. In the evenings Eddy and Jim sat side by side in front of the fire in a pair of Chinese Chippendale chairs working at their knitting and ripping to pieces the reputations of their friends, egged on by Nancy, mocking everything and everybody in her witty, restless, high-pitched way. She revived a girlhood passion for Captain Scott, reading everything she could lay her hands on, and insisting that the others should read about

[1] Novelist, critic and musician, he succeeded as Lord Sackville in 1962.

him too. ('Thank goodness I have at last finished Scott's lengthy journals,' Jim wearily recorded in his diary.) The polar expedition was her favourite topic of conversation: she christened the upstairs lavatory the Beardmore after the famous glacier, as it faced north, the window was jammed permanently open, and there was often snow on the floor. 'Must dash to the Beardmore,' Nancy would say before lunch, a joke that quickly palled with Helen. But it helped to pass the time.

In March 1942 Nancy, recovered in body if not altogether in spirit, returned to London and, at the suggestion of Jim Lees-Milne, took up a new job, working as assistant at a bookshop in Curzon Street for a salary of £3.10s a week. Heywood Hill was a bookshop of distinctive character specialising in early Victorian toys and automata, in embroidered pictures and unusual prints, rare first editions and old folios, as well as offering a good selection of recent publications. The books were displayed almost as if in a private house, not only on the shelves but piled in disorder on a couple of tables, and collapsing in heaps on the carpet. Conveniently placed in the centre of Mayfair, an easy walk from the clubs of St James's and, a short way down the street, from Trumper's, the gentlemen's barber, it had become a favourite stopping-place among the fashionable and literary intelligentsia for browsing and gossip, even more since the arrival of the new assistant, whose enthusiasm for the latter pastime occasionally annoyed those rare customers who came in only to buy a book – 'A little less "darling" and a little more attention, please!' a cross voice could now and again be heard cutting through Nancy's drawling tones. Evelyn Waugh, when in London, was a regular patron, so was Raymond Mortimer[1], the Sitwells ('my spiritual home', Osbert called it), Gerry Wellesley[2] and Gerald Berners[3].

When Heywood Hill was called up in December 1942,

[1] Literary critic and author.
[2] Gerald Wellesley, succeeded as seventh Duke of Wellington in 1943.
[3] The fourteenth Baron Berners, author, painter, composer, eccentric and wit.

Heywood's wife Anne and Nancy ran the business on their own.
Nancy, in a neat uniform of black velvet top and woollen skirt, was
surprisingly proficient: she enjoyed the business of selling and
not only had an excellent memory for titles, publishers and prices,
but was more than willing to do her share of the hard labour,
packing and unpacking books, sorting out orders, and lugging
heavy parcels to the post office. She walked to the shop every
morning from Blomfield Road, a distance of over two and a half
miles – down the Edgware Road, across Oxford Street at the
Marble Arch, down Park Lane – and very often walked back again
in the evening. As she and the Hills lived near each other in
Maida Vale, Nancy and Anne took it in turns to arrive first at the
shop in the morning, the one whose turn it was not dropping the
key into the letter-box of the other on her way home at night. It
was not an entirely fool-proof system. 'What *do* you think I did?' a
horrified Nancy wrote to Muv one weekend. 'I decided not to
come here Sat: morning as I was really tired, & forgot to lock the
door on Friday so the shop was full of wandering people trying to
buy books from each other. Wasn't it a nightmare. By the mercy
of Providence Heywood was passing through London & happened to look in HE WASN'T BEST PLEASED. And I don't
blame him.'

On the occasions when Anne Hill had to be away from the
shop, Nancy remained in charge, running the business with the
help of a new assistant, Mollie Friese-Greene, who had been taken
on mainly to cope with the accounts, for which neither Nancy nor
Anne showed much aptitude. 'All is much slacker,' Nancy wrote
to Diana, '& Miss Freeze-Greene (well named I consider when
you think where she's going to sit) will provide further allevia-
tion.' Nonetheless the work was hard and Nancy, never strong,
began to feel run down. 'I feel very old, going grey & bald & look
terrible. I've been doing far too much & need a week in bed.' Her
only break had been a few days in August helping to look after
Unity at Swinbrook. It had been bliss to be out of London and
away from the stuffiness of the shop, away from the bombs and
the bad food and the endless queueing, but it could hardly be

described as a holiday. The news from abroad was not encouraging either: Tom was fighting in Libya, Mark was now a prisoner of war, and Hamish had just been captured after an action of outstanding bravery resulting in the blowing up of a German tank at Tobruk. Now he was in a prison camp in Italy (the story going round was that the one message he had been able to get through was an urgently scribbled note to his mother, 'Send Almanach de Gotha')[1]. In November, in order to give Muv a few days' respite, Nancy had the obstreperous Unity to stay with her in Blomfield Road, and exhausted though she was pulled herself together sufficiently to throw a party, which she afterwards described to Diana. 'Bobo enjoyed my party. She brought a ghastly old dress full of moth holes so I crammed her into my only good black one which we left undone all the way down the back & she kept on a coat so all was well but it was rather an awful moment when I saw what she did propose to wear. Then she refused to make up her face but the adored Capitaine Roy took her upstairs & did it for her. So in the end she looked awfully pretty.'

For the adored Capitaine Roy the evening may not have been so agreeable. Nancy had recently met someone else, a man who appeared to be making a considerable impression on her, a few years older than Roy and a Colonel in the Free French Forces. His name was Gaston Palewski.

---

[1] Hamish's courageous war continued with his escape from the camp just before the Germans arrived to take it over; dressed as a woman – 'the Marchesa della Piccola Mia, I suppose,' Nancy knowingly remarked – he made his way up through Italy, moving from one ducal house to another until he was eventually picked up by the British and repatriated, whereupon he immediately returned to Italy to organise an escape route for other prisoners on the run.

CHAPTER SEVEN

The Colonel

Gaston Palewski was possessed of all the qualities that, to an English eye, epitomise the sophisticated Frenchman: he was charming, he was amusing, he was a great lover of the arts and an incorrigible womaniser. He was also a shrewd politician, with an unswerving loyalty to his country and his cause.

Born in 1901, he came of a Polish family which had been settled in France since the middle of the nineteenth century. His parents were clever, cultivated people, Palewski père an engineer and one of the pioneers of the aerial navigation industry. Gaston himself was educated at the Ecole du Louvre, the Ecole Libre des Sciences Politiques and the Sorbonne, after which he came to England for a year's postgraduate study at Oxford. His political career started early. At the age of twenty-one he was appointed attaché to Maréchal Lyautey in Morocco, and then worked with Paul Reynaud during his time as Minister of Finance under Daladier. It was this period that saw the beginning of Palewski's lifelong association with Charles de Gaulle, then, in 1934, vainly trying to promote the establishment of a professional army with which to counter the highly mechanised German forces already mobilizing with such sinister intent on the other side of the Maginot Line. At their first meeting Palewski had been over-whelmed by what he saw as de Gaulle's mastery and vision, and it was he who at once urged Reynaud to recognise his genius. From that moment Palewski's faith in de Gaulle never wavered, and de Gaulle never forgot what he owed him. (In a letter after the war, the General, not one easily to express emotion, wrote to his faithful supporter, 'Vous savez combien j'ai d'affection pour vous, sous la cuirasse.')

When war broke out Palewski, unable to countenance the pacifist policies of Reynaud, volunteered for the French Air Force's 34th Bomber Squadron, where he distinguished himself by winning a mention in despatches for valour at Sedan. At the fall of France in June 1940, he was in Tunisia with his squadron and telegraphed at once to de Gaulle in London offering his services. De Gaulle replied with an immediate summons, and from August 1940 to March 1941 Palewski scarcely left the General's side, his knowledge of the English and his diplomatic skills making him an invaluable keeper of the peace between the somewhat overbearing Allies and his touchy and intransigent chief. In the spring of the following year Palewski left London to return to Africa, this time to Ethiopia, believing that the interests of his country were better served fighting on the field of battle than in the quarrelsome atmosphere of Carlton Gardens and in the organisation of a resistance movement that then seemed premature. He spent six months in Ethiopia commanding the Free French Forces of East Africa before again being recalled to London, arriving in September 1942 to take up the post of de Gaulle's directeur de cabinet.

In London Palewski performed an invaluable service. He was a man of the world, at ease in society, accustomed to the manners of the English ruling class. He was delightful company, his conversation brilliant, his knowledge of political affairs profound. He understood the world in which he moved. A subtle and accomplished diplomat, his love of France was fierce, his loyalty to the General absolute. Known among his colleagues (behind his back) as Eminence Grise for the influence he was thought to have with the General, Palewski was careful always to detach himself from the internecine rivalries that were carried on incessantly among the staff and officers of the Free French. Thus he was able to act as a buffer between the General and his quarrelsome compatriots, and also as an emollient between the General and his English Allies.

When Palewski came back to London he made a point, as he had the year before, of conducting his social life as far away as possible from the enervating dramas at Carlton Gardens. His working day was long (the General arrived at his office at 9.30 every morning and was usually still there at midnight); the news was frequently depressing; the outlook bleak. Moreover the gallant French Colonel, an old habitué of the dining-tables of Ladies Colefax and Cunard, had friends in all the most sophisticated circles in the capital. Shortly after his return it came to his ears that there was a certain Mrs Rodd whose husband was in Ethiopia and who would no doubt be grateful for news of him. It so happened that the Colonel had met both Francis and Peter when he was in Addis Ababa, all three of them having been involved in the Anglo-French negotiations over the Djibouti-Addis Railway. He would be more than happy to make a rendezvous with Mrs Rodd and tell her what he could of her husband's situation.

They met on a warm September evening in the garden of the Allies' Club, that most congenial meeting-place for officers in exile established in the old Rothschild house at the corner of Hamilton Place and Park Lane. They talked first about Peter and Ethiopia, and then of France, of French literature and history, for which this pretty grass widow had a most gratifying enthusiasm. The Colonel was very taken with her, so amusing and high-spirited; her clothes (though clearly not expensive) were (for an Englishwoman) elegant, and most beguiling of all was her evident love of France and in particular of Paris, that lost paradise, 'la cité du bonheur parfait'. Nancy was equally entranced. She saw before her a small, stocky Frenchman in early middle-age with a face like an amiable toad, dark hair and moustache and a badly pitted skin, by whom she unaccountably found herself powerfully attracted. He charmed and flattered her; he gossiped, joked and made her feel every minute she was with him that she was the centre of his undivided attention.

A few days later she invited him to dine with her in Blomfield Road. The Colonel enjoyed himself; as an enthusiastic *amateur des jolies femmes* he knew very well how to conduct a flirtation. Women were his greatest weakness; he could not see a pretty woman without wanting to make love to her and Nancy was no exception. As far as Palewski was concerned, charming Mrs Rodd – so sophisticated on the surface, so delightfully naive beneath – provided the opportunity for a most agreeable interlude, a welcome respite from the austere atmosphere surrounding his single-minded chief. The pattern was quickly established between them that several evenings a week he should dine with her at Blomfield Road, arriving usually very late straight from Carlton Gardens in a taxi, and signalling his presence by whistling a few bars of a Kurt Weill song popular that year. Sometimes they dined at the Connaught, where the General always ate his luncheon, or at 25 Eaton Terrace, the house Palewski had taken, belonging to Anne Rosse, sister of Nancy's old friend Oliver Messel – a most unlikely setting for a Colonel of the Free French Forces, who often woke in the morning bewildered to find himself in that very pretty lady's bedroom with its pink walls, frilled pillows, and all the little devices to protect the sleep of a fashionable young woman. Nancy enchanted and entertained him. He adored her stories about her eccentric family: 'Racontez, racontez,' he would say, his dark eyes shining with amusement, 'la famille Mitford fait ma joie.' Whenever he could, he spent the night with her ('J'ai horreur de coucher seul'), getting up at seven, dressing and returning to Eaton Terrace in time to be brought his breakfast and the papers at eight o'clock. Then he telephoned Nancy to chat for a few minutes – 'Allons, des histoires!' – before he left for his office and she for the shop. Sometimes he dropped into the shop during the day: for the General's birthday she sold him a copy of the *Memoirs of Saint-Simon*.

But what was a pleasant pastime for Palewski soon became the very breath of life to Nancy. Like her heroine Linda, she was filled with a strange, wild, unfamiliar happiness, and for the first time in her life knew that this was love. She was drunk with excitement, lived only for her meetings with the Colonel, and in between those meetings for their long, teasing chats on the telephone. Thanks to his year at Oxford the Colonel spoke excellent English and had an easy familiarity with English literature, giving him immediate access to Nancy's terms of reference. 'Do I not know wonderful English? Do I not know a lot of English poetry? . . . Season of mists and mellow fruitfulness – am I not brilliant to know that?' There was nothing in the least effeminate about this small, swarthy Frenchman, but as up to now had been the case only with her homosexual men friends he was a lover of art and beautiful things, witty, worldly and frivolous, with an insatiable appetite for gossip, an ebullient joie de vivre, and a pleasure in the company of women incomprehensible to the average Englishman. For Palewski adored women, preferably young, preferably pretty, but almost any woman was better than none. He awoke Nancy, whose sexual nature had until then lain restfully dormant, to a profound awareness of sexual love. She felt for him a deep and overwhelming physical attraction which at times frightened her, in a way almost shocked her, and she had never in her life been so happy.

The first person to be told of this new love affair was the widow on the Isle of Wight, who took it to be no more than a passing fancy, another admirer to make miserable, all part, was it not, of the tantalising game? 'Colonel Palewski sounds enchanting,' wrote Mrs Hammersley, 'and very entreprenant – But what of Roy?' It was no game, however. Just before Christmas 1942, spent with Maurice Bowra in Oxford, Nancy brought to an end her affair with Roy. She wanted no one but the Colonel.

In January they dined together several times before Palewski left on the 21st to accompany the General to the Allied Conference in Casablanca. In Nancy's appointment diary for that day is written, 'Bridget's party. Gone.' A month later he was back, now referred to in the diary not as Palewski, but as Colonel, his rank in the Air Force but also Nancy's private name for him. They had dinner together on February 21, lunched on March 7, visited Hampton Court on the 13th, a Saturday, and the Sunday Colonel spent according to established custom at Blomfield Road. The following weekend, they dined at the Connaught on Saturday, were together all Sunday, lunched the following Tuesday and Wednesday, and were together from dinner on Saturday at Eaton

Terrace to seven o'clock on Monday morning when Colonel left Blomfield Road for his own quarters. This blissfully happy state of affairs continued until the end of May 1943, when, on the 28th of that month, Colonel left to join General de Gaulle in Algeria. He was unable to tell Nancy when, if ever, she would see him again.

By this time most of Nancy's friends knew that this was something serious. Mrs Hammersley, worried that she might in desperation take some irrevocable step which she would later regret, offered a word of caution. 'I feel rather anxious about you darling. I must tell you that I never would have thought your heart would prevail over your reason. I still can hardly believe it, not because you haven't got a heart, but because just something (I hoped) in your temperament. Also of course your humour gets in the way . . . Perhaps its a good thing P. will be absent for a bit. I don't mean to be harsh but, at one remove, you will be able better to take stock of the future and of your own feelings. It's important in life to keep balanced.' Mark, too, having heard of the Pretty Young Lady's situation, wrote reprovingly from his prison-camp in Italy: 'I am glad your Frogs are friendly – there is one in my room, though not, Alas, Free – But I am not sure that I can approve the gay goings on in the P.Y.L.'s[1] bed . . .' Only Peter was cheerfully unaware of his wife's affairs, writing from Asmara with typically Proddish swagger: 'I am doing or trying to do everything myself and am now a building contractor and a farmer as well, as I have had to make sure of my meat supply by buying a lot of live cows, rather nice cows with humps. Besides that I am Cooks Tours, Carter Patterson, Somerset House, the Passport Office and Customs and Excise, with a spot of Treasure Cot, Heppels and Fortnum and Mason thrown in.'

Meanwhile Nancy, careless of the advice of well-meaning friends, went on from day to day as best she could, waiting for those letters from Algiers on which it seemed her life depended. They arrived at long and infrequent intervals, a meagre ration on

[1] Pretty Young Lady.

which to support existence. Every morning she looked for that longed-for envelope with the General's stamp forwarded from Carlton Gardens and enclosing another envelope, inside which was a single sheet of the thinnest airmail paper, paper so thin it was almost transparent. Sometimes the contents were typed by a secretary, sometimes, much worse, written by Colonel himself apparently using a rusty pin – 'l'épingle d'Alger', she called it despairingly – and in a tormentingly illegible hand. The letters, those that she could decipher, were friendly but cautious: in no sense could they be described as love-letters. But then the Colonel was not in love. Moreover he had his position to consider: any scandal concerning a married woman, a married Englishwoman, would not be regarded with favour by the General. He was careful always to address her as 'vous', usually beginning 'Ma chère amie', so much more impersonal than 'Chère Nancy', and signing himself with all the elaborate epistolary flourish in which the French delight: 'Agréez, je vous prie, ma chère amie, l'hommage de mes sentiments bien fidèlement dévoués et respectueux Gaston Palewski.' He wrote of the terrible difficulties facing the General; of the discomfort of Algiers, 'ce trou méditerranéen'; of the 'climat étouffant; gens horribles; bourgeois repus ... Horrible war'; of how he dined once with Prodd: 'Il est en bonne forme'; of the exigent nature of his work and of his long hours: 'Je travaille depuis 7h du matin jusqu'a 8h 30 du soir et je prends tous mes repas avec le gén. Je n'ai donc jamais un moment de liberté.' Now and again there is a glimpse of a fondness to which in the circumstances it was difficult to give expression: he had to be wary of what he might inadvertently reveal in the way of war news, and dictation to a secretary was hardly conducive to intimacy. 'Je m'excuse de cette lettre pratique et dactylographiée. Les interlignes sont écrites à l'encre sympathique,' he added once in his own hand. If he were feeling particularly warm towards her, he would add after his signature the words 'Connaught Hotel', a private reference to an occasion when he had tried to take her upstairs after dinner at the Connaught. To Nancy's embarrassment, they were stopped by a stern-faced receptionist who told them that ladies who were not guests of the hotel were *never* allowed in the bedrooms.

But Colonel was under no obligation to conceal how much he enjoyed Nancy's letters to him. 'Ecrivez, écrivez' was the constant cry, 'vos lettres sont mes ballons d'oxygène . . . Rien ne donne la température de Londres comme vos lettres, et j'ai besoin de pouvoir évoquer le passé pour me consoler du présent . . . Surtout continuez à m'écrire.' And continue she did, entertaining him with funny stories and all the gossip of the town. Already she was beginning to realise that, if she wanted to hold on to this very fascinating, very slippery man of the world, she must, like Scheherazade, beguile him with stories: her hold on him depended on her ability to entertain; she must be gay, always there must be something amusing to recount. The Colonel did not care for the melancholy nor the mundane; he did not wish to know if she were sad or cold or worried about money. That was not what life was for. And so she spun her tales, regularly posting off her grey Harrods envelopes to their unseen destination. Colonel made the error once of light-heartedly referring to 'la charmante avalanche grise', a phrase which wounded Nancy and for which he was obliged hastily to apologise: 'J'avais employé le mot "avalanche" pour des raisons de style mais non pour me plaindre de l'abondance de vos lettres . . .'

All this was meagre enough, and on her near starvation rations Nancy came close to despair. She was pining for the Colonel, to such an extent that for one wild moment she even considered trying to get to Algeria – before commonsense and Mrs Hammersley prevailed. 'Venez donc pour l'hiver,' he had casually thrown out, knowing he was safe, for how could she possibly leave the country, let alone travel to North Africa? 'On serait ravi de vous voir.'

Meanwhile there was little to look forward to at home. The only pieces of good news were the release of the Mosleys in November (Diana now received letters from her waggish sister sealed with stickers issued by the *Daily Worker* reading 'Put MOSLEY back in GAOL!'), and the arrival of Hamish, returned

from Italy in time for Christmas, very thin but otherwise well. The
work in the shop was becoming more and more arduous – 'I'm
going to try & leave the shop if the Labour Exchange will allow,'
Nancy wrote to Muv in a thoroughly bad mood. 'I think its making
me ill & I shall have a breakdown if I go on never seeing daylight' –
and the money shortage was once again acute, with nothing at all
coming in from Peter. He and Francis were now together in
Calabria working for AMGOT[1] after the collapse of Italy
('AMGOTterdämmerung, the Twilight of the Rodds' was
Maurice Bowra's joke on the subject). Here he was having a
wonderful time reconstructing life for thousands of destitute
peasants to whom, naturally, he was able to speak in their very
own dialect, while rebuilding their bridges, organising boar-
hunts to provide them with food and, under the Rodd family
ensign, running a pirate fleet up and down the coast plundering
the German fuel supplies. Peter was of course the only man on
the spot who knew what he was doing: the British, a lot of
rip-snorting shits buggering about and getting in the way; the
Americans, prep-school children, a far greater handicap to the
troops than the enemy; and the Italians, 'a band of wets. I am sick
of teaching them to blow their noses and wipe their bottoms.'

    This was all a tremendous lark but little consolation to Nancy,
tired, depressed and suffering almost physical pain from the
absence of Palewski. The New Year of 1944 saw her at her lowest
ebb. It was the fourth year of the war and the shortages were
worse than ever. There was almost nothing to buy in the shops,
travel virtually impossible, everyone suffering from cold and
exhaustion. There were times when there was not actually
enough to eat, and even the ducks in Hyde Park looked appetising
on her walk to the shop in the mornings. (When in later years she
used to boast of how much she had enjoyed the war, this period
cannot have been uppermost in her mind.) In January she wrote
to Muv, 'You never saw anything like the burning – I pack a suit
case every night & always dress which I *never* did before, but the

---

[1] Allied Military Government of Occupied Territory.

raids are very short, exactly one hour so that's no great hardship only chilly . . . I spent the morning looking at clothes – the most utter horrors (dresses) you ever saw for £23 cheap & dreadful looking what is one to do. Then I tried to get a suspender belt – they have wooden suspenders. So the squander bug went hungry away. It makes the burning even more of a bore doesn't it. The last straw is Harrods don't stamp ones note paper any more.' And always, as for everyone else, food was very much on her mind. 'Picture my joy when I found a chicken chez Jackson & my despair when on presenting this much heralded fowl to Gladys she immediately discovered it to be *crawling* with maggots! Really you wouldn't expect Jacksons to sell you a maggotty hen. So we all cried a great deal, the disappointment was dreadful.'

The work at the shop was more than usually tiring now that every ten days Nancy and the other assistant, Mollie Friese-Greene, had to spend the night fire-watching, one of the dreariest of all war-time duties. After they finished their day's work they changed into slacks and jumpers and, having dumped tin hats and gas-masks on a couple of camp beds, settled down on the roof of Crewe House, half-way down Curzon Street, to wait for incendiaries. They got one once in Hill Street, Nancy displaying a courage of which Farve would have been proud, dashing up the stairs with her bucket while Mollie followed behind with the stirrup-pump. On the strength of this Nancy was asked to lecture on fire-watching to trainees, but had to give it up almost at once; the trouble was the affectation of her voice: it irritated the class so much, said the lady in charge, embarrassed, that it was Nancy they all wanted to see put on the fire.

No one, not even Mrs Hammersley, realised the extent of Nancy's unhappiness. She went on as usual seeing her friends and going to parties – there was a party at Cecil Beaton's in Pelham Place, at which she spent the evening sitting on the sofa with Eddy Sackville-West, the pair of them hooting with laughter as they dissected each guest in turn. She herself gave a dinner-party at Boulestin at which the guests were Raymond Mortimer, Jim Lees-Milne, Clarissa Churchill, Alice Harding, Gerald

Berners and Stuart Preston, the ubiquitous American service-
man known as 'the Sergeant'. At a luncheon at Emerald Cunard's
Nancy startled the company by turning on the Greek Ambassador
with uncharacteristic ferocity and attacking him for referring to
the French as 'rotten'. This was a new habit of Nancy's which
people were beginning to remark, an unshakable conviction that
France and the French were in every way *perfect*. Some of her
closer friends thought, too, that they detected a note of hysteria in
her laughter, a more than usually mocking tone in the banter. She
made a great point of being indifferent to the bombs, an indifference that Osbert Lancaster among others interpreted as a direct
consequence of a new-found unconcern for Peter's misbe-
haviour. But nothing Peter got up to could affect her now: her
unhappiness had nothing to do with her husband.

And the envelopes from Algiers continued to arrive from time
to time, mainly in thanks for the unfailing flow of letters and the
parcels of books sent from the shop. 'Je commence à être un peu
honteux de recevoir et de ne jamais donner . . . comme je vous
suis reconnaissant de veiller à mon entretien cérébral . . . Je
trouve que Peter Quennell a fait une tres brillante réussite avec le
Cornhill [magazine]. L'essai de Max Beerbohm est parmi les
meilleurs que j'ai lus . . . vous me comblez de gentillesse, mais
surtout comblez-moi de lettres.' There was little he could offer in
return, except for the occasional item of news to be sent over in
the Bag, as, for instance, the arrival of the Coopers, Duff having
been appointed British Representative to the French Committee
of Liberation. 'Diana est arrivée. En voyant le chambre de sa villa,
Louis XV et miroirs, elle a dit: "It is very nice, but, Olga, isn't it a
little too much like a b . . ."'

Then in February 1944 yet another member of the Free
French Forces came into Nancy's life. Marc, Prince de Beauvau-
Craon, was young (in his early twenties), rich, good-looking and
brave, having just escaped through Spain having been captured
while working as a 'passeur' in Andorra. More important, he
knew the Colonel: his mother, Minnie de Beauvau, was a close
friend of Gaston, and so he was able to talk to Nancy about her

longed-for lover. For this reason she saw as much of Marc as she could. They dined together nearly every night either at the Savoy, Claridges or the White Tower, after which they would go dancing at the Hungaria. During the day Marc joined in with enthusiasm the constant cocktail-party atmosphere at the shop. Mrs Hammersley, when she was told about this new development, was quite shocked. 'Of course Beauveau has ousted Col. In fact you've become fickle to use a polite word . . . The truth is you . . . are fast becoming femme fatale. Perhaps he and Col will fight a duel on your account. Little Prince will I suppose kill the Col and break your heart.' But there was no danger of that. Nancy enjoyed Marc's company, happy to be able to talk about Gaston and flattered by his attention, but there was no question of a rival to the Colonel. And in a month Marc was gone – off to Algiers to join de Gaulle. From there he wrote to Nancy in a far more affectionate manner than the man she loved was ever to do: 'Nancy darling . . . do you think of me a little bit, if so how much? . . . écris moi et dis moi, comme dans la chanson, si tu m'aimes, je t'aime!'

No sooner had Marc gone than a letter arrived from Peter announcing his return. He was still in Italy, 'cruising round just now looking for a nice cosy battleship to give me a lift . . . Build up a small supply of cigarettes whisky and other delicacies for me there is a kind wife.' He arrived in March, laden with cheeses, oranges, brandy and a ham, bronzed and fit and full of his adventures. He and Nancy had a celebration dinner at the Ritz, and then he disappeared again almost immediately to prepare for the invasion. Nancy, running into Jim Lees-Milne and Billa Harrod at a wedding reception, was able to tell them that 'Peter actually knows which beaches they are to land on'. Jim was a great comfort, an old and trusted friend who did not enquire too closely into Nancy's private emotions, and who was often available to lunch with at Gunter's or to chat with at Sibyl's or Emerald's. One warm, sunny Sunday at the end of April he drove Nancy and her dog Millie down to Polesden Lacey, one of the National Trust properties under his care. They picnicked on the verandah;

then, while Jim carried out his work of inspection, Nancy lay in the sun, after which they strolled across the fields together picking cowslips.

One morning at the beginning of May Nancy answered the telephone to hear the voice of the international operator: it was the Colonel in Algiers. Nancy was so taken by surprise that she was quite unable to put what she felt into words. The telephone was such a bitterly unsatisfactory medium, and the distance between them too great for her instantly to summon up the gaiety he had been expecting. As soon as he had rung off she sat down miserably to write him a letter. 'Je suppose que vous avez dû me trouver assez bête ce matin – ce n'est pas une indifférence aux événements mondials mais plutôt une espèce d'absence d'esprit qui me prends lorsque j'entends la voix Coloniale. Oh isn't French a difficult language, you *are* clever to know it so well.'

But this unsatisfactory exchange was forgotten a month later when, one Sunday at the beginning of June, the Colonel appeared in person. 'At 7.30 this morning ...' Nancy wrote to Mrs Hammersley, 'I was woken up by my Col telephoning, & soon afterwards he appeared in a royal car, lent for his visit. It is supposed to be a great secret but no doubt will have been announced long before you get this. So you can imagine if I am pleased He spent the whole day here & has just gone ... He looks extremely well, thinner & younger looking & is *very* important, as you can imagine. What heaven it is to see him again & oh the jokes!' That was her account of it to Mrs Ham. This is what happened to Linda in *The Pursuit of Love*, also lying in bed one summer Sunday morning, dreaming of her absent lover.

'On a sunny Sunday morning in August, very early, her telephone bell rang. She woke up with a start, aware that it had been ringing already for several moments, and she knew with absolute certainty that this was Fabrice.
"Are you Flaxman 2815?"
"Yes."
"I've got a call for you. You're through."

"Allô – allô?"

"Fabrice?"

"Oui."

"Oh! Fabrice – on vous attend depuis si longtemps."

"Comme c'est gentil. Alors, on peut venir tout de suite chez vous?"

"Oh, wait – yes, you can come at once, but don't go for a minute, go on talking, I want to hear the sound of your voice."

"No, no, I have a taxi outside, I shall be with you in five minutes. There's too much one can't do on the telephone, ma chère, voyons –" Click.

'She lay back, and all was light and warmth. Life, she thought, is sometimes sad and often dull, but there are currants in the cake and here is one of them. The early morning sun shone past her window onto the river, her ceiling danced with water-reflections . . . Sun, silence and happiness . . . Early the next morning another beautiful, hot, sunny morning, Linda lay back on her pillows and watched Fabrice while he dressed, as she had so often watched him in Paris. He made a certain kind of face when he was pulling his tie into a knot, she had quite forgotten it in the months between, and it brought back their Paris life to her suddenly and vividly . . .

"And how soon shall I see you again?"

"On fera la navette." He went to the window. "I thought I heard a car – oh yes, it is turning round. There, I must go. Au revoir, Linda."

'He kissed her hand politely, almost absentmindedly, it was as if he had already gone, and walked quickly from the room. Linda went to the open window and leaned out. He was getting into a large motor-car with two French soldiers on the box and a Free French flag waving from the bonnet. As it moved away he looked up.

"Navette – navette –" cried Linda with a brilliant smile. Then she got back into bed and cried very much. She felt utterly in despair at this second parting.'

Fabrice stayed in London for one day, Colonel for just over a week. On June 14 he and the General embarked on a destroyer at Portsmouth, and sailed for France. Nancy wrote to Mrs Hammersley, 'Yes I do feel gloomy without the Col but I don't believe it will be another year before I see him again & I must say it cheered me up – all the jokes you know & they are in *such* spirits ... The Colonel knew all my letters by heart (flattering?).'

And to Palewski himself:

Colonel I have begun to miss you most dreadfully again you wicked Col. Do you get my letters? Please please say ... Now where am I sitting? In Mr Luxmoors garden, waiting for Jonathan[1] to finish his Sunday lesson. Two boys have just wandered by & I thought I heard one of them say 'Oh, Eddy DO let's' It all reminds me of *20 years ago* when I used to visit Tom – toi que voilà qu'as tu fait de ta jeunesse? Is one's failure in life always absolutely one's own fault – I believe it is Everything really happens inside one's head doesn't it & Verlaine couldn't have felt more enclosed in a prison cell than I do.

I went yesterday to see a news reel of the Gen & got one glimpse of my dear col looking very happy – Oh col I hope soon you'll look like that all the time ... I seem to make the worst of every world but then as I'm always trying to explain to a doubtful Colonel I really am not cut out for *this sort of thing* at all.

Osbert Lancaster said at Luncheon on Fri: that Aly F[2] told him you were so frightened in that raid on Thurs: that you kept ringing him up – I said furiously that is a total lie. I was with Palewski *all night*. Sybil Colefax: *all night*? N.R. Well, you know what I mean.

With the liberation of Paris in August, Nancy felt the Colonel was further away from her than ever, further than he had been in

---

[1] Diana's eldest son, Jonathan Guinness.
[2] Alastair Forbes.

Algiers, now that he was restored to his beloved city, reunited with his friends, and working night and day with the General to put France on her feet. In London Nancy felt increasingly cut off. She was tired and dispirited and hating her job at the shop: the Hills were 'hell', her salary barely enough to support life, and, as she told Muv, 'I am so tired, simply limp. I must leave the shop or I shall look 100 soon.' Even more to the point she was charged with emotion and longing to start work on a book. This had been diffidently suggested to Hamish Hamilton ('I expect your list is enormous, & you may not want it') who had jumped at the offer, but how to get permission from the Ministry of Labour for leave of absence in which to write it? Keen though he was, Hamilton knew that the writing of a novel by a little-known author was unlikely to be considered essential war-work. Nancy told Evelyn Waugh, now in Yugoslavia, that she longed to start work, 'but £sd rears its ugly head – I write so slowly & my books always come out at moments of crisis & flop (my last 2 never covered their advances & as you know that is not encouraging. And one was a loss to C & H)'. Then the project had to be further postponed because of the Christmas rush at the shop, 'complicated this year by the fact that there are no other presents to be given but books. Today two quite separate people came in & asked me to think of a book for the Duke of Beaufort "he *never* reads you know" If somebody could write a book for people who never read they would make a fortune.' But Evelyn encouraged her not to give up. 'It is good news that you may take up the pen again. Please give the results to Chapman & Hall. They love losing money and I will get you a substantial over advance.'

He himself had just finished *Brideshead Revisited*, which he had sent Nancy to read in proof. 'A great English classic in my humble opinion,' she told him. 'Oh how I shld like to chat about it, there are one or 2 things I long to know. Are you, or not, on Lady Marchmain's side. I can't make out . . . One dreadful error. Diamond clips were only invented about 1930 you wore a diamond *arrow* in your cloche. Its the only one, which I call good – the only one I spotted at least.' When it came out in May 1945 he asked her to report back on its reception. Colonel, she was able to tell him, had telephoned from Paris to say that 'people are giving luncheon parties to discuss the book & the Windsors have given it to everyone for Xmas. Rather low-brow circles I fear but still!' And she herself had 'a great deal to say – 2 air letters (1/-, agony) if necessary & the whole evening before me . . . I am answering your letter about Brideshead. I quite see how the person who tells is dim but then would Julia & her brother & her sister all be in love with him if he was? Well love is like that & one never can tell. What I can't understand is about God. Now I believe in God & I talk to him a very great deal & often tell him jokes but the God I believe in simply *hates* fools more than anything & he also likes people to be happy & people who love each other to live together – so long as nobody else's life is upset (& then he's not sure). Now I see that I am absolutely religious. I also see this because what is a red rag to a bull to several people about your book is the *subtle clever* Catholic propaganda & I hardly noticed there was any which shows I am immune from it Now about what people think:

> *Raymond*: Great English classic
> *Cyril*: Brilliant where the narrative is straightforward. Doesn't care for the "purple passages" ie death bed of Lord M. thinks you go too much to White's. But found it impossible to put down (no wonder)
> *Osbert*: Jealous – doesn't like talking about it 'I'm devoted to Evelyn – are you?'
> *Maurice*: showing off to Cyril about how you don't always hit the right word or some nonsense but obviously much impressed & thinks the Oxford part perfect.
> *SW7 (European royal quarter)* Heaven darling
> *Diana Abdy*: like me & Raymond, no fault to find
> *Lady Chetwode*: Terribly dangerous propaganda Brilliant
> *General view*: It is the Lygon family. Too much Catholic stuff.'

At the end of the letter is this modest paragraph: 'I am writing a book, also in the 1st person. (Only now has it occurred to me everybody will say what a copy cat – never mind that won't hurt you only me) It's about my family, a very different cup of tea, not grand & far madder. Did I begin it before reading B.head or after I can't remember. I've done about 10 000 words & asked Dearest [Heywood Hill] for a 3 month holiday to write it which I believe I shall get – I'm awfully excited my fingers itch for a pen.'

Heywood Hill gave her the three months, and in March she went up to Ashford in Derbyshire to stay with Andrew and Debo. 'You can't imagine the heaven of hols,' she wrote to Diana, 'after a 3 year solid grind in that shop.' From there she moved on to Faringdon to stay with that remarkable eccentric, Gerald Berners. Having originally met him with Diana, they had become great friends, Gerald's iconoclastic sense of humour, often subtle and sardonic, at other times extremely childish, enormously appealing to Nancy. He was a Master Tease, and his elegant eighteenth-century house near Oxford was full not only of magnificent pictures and furniture but also of jokes, jokes of an undeniably schoolroom nature: a notice on the dining-room two feet from the floor reading 'No Dogs Admitted', a flock of pigeons fluttering about the garden dyed all the colours of the rainbow. He was, too, the perfect host for a working writer: Faringdon was luxuriously comfortable (while Nancy was shivering on the roof of Crewe House fire-watching, the red bedroom at Faringdon was always the place she longed most intensely to be), the food was delicious, and Gerald, himself a serious painter and composer, understood the creative artist's need for discipline, refusing to allow Nancy out of her room until she had fulfilled her quota for the day.

It was while she was at Faringdon that she heard the news that Tom had been killed fighting in Burma. Gerald took the telephone call, and, appalled, went upstairs to tell Nancy what had happened, begging her to stay in her room, not to think of coming downstairs for dinner. But Nancy wouldn't hear of it: she insisted on behaving as though nothing had happened. It was nonetheless a fearful blow. Tom, her earliest confidant, 'Civilization's Fattest Boy', had been the most delightful and charming companion, her link to the world outside, the only member of the family for whom

her feelings were unclouded by jealousy. 'It is almost unbearable,' she wrote to Decca. 'Oh *Tud* & if you knew how sweet &
nice & gay he has been of late & on his last leave.' But, although
she was deeply grieved by his death, it did not mean for her, as it
did for her parents, that all pleasure in life was over. Tom and
Nancy had seen less and less of each other over the past ten
years. Their interests were very different: Tom was a lawyer, a
Germanophile and deeply musical. Ever since their difference
of opinion over Hamish, they had remained, although fond, at
a distance from each other. And now Nancy was in love with
Gaston. As long as Gaston was safe, nothing really could touch
her.

In June Nancy returned to the shop with her book finished. It
was summer, the war was over, restrictions were being relaxed
and friends starting to return from overseas. Peter was back,
happily organising German prisoners, and Mark had been re-
leased from his prison-camp. Nancy wrote to Muv, 'He looks like
a horror photograph, his knees are enormous lumps & his arms
like sticks, but alive & well & *immensely* cheerful. He says in
prison they dreamed of nothing but food & *his* dream was – do
you remember that layer-cake with jam you used to have? well
that! Isn't it too funny. I'd quite forgotten it but of course it used
to be a feature of our lives. He has been in 13 prisons.' For the
first time since the beginning of the war Nancy had a little money
of her own – Hamish Hamilton had given her an advance of £250
('which I call enormous') and she was longing for some new
clothes. Good clothes were a necessity, almost a matter of health,
and Nancy had suffered more than most from the make-do-and-
mend policy of the Duration. Mme Massigli, the newly-arrived
French ambassadress, was a source of great torment on this
count. Mme Massigli's clothes, she told Diana, 'make one feel
Cinderella in the cinders . . . She comes into the shop & I can't sleep
on account of her clothes, wondering how mine could be made
over but of course they couldn't It is a different shape altogether. I
really stayed awake all one night, it simply bothers me – I hadn't
realized how utterly dowdy we all are, & of course my Worth suit,

which has just arrived is no pleasure at all now! What a horrible bore!'

With all this going on, and the general atmosphere of change and excitement in the air, the job at the shop seemed more than ever arduous: it tired and bored her, and she had worked herself up to a strong feeling of resentment against the Hills. It was the Hills whom she made into the target for her unhappiness and frustration, complaining that they were mean and drove her too hard. But Heywood and Anne were not mercenary; it was just that in business matters they were naive and impractical, barely managing to keep their own heads above water. Nancy worked hard, but so did they; her salary was small, but Anne Hill's was smaller. The truth was that Nancy longed to be away: she was pining for Paris and the Colonel.

The Colonel had returned to Paris in August 1944, walking by the General's side on the famous progress down the Champs-Elysées. He was beside himself with happiness, home at last in the centre of the civilised world: 'Paris est admirablement beau. Les fumées des usines ont disparu. Le ciel est ravissant.' And then, 'Quand venez-vous à Paris?' If only she could! But although Colonel was liberal in his invitations, he did not seem prepared to make any practical suggestions. While the war continued he knew very well there was no more possibility of Nancy coming to Paris than there had been of her joining him in Algeria. He was delighted to continue their correspondence; he was more than grateful for the presents she showered on him: 'Après les lettres, le café. Après le café, le jersey . . . J'ai jauni de plaisir en voyant les oeufs en poudres.' But if ever it began to look as if Nancy might after all be able to come, his genial offers of hospitality turned cold: he would try and find her a room in a hotel but there could be no question of her staying with him: 'Vous connaissez notre froide respectabilité'; he would of course be pleased to see her, but she must understand that he was a very busy man, concerned with 'le poids écrasant de mes occupations, dont vous ne semblez pas apprécier le caract̀re tout sérieux'.

But with the coming of peace, it suddenly began to look

possible. Farve, for once sympathetic to Nancy's state of penury and her wish to do more with her life than work as a sales assistant, gave her £3,000 with which to buy a partnership in the shop, the idea being that she should concentrate on building up a strong line in French literature, giving her the excuse of going over, often, to Paris. Heywood approved the project, a licence was obtained from the Board of Trade, an exit permit from the Foreign Office, and by August in soaring spirits she was making ready to leave. 'Went to Drummonds about my passport wearing my new hat,' she told Muv. 'The typists & clerks got such terrible giggles they were paralized & couldn't attend to anything it must have made their day. Did I tell you a woman on a bus said if she could see herself as others see her!' On September 2 she wrote to her mother again: 'I'm off at last, on Wed: I think Should you care to do so, it would be a great kindness if you could send my butter to M. Gaston Palewski, (Cabinet du General de Gaulle) 1 Carlton Gardens SW1 & put *from* Mrs Rodd 12 Blom & in large letters VALISE. Ava Anderson says the breakfast one gets is terrible, insufficient & the bread gives you diarhea all day, so I am taking dozens of oatcakes.'

Paris, in that first autumn after the war, was a city pared to the bone. Conditions were far more austere than in London: accommodation was almost impossible to find, fuel shortages were acute and, because there was no system of rationing, only the rich who could afford the exorbitant prices of the black market had anything except vegetables to eat. Through the Colonel's influence Nancy was installed in a small left-bank hotel in the rue Jacob, 'the kind of hotel O Wilde died in – aucun confort, no bathroom, or loo except dans le couloir . . . washing is rather dreadful, a pint of hot water once a day! . . . Breakfast here is 2 pieces of dry black bread & hateful acorn coffee, black, 8/6 so now I eat oatcake, of which luckily I brought some, & water . . . I eat in workmens' restaurants mostly little bits of cat I think & feel alternately very hungry & very sick. Like this I can live on £1 a day for everything – rather wonderful I suppose when the weather gets cold I shall die, like a geranium.' But all through September and October the weather continued perfect, a true Indian summer, brilliant blue sky day after day, the leaves on the plane trees yellow and gold. To Nancy, her perceptions heightened by emotion, the capital of France was the most beautiful place on earth. 'I must come & live here as soon as I can,' she wrote to Muv. 'I feel a totally different person as if I had come out of a coal mine into daylight . . . It is such a holiday – getting up when I like (shamefully late) sleeping all the afternoon & reading a book in the boiling sun by the river . . . I'm doing a lot of business of various kinds – getting my book translated I think, giving an interview to a French paper & so on besides books business. All great fun. I am as happy as can be.'

The cause and root of her happiness was of course the Colonel. To be in the same city, living in the very next street, talking to him every day on the telephone, holding herself ready to run round to his office in the rue Saint-Dominique whenever he had half an hour to spare, all this was now the essence of life to Nancy. To Gaston himself it was nothing of the kind. He was pleased to see his chère amie of those few hectic months in London, author of that charmante avalanche grise, amused as always by her wit and her outrageous stories, but far too busy to give her much time. He was now in a position of considerable power, heading a Cabinet in de Gaulle's Gouvernement Provisoire which included among its members Michel Debré and Georges Pompidou. He was one of the few members of the government given the use of an official car, and it was Palewski, all the world knew, who had the ear of the General. If it was a question of having a telephone installed, or a collaborating member of the family sprung from gaol, it was Palewski whom one petitioned. On those occasions when he was free to arrange to meet Nancy for dinner, more often than not he telephoned at the last minute to cancel, leaving her in floods of tears to face an evening alone in her bedroom.

But this was never admitted. Nancy lived in 'a whirl of happiness', her one terror, as currency restrictions were stringently enforced, running out of money and having to return home. She was doing well in her book-buying, attending sales at the Hôtel Drouot and making friends with all the most reputable booksellers – M. Camille Bloch in the rue Saint-Honoré, Mlle Jeandet in the rue de Verneuil, M. Caillandre on the Quai Malaquais whose unvaried greeting was so particularly gratifying: 'Ah! voici la Parisienne!' Unfortunately, although Nancy worked hard both buying and selling, 'Nobody in London takes the slightest interest in my activities, Dearest doesn't answer my letters & Mollie just says it makes more work for her – I see her point vividly but it's all rather discouraging I must say. What I've done in fact is to establish a branch of HH here which will take up to any amount of books from us at 30% more than we pay for them which must be quite a cop.' Then Evelyn came up with a scheme to make a little money: Randolph Churchill had been commissioned by a group of American newspapers to write a column on Paris; would Nancy, for two guineas a time, send him a Paris letter every week to appear under Randolph's by-line, to be read only by Americans. 'No shame, no effort,' as Evelyn pointed out. At first demurring, for the mysterious reason that 'social gossip [is] not my strong point', she soon agreed, keeping Randolph supplied with chatty paragraphs on fashionable Parisian life – the black market, a musical soirée, the pathetic situation of the writer Henry de Montherlant. 'Montherlant is hiding in Paris but nobody bothers to look for him. Rather humiliating, like when one hides for sardines & nobody comes!' Whenever she could she worked in a reference to the Directeur de Cabinet: 'The elections are of course the great topic . . . All the attacks & they are many & venomous, are directed against Palewski, who is presented as a sinister Eminence Grise – l'ennemi du peuple. GPRF (Gouvernement Provisoire de la Republique Française) which is on all their motor cars etc, is said to stand for Gaston Palewski Regent of France.' Randolph repaid Nancy's efforts on his behalf by writing 'an absolutely hateful article' about Palewski in a French Communist Paper. The Colonel saw it and was seriously annoyed, more, it is true, for fear of what the General would say than on his own account. 'Voulez vous lui dire de ma part qu'il n'est pas d'usage en France d'écrire sur les gens avec lesquels on est en relations d'amitié ou de camaraderie, sans leur avoir montré au préalable ce qu'on veut publier, et que dans ces conditions je renonce a toute idée de chasser le tigre avec lui.' 'How I wish none of my friends could hold a pen,' Nancy wailed. 'I've now got what I haven't had for years, an ENEMY, & have ranged myself on the side of the hottest Randolph haters.' Nancy's relationship with her obstreperous cousin continued in this pattern for several years. 'You see he rings up, sounding like a rusty old bicycle going up a hill, & is very disarming – then one goes to see him & is subjected to an hours bellowing roaring unpleasantness. I always say never again & always succumb.' The point was finally reached, however, when Randolph went too far to be forgiven. One evening in May 1947, Nancy and Gaston with Momo Marriott, a wealthy American friend, met Randolph for dinner. 'Dinner wasn't ordered, in a crowded restaurant, before Randolph began bawling insults about Gen de G & this continued until coffee. Everybody listened with fascination. The Col tried to laugh it off, then became angry couldn't get up & go because hemmed in by the table & Momo & because it would have made more of a thing you know . . . When we got into the street . . . [Col] said Ma chère Nancy! to which I replied Ma chère Colonel! Indeed I was almost in tears. Never never again. Odious little creature – spitting, sweating, shrieking, oh the horror of him.'

Nancy returned to London in the second week of November filled with a determination to go back to Paris as soon as she possibly could. 'Oh my passion for the French I see all through rose coloured spectacles . . . Apart from love or anything, I must come & live here, & if one makes up one's mind things generally happen don't you think,' she asked Diana. But there was another matter to be attended to first. Her novel, *The Pursuit of Love*, was published on December 10. It was an instant and phenomenal success. If ever there were a case of the right book at the right time, this book was it. Funny, frivolous, and sweepingly romantic, it was the perfect antidote to the long war years of hardship and austerity, providing an undernourished public with its favourite ingredients: love, childhood and the English upper classes.

Far more even than Nancy's previous novels, *The Pursuit of Love* is intensely autobiographical. The heroine, Linda Radlett, is beautiful, feckless and tender-hearted, one of the seven children of Matthew Alconleigh, an eccentric backwoods peer known for his defiant philistinism and the terrible force of his temper. The story is told by Linda's cousin, Fanny, who comes frequently to stay at Alconleigh (a composite of Batsford, Asthall and Swinbrook), rapturously joining in the Radletts' thrilling, savage family life – the feuds with Uncle Matthew, days out hunting on the Cotswold uplands, the cosy conversations about sex in the linen cupboard known as the Hons' cupboard, after the Radlett children's secret society.

As Linda and Fanny grow up they start to dream longingly of love, yearning for the day when they will be swept off their feet by some dashing and romantic man. But it isn't quite like that. Linda marries straight out of the schoolroom, first a handsome, complacent bore called Kroesig, then a dedicated Communist, Christian, devoted to his cause and with little time to spare for his wife. Both times Linda believed herself to be in love, and both times it had proved an illusion. Then, on her way home from the south of France, she is picked up – no other word for it – by a Frenchman in the Gare du Nord: a short, stocky, very dark Frenchman in a black Homburg hat. And thus begins the one true love affair of Linda's life. Fabrice, duc de Sauveterre, is one of the great fascinators, clever, funny and amorous, a man of the world and French to his fingertips. He installs Linda in a pretty apartment in Paris, and here for nearly a year she lives a life as near perfect happiness as it is possible to attain. Then comes the war: Linda has to return to England while Fabrice disappears into the Resistance. She sees him only once more, when he suddenly appears for twenty-four hours on a brief mission to London. In the end Linda dies giving birth to their child; and at about the same time Fabrice is caught by the Gestapo and shot.

It is all here, all Nancy's life, in this novel, exaggerated in parts, circumstances changed, fantasies fulfilled (Fabrice tells Linda he loves her), but as a testament of her heart and mind it is true to the last letter. The hero is, of course, Colonel as Fabrice, down to the smallest detail, from his demands to be entertained – 'Alors, racontez!' – to his habit of bursting into little snatches of song, and even the face he makes when knotting his tie. Prodd is divided into two as Linda's two husbands, Christian who cares only for causes and is 'so detached from other human beings he hardly notices whether they are there or not'; and Tony Kroesig, pompous and clever, his head full of a 'vast quantity of utterly dreary facts, of which he did not hesitate to inform his companions, at great length and in great detail, whether they appeared to be interested or not'. Eddy Sackville-West appears thinly disguised as Fanny's hypochondriacal Uncle Davey; and Gerald Berners as Lord Merlin, with his expensive, cultivated taste, his diamond-collared whippets and his love of ingenious teases (Merlinford's telegraphic address is 'Neighbourtease').

But the character who dominates all the others, just as he dominates his own large family, is Lord Alconleigh, Uncle Matthew, a portrait of Farve in all his glory, drawn with that devastating combination of caricature and unerring psychological accuracy which is one of Nancy's greatest gifts as a novelist. Irascible, unreasonable and tender-hearted, there he is cracking his stock-whips on the lawn, up at dawn and roaring at the housemaids, his eyes flashing a furious blue as he repeats his unshakable conviction that, 'abroad is unutterably bloody and foreigners are fiends!' There is his favourite epithet 'sewer', his favourite records ('Fearful the death of the diver must be, Walking alone in the de-he-he-he-he-epths of the sea') and his habit of falling asleep at the dinner table. Although in middle age she became convinced that she had never been fond of either of her parents, Nancy's depiction of her father as Uncle Matthew is deeply affectionate; frightening and funny, he is also endearing, and there is no question but that Nancy was speaking her own mind in these words of Fanny's: 'Much as we feared, much as we disapproved of, passionately as we sometimes hated Uncle Matthew, he still remained for us a sort of criterion of English manhood; there seemed something not quite right about any man who greatly differed from him.'

Nancy wrote the novel from beginning to end in three months. Never before had she found a book so effortless to write, and never would she do so again. It was as though falling in love had given her access to a creative source of which previously she had barely skimmed the surface. Evelyn read the manuscript, and it was Evelyn who suggested the title. Hamish Hamilton had no hesitation in declaring his enthusiasm for *Pursuit* ('the word brilliant has been used'). He recognised it as a winner from the first, asking only for a few, very minor, editorial changes: 'p. 252 – re Dunkirk. I know exactly what Linda means and I think she would probably have said it, but I have a hunch that Miss Mitford ought to tone down line 6. There are just too many people who didn't think it Heaven.' His faith in Linda was amply repaid. The critics praised it – 'Highly diverting from the first to the last page', 'More truth, more sincerity, and more laughter than in a year's output of novels' – the public bought it, read it and, it sometimes seemed, talked of little else. It was the Book Society Choice for December, with 200,000 copies sold in the first twelve months. Hamilton had told her that in the end Linda might earn as much as £750, but she made more than that (£798) in the first three weeks, and in six months over £7,000. From all sides the congratulations poured in. 'Clever, clever Nancy,' wrote John Betjeman, 'I am proud to know you.' Uncle Matthew, whose opinion was awaited with some trepidation, 'sat with his nose in the book & grunted out various corrections: "Never got the stock whips in Canada, a bloke from Australia gave them to me" & so on. He was delighted with it but cried at the end.'

There was a dissenting faction, of course, led by Cyril Connolly and the Bloomsbury Home Guard who 'think my book utterly indecent on acc/ of not being about cabmen's shelters & Hons Cupboard makes them vomit & they are all the more annoyed because they think its quite well written. I've just had this month's Smarty's[1] Own Mag [*Horizon*] & of course the great

[1] Cyril Connolly.

joke is one does write better than all of them (not SB himself[1])
because even when they quite want to be understood they can't
be. As Tonks used to say "Why don't they stick to cooking?" '

The opinion that mattered most was that of the book's be-
getter: Colonel was pleased with his portrait as the duc de
Sauveterre, although constrained to point out that French dukes
were not in life like that; 'he then introduced me to one & indeed
he can hardly have been more like the late Hartington & less like
Fabrice. Still – fiction.' He had been flattered, too, by Nancy's
dedication 'To Gaston Palewski' ('Avec la dédicace, je dois
entrer dans la gloire'). But then at the last moment, with the book
already at the printer, he panicked, frightened that the Communist opposition would scent a scandal in his association with la
soeur d'Unity Mitford, l'amie de Hitler. There was a flurried
exchange of telegrams between Nancy and her publisher –
'DELETE DEDICATION SUBSTITUTE LORD BER-
NERS', 'LEAVE GASTON IGNORE INSERTION PRINT
AWAY' – before Colonel calmed himself and allowed the dedication to stand. '*Please* never let Gerald know,' Nancy implored
Hamilton. 'I count on you to be like a doctor & never tell tho it's
almost more than I can expect.' No sooner was that panic over
than another cause of annoyance came to light. In the last chapter
Fanny's mother says to her daughter about Fabrice, 'He seemed
to have settled down for life with that boring Lamballe woman;
then she had to go to England on business and clever little Linda
nabbed him.' Now the Colonel had had a serious liaison with a
lady of that name, as Nancy knew very well; 'that boring Lamballe
woman' was put in expressly to tease; and tease it did. 'Gerald
says Diana [Cooper] says you are cross with me about the boring
Lamballe woman. Don't be cross, I can't bear that. As for the
BLW herself, tell her to write a book about *me* – I am very
vulnerable. I hate her – hateful Lamballe who deserted you when
you were a lonely exile & ran off with her own sort. It was a mean
& shabby trick. All the same I will take anything you tell me out of
the American edition.' But it was too late: the Americans had

[1] Smarty-Boots, a name originally given to Connolly by Virginia Woolf.

already printed. All Nancy could now do was offer to delete the offending line before the book was published in France. And with that the Colonel ('il est vain de pleurer sur le lait répandu') was forced to be content.

Much as Nancy had been gratified by Linda's enormous success, she could not feel happy while the cruel grey English Channel separated her from all she loved best. Her own idea was to get back to the Colonel as quickly as possible, for not only did she miss him but she knew very well that if she were away from him for long she would lose him. There was that terrible roving eye of his, and she had been badly frightened by how hard she had had to work to re-establish herself after their year's absence from each other during the war. The Colonel was out of power now, the General having resigned in January, and his future was uncertain.

'Colonel I know of nothing worse than when somebody one loves is far away & unhappy & one is quite quite incapable of helping them. Not only do I love you very much but also the Gen – & the hateful way in which he has been treated wounds me to the heart . . . I liked you being where I knew the set-up. When I felt sad I used to go past those men at the gate, past those men at the table, up the stairs, past that little squinting man & into the room where my darling colonel was working & working, & I felt well there he is, I know. Now it is all a mist – & then there are those hateful nieces. Don't laugh & don't say I know . . . there will be a long long silence now, no petite chose noire[1], seulement l'épingle d'Alger – & I don't like long colonial silences.' When he did write or telephone it always gave her joy. 'Your darling voice & your darling hand writing within an hour of each other is almost *too* much happiness. And I suppose the next best thing to having one's sentiments returned is to have them appreciated.' But when she did not hear, she was miserable. 'Dear darling Colonel I think of you all the time don't leave me for ever without a word of what is happening to you. I went yesterday to send you a telegram but then thought it would perhaps be a bore.'

[1] The Colonel's phrase, trying to find the English for 'typewriter'.

Being a bore was the one thing she knew she dare not risk: she was often sad but her sadness must never be allowed to weigh upon the Colonel. 'I've just written you a long sad letter which I've torn up – I don't think you like being invited to regard me as a serious character . . . this is my Sunday letter – I've been writing to you for hours because the letter I tore up as well as being *very* sad was also *very* long. What will happen to me on Sunday mornings when I have to stop writing to you? Oh darling Colonel.' It was clear then that the Colonel must at all costs be amused, and Michael Duff's ball provided the ideal subject for just the sort of performance Gaston most enjoyed. This was the first big party Nancy attended since the beginning of the war and, having no suitable dress, she sewed an old nightdress on to the top of a discarded satin ball-gown. 'I think at balls it is better to look a joke than dreary don't you,' she anxiously asked Diana. 'I must say,' she wrote to Colonel, 'it was great great fun . . . I felt like a drowning man, the whole of my past life was there Chips [Channon] said to Emerald, surveying the scene "This is what we have been fighting for" to which clever old Emerald replied "Why are they all Poles?" . . . Prince Peter [of Greece] invited us to dinner in a kind of Chinese swimming bath (I do think foreign royalties are extraordinary) There were two *horrible* little Greek insect-women, one called Mrs Sitwell (I told Osbert & he said "Oh yes, those are the Jigga-Jigga Sitwells") Prince P has a Norwegian girl friend who seems to wait faithfully for him & sees him once every 6 years, exactly like me. I felt for her . . . A friend of mine called lady Pat Russell writes from Austria that she was raped by 6 Cossacks (Hard cheese as she is a Lesbian) Very topical & in the swim of her isn't it . . . I saw Penelope at the BALL she is going back to Paris lucky her. You would have loved the ball & oh the pretty young women back from running away to the country, now the war is over – come to London darling Colonel *do* & I promise you can *see* them (mustn't touch).'

London was full of French Society – the Tour du Pins, the Massiglis, even Marc with his mother the Princesse de Beauvau. 'I'm afraid I wasn't very nice to poor Marc but he has a proprietory attitude as if he had been my lover for 25 years which I find impossible to bear.' Every other person Nancy met seemed either to have just arrived from Paris, or be on the point of going there. It was too much to bear. 'Can't I come to Paris?' she asked the Colonel. 'You are the door-keeper of Calais to me.'

And really what was there to stop her going? She had given up working at the shop in March, and Peter was on the point of leaving for Spain to make a film. He and Nancy were on the friendliest terms but Prodd was the same old Prodd and nothing was going to change there. ('We are dining on Tues to meet the Duchess of Kent,' Evelyn was informed. 'I've offered Prod 2/6 not to embarrass me, as I used to do with my sisters when my young men were coming to stay but I fear Prod is less venal & I dread his views on monarchy being aired.') The marriage existed in name only, and Nancy's longing to be in France was far stronger than any desire to keep up appearances with her husband. It was France she wanted, 'all that bubbling & cheerfulness & endless flattery which goes on ceaselessly there. They never seem to want to take one down a peg, like English people do, & they *seem*, which is all that matters, to love one so much. Angels.' And in April she was off.

CHAPTER EIGHT

Paris

Nancy arrived in Paris in April 1946 knowing that she would never live in England again: from now on she was to devote herself to the pursuit of her love affair with the Colonel and with France. England represented everything that was ugly, hostile and cold: France was light and warmth. The unhappiness in her past – a lonely childhood, the sterile relationship with Hamish, her unsatisfactory marriage and failure to have children – were all represented by the bleak and barren British Isles. France, on the other hand, contained the Colonel, and it was on the Colonel that her happiness depended. Nancy was always inclined towards hero-worship, and Colonel was her hero. She knew in her heart that he was not and never would be in love with her; but the nature of her love for him, almost like a schoolgirl's crush, allowed her to live with this knowledge. She lived for his whirlwind visits, for the hasty telephone calls between appointments, for the last-minute summons to run round and chat for fifteen minutes before he went out for the evening. Always she was expected to perform, to be at her best, to amuse and entertain. It was exciting because Nancy could never be sure when she would see him, when she would get the call to go on stage. But the excitement concealed a great emptiness: there was no ordinary life with the Colonel, none of the daily humdrum give and take, no waking up together in the morning or going out at night, no crossness or tiredness, none of the boredom, even, of married life, none of the emotional fulfilment of mutual love. Something had to take its place, and as she could not concentrate the powerful beam of her affection on one man, she increased its span to embrace the entire country. France itself, its people, its history and culture, its delicious food and pretty clothes, was bathed in a golden light, a light which, as in the pantomime, brilliantly illuminates the Good Fairy on one side of the stage, while on the other the Demon King (brandishing a Union Jack) is immersed in evil green. Thus Paris was the most beautiful city in the world, London so hideous it made one physically ill to go there; the weather in France was sunny and warm, in England one froze to death in those unheated houses and it never, ever stopped raining. Even the smells characteristic of the two countries exemplified the contrast: France was women's scent and chestnut flowers and rich garlicky cooking, while in England one was made literally to retch by the smell of stale sweat, cold mutton, dirty clothes and unwashed hair.

None of Nancy's friends was left in any doubt as to her feelings for her newly-adopted country. To Evelyn she wrote, 'The day one sets foot in France, you can take it from me, PURE happiness begins . . . every minute of every day here is bliss & when I wake up in the morning, I feel as excited as if it were my birthday.' Evelyn was unpersuaded – 'I have long recognized your euphoria as a pathological condition . . . You have made great friends with a Pole who has introduced you to a number of other Poles . . .' – but then Evelyn was not fond of the French. To her mother she described at greater length her reasons, leaving out the main one, for preferring to live in France: 'For one thing I really can't stand the English climate any more & in a world where the sun can shine on you all day see no point in continuing to live at the bottom of a well . . . Then there is an intellectual life here which has no counterpart at home & which I love. Then eating is a recurring delight here & so is walking about the beautiful town & so is the fact that real deep country is within ½ an hour, & a country where you can walk & then deliciously dine. Everybody is cheerful, nice to you, anxious to please. They wash & iron to perfection – there are none of the minor pin pricks of life everything goes on oiled wheels. You can drink wine at every meal. In fact, except for leaving a handful of friends who anyhow can come over here whenever they want to now, & relations who

anyhow all live in the country & whom I only saw intermittently, I
have no doubt at all that life here, for me is far the most agreeable
life. I can come home for 3 months every year which will be quite
enough . . . !'

Nancy's move to Paris was important in another way, which
had nothing to do with Gaston nor with the rival merits of the two
countries. Away from home and divided by the Channel from
family and friends, she had every opportunity for that form of
communication at which she excelled – writing letters. Many of
her friendships developed further on paper than they would have
done in the ordinary course of meetings on social occasions and
exchanging a few minutes' gossip. Heywood Hill, to whom, once
she had left the shop, Nancy turned back with affection, was one
of these friends; Evelyn was another. Evelyn had particularly
regretted Nancy's departure ('Nancy has gone to Paris leaving a
grave gap in my morning's routine,' he noted in his diary in
September 1945), but in fact their correspondence became as
important to them both as any more contiguous relationship. To
his many enemies Evelyn was the nastiest-tempered man in
England, but Nancy saw past that and loved him, 'knowing as I do
the real bonhommie behind that mask of iron'. They quarrelled,
of course, mainly about religion, a subject on which Nancy
irritated Evelyn by preserving an incorrigibly flippant attitude;
but they moved in the same world, found the same jokes funny,
both revelled in gossip, and Nancy relied very much on Evelyn's
critical judgement. While in the process of writing a novel, she
discussed every stage with him, and always sent the manuscript
for his approval before showing it to her publisher.

And at first Nancy was gloriously happy. Gaston, out of office
and with time on his hands, was much more accessible than
before. 'The Col is no longer governing France, so instead of
always waiting about to be rung up & then hurrying round for ½
an hour I can see him for hours every day.' The difficulty was that
he was extremely hard-up, whereas Nancy for the first time in her
life had money to spend, and could afford to do much as she
pleased. Linda was still bringing in a healthy income, the film

rights had been sold, there was the American edition and translations into several European languages.[1] But so many of the pleasures of Paris – going to the theatre, eating in restaurants – were disappointing on one's own, and the only company Nancy wanted was that of Gaston who absolutely refused to let her pay for him. 'I've begged & implored him to have some of my millions but it simply makes him cross so I've had to desist,' she told Diana. 'When he isn't asked out he eats things in tins which have been sent him from time to time by American friends & luckily conserved by his faithful Pierre – High Grade pork etc. Yesterday morning he rang up & said "franchement ma chère j'en ai assez du High Grade". Isn't it dreadful.' Evenings which they spent together always began with Colonel opening a tin of High Grade in the rue Bonaparte where Nancy would join him after eating on her own in a bistro. Only if she were entertaining several people to a meal would he agree to be her guest. She described her first luncheon party to Diana: '2 bottles of champagne & 2 of red wine – lovely snails, chicken & port salut (don't cry) which with tip came to £9. You must say that's pretty cheap if one thinks of London. I had Maurice Bowra, Col, Marie Louise Bousquet, Paz Subercazeaux (Gerald's enemy) & Marc de Chimay . . . Maurice is wonderful here, he launches unashamed into the most extraordinary French, never draws breath, & the frogs utterly love him.'

The Colonel, of course, had an extremely busy social life of his own: he had a wide acquaintance, was much sought after as a diner-out, and evenings alone with the tin-opener did not feature often. It was he who introduced Nancy into Paris society. Most of her friends in Paris were English whom she had known for years, like Geoffrey Gilmour, first met as a friend of Hamish in the twenties, now living in the rue du Bac; Alvilde Chaplin at whose house in Jouy en Josas Nancy often spent the weekend; and Violet

---

[1] About one of these, Muv snorted to Diana, 'My Swedish friend sent me a publisher's notice of Nancy's book it says "Everywhere in Europe men lost their heads when the beautiful elegant Mitford sisters dominated the salons" Oh dear what nonsense.'

Trefusis, that clever, tiresome woman, daughter of Mrs Keppel, who mesmerised a large circle of friends by her impulsive generosity[1] and her habit of telling the most terrible lies, lies of mythological proportion always with herself in the starring role. (One of her favourites was that her real father was not Mr Keppel but King Edward VII himself, and at Buckingham Palace *she clearly remembers* being sent into the garden to play with the sceptre and orb.) Like Nancy, Violet, too, was a writer, and as such took herself very seriously indeed: after her name in the Paris telephone directory, as it might be 'épicier en gros', was the entry, 'fmm de lttrs'. The people whom Nancy now came to know through Gaston were not so much 'gratin', the old grand French with their pre-Revolutionary titles, but a sort of café society, people like Princesse Dolly Radziwill and her Danish husband Mogens Tvede, the Prince and Princesse de Caraman-Chimay, Marie-Louise Bousquet and Princesse Sixte de Bourbon-Parme. He was very careful, was the Colonel, that among his friends he and Nancy should never be regarded as a couple: if invited to the same occasion they must make their separate ways; Nancy was not allowed to 'tutoyer' him, nor did he care for her to address him by his first name. In the eyes of the world, they were no more than good friends from his days in London during the war; the world knew nothing of Nancy's passion, nor of her anguish, nor of her tears on those many occasions when the telephone rang at the last possible moment with the Colonel cancelling the evening's plans.

Her entrée into this glittering society made it essential that Nancy should equip herself with a couture wardrobe. One of the most painful disciplines of her visit to Paris the year before was denying herself the pleasure of buying clothes. But that was before the publication of her book, and prices then were far out of her reach. 'The pre-war price of about £40 I could now afford,' she had written to Muv, 'but £100 really is out of the question. Oh

---

[1] She had promised so many people that she was leaving them treasures – houses, jewellery – in her will that Nancy suggested they form a trade-union.

I had to make an effort though! the devil whispers get it – you'll never see anything pretty again for years & years, & you'll wear it for 10 years, & that's only £10 a year.' Her one small extravagance was a hat but 'I'm sorry to say the hats really are smaller again (mine is huge, but I got it a bit too soon) the really smart women all have lovely little ones with feathers, not ostrich, & bows … Maddening that one just missed the fashion, so becoming to one. Never mind, gallant old London won't know this – except that gallant old Eng: ladies so love to pose a dolls hat over their gallant old huge yellow faces, that they will probably snatch at the news.'

Now, however, she could afford to indulge herself. Good clothes were of immense importance to Nancy. 'It's terrible to love clothes as much as I do, & perfectly inexplicable because I'm not at all vain & Col who is the only person I care for doesn't know sackcloth from ashes.' Clothes were almost an essential part of life: she loved looking at them, she loved wearing them and she loved the whole business of having them made – the cutting of the toile, the lengthy fittings, the detailed discussions over the set of a shoulder or the placing of a dart. Her narrow English figure was much admired by the fitters and vendeuses: it was a pleasure to fit clothes on a figure such as Mme Rodd's, 'one in 100,' they told her at Grès. But, even more than this, Nancy's love of fashion was part of the shop-front, part of showing to the world an image of polished perfection, of immaculate chic. Nancy in her Paris clothes presented the very picture of elegance, but her boned bodice, padded hips and huge skirts lined in stiff buckram invited one to look, not to touch. She was one of the first to wear Dior's New Look in London: the showing of his original collection in February 1947 acted on Nancy, as on most of the female population of Paris, as a magic potion. After years of short, skimped skirts and brutal, square-shouldered jackets, the softness and fluidity of Dior's line, the rustling petticoats and wasp waists, the yards and yards of swirling stuff in his full skirts were frankly irresistible. 'Dior, oh darling,' she wrote to Diana, 'made for you & me, absolute Anna Karenina clothes. The coats – to the ankle literally & mountains of loovely stoof. Oh me, my brain is in a whirl.' But Dior was still just in the future. Nancy bought her first couture wardrobe from Mme Grès – a dress and coat, a suit with a sealskin collar, a pink wool dressing-gown, two hats (one a white satin boater with aigrette, the other a pair of birds, one pink and one green, perched on a base of black velvet) and, the pièce de résistance, a ball-dress in black velvet with a huge skirt and a wide band of black transparent chiffon round the midriff. 'I wish to constater here & now,' she wrote to Muv, 'that I am *not* repeat *not* going to lend it to Miss Deborah under any circumstances Let there be no misunderstanding on this piont . . . You never saw such a dress – who was that friend of Farves who had £12 a year? Not for her.'

Nancy first wore this wonderful dress at a ball, an event much looked forward to but which turned out something of a disappointment, as she explained in a letter to Evelyn. 'I went to a ball at Princess de Bourbon-Parme's, duly binged up as one is before balls with champagne, black coffee & so on. Well we hadn't been there 2 minutes before the Colonel said we couldn't stay on acc/ of the great cohorts of collaborators by whom we were surrounded, & firmly dumped me home. I perceive that I have made enemies for life of Pss Radziwill who took me & Pss B-P because there was only one entrance over which they were both hovering. I know you are pro-collaborators anyway & probably think the Col was being babyish. Anyway here I am wide-awake for hours.' To this Evelyn unsympathetically replied, 'Collaborationists my foot. Does it not occur to you, poor innocent, that the continental Colonel went back to the aristocratic ball and that while you lay sleepless with your fountain pen, he was in the arms of some well born gestapo moll?'

Dazzling as was this Proustian world, the pinnacle of Nancy's social life was not French but English – its focus the British Embassy, that large, beautiful, honey-coloured house on the rue du Faubourg Saint-Honoré. Duff Cooper after leaving Algiers had come as Ambassador in September 1944, and his wife Diana had made the Embassy a centre for the most amusing society in Paris. She herself, with her great beauty, charm and originality, possessed a genius for creating an alluring atmosphere. With the help of Cecil Beaton she had brought a personal touch to the great state rooms, placing family photographs and favourite Victorian portraits among the grand Napoleonic furniture. Diana could not tolerate boredom, and she was accustomed to getting her own way: rules were for other people. If there was something Diana thought she should have, there was little to which she would not stoop to get it, with the result that the British Embassy was one of the few houses in Paris that was properly heated, and where the food (all bought on the black market) was plentiful and rich. Diana showed not the faintest interest in furthering British interests, and was far too special to concern herself with the ordinary, tedious duties of an ambassadress. Instead she directed her energies towards the entertainment of what she called her 'bande', a little group of habitual diners-out who were considered by Diana good-looking, amusing, or both. She did not much care for France nor for the French; she knew little about them, and spoke their language badly; the members of 'la bande' were either friends from England, such as Cecil Beaton, Peter Coats, Chips Channon, Evelyn Waugh and Raymond Mortimer, or English-speaking Anglophiles mainly from the world of the arts. She was supremely indifferent to questions of politics, and it mattered not at all to her whether she sat down to dinner with a hero of the Resistance or with an arch-collaborator, as long as he could pull his weight at table – an attitude which may have done little to foster the entente cordiale, but was terrific fun for 'la bande'.

Nancy was mesmerised by Diana, who now took her up and into her innermost circle. In the intimacy of the Salon Vert or at big parties in the Salon Jaune Nancy met many well-known faces: 'Chips [Channon] & Petticoats [Peter Coats] are here. The pansy world has been in a ferment for this event, half longing to see Petti whose fame has preceded him & half terrified that the particular loved one will be bewitched by him!'. She met, too, some of the most fashionable French artists, writers and musicians of the day – Cocteau, Drian, the stage-designer Bébé Bérard, Edouard

Gerald Berners

Eddy Sackville-West

Evelyn Waugh. Photo: Mark Gerson

Hamish Hamilton

Nancy

The six Mitford sisters drawn by William Acton

From the collection of the Hon Desmond Guinness

Pam

Diana

Unity

Decca

Debo

Nancy with Anne Hill outside the shop

Marc de Beauvau-Craon

Gaston Palewski with the General
in Algiers, 1942.
Photo: Institut Charles de Gaulle

Nancy (wearing the New Look) with
Alvilde Chaplin in the courtyard of the
British Embassy in Paris

Duff and Diana Cooper

Marie Renard, Nancy's cook-
housekeeper

Colonel what does it mean? Rather
...did for me because now I shant
...r to come   3. EARTON STREET.   back to Paris —
              WESTMINSTER. S.W.1.
              WHITEHALL 3673   I shall buy a
                        little house
                      in Maidenhead
                    I find some
                  faithful English
colonel. When is the
wedding day? (I
must say you look as
if about to fell her
with a blow)

...etter from Nancy to the Colonel showing him in
suit of his favourite pastime

Portrait of Gaston Palewski, 'Homme au Gant', by Nora Auric. Nancy bought it, and in order to make it fit the frame cut several inches off the bottom of the canvas, including the glove of the title and the artist's signature. She then made matters worse by painting in the signature herself, wrongly spelt, a desecration which caused Mme Auric considerable annoyance when she discovered it some years later

Mrs Hammersley at Chatsworth

Muv on Inch Kenneth

Nancy and Debo on the Venetian Lagoon

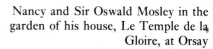

Nancy and Sir Oswald Mosley in the garden of his house, Le Temple de la Gloire, at Orsay

Nancy at a party in London in 1959

Diana, Pam and Debo at Nancy's funeral
Swinbrook on July 7, 19
Photo: David Newell-Smith, the *Obser*

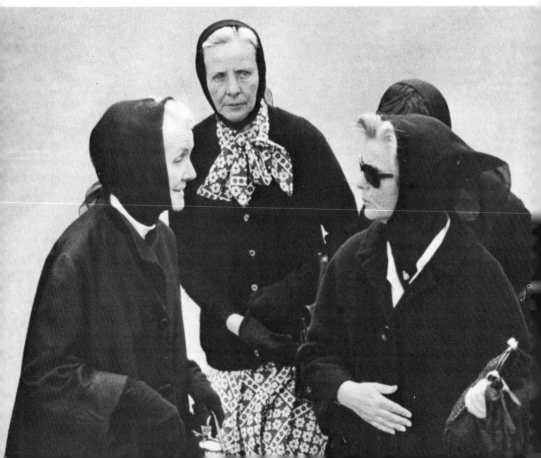

Bourdet director of the Comédie Française, Poulenc, the pianist Jacques Février and the composer Georges Auric and his painter wife Nora ('exactly like Oliver Messel dressed as a woman'). Diana appointed Gaston, an old friend from his time in Algeria, to be her unofficial censor, her pilot-fish, to advise on whose war-time activities should debar them from swimming into her net. But the advice once given was usually ignored, and Gaston himself, so sensitive to any whiff of collaboration elsewhere, sat down without a murmur to eat his (excellent) dinner in the company of such as Marie-Laure de Noailles[1] and Louise de Vilmorin[2]. To Nancy it was all perfect, the very height of civilisation. Diana's rudeness couldn't be funnier, her intolerance of bores even more ruthless than Nancy's own.

It was a great blow when at the end of 1947 Duff Cooper was recalled by a Labour government to be replaced by Sir Oliver Harvey, a career diplomat who, after the charismatic Coopers, was bound to be a sad come-down, 'utter ghastly drear personified'. Diana, suddenly realising, now she was on the point of departure, what she was leaving behind, discovered in herself a deep love of the city where she had reigned like a queen, and in a spirit of romantic gloom threw a great valedictory ball. Nancy, with her black velvet ball-gown updated for the occasion, was alight with excitement: 'All the people beginning to arrive for the Ball, its so exciting, like a house party for a hunt ball when one was young & loved them only magnified a hundred times. Also made more strange by the streets – black out, search lights playing, huge mounds of refuse everywhere & armoured cars dashing through the serried ranks of limousines.' It was a magnificent set-piece, the 'Waterloo' ball, with the Embassy lit entirely by candles, every piece of the historic gilt dinner-services gleaming

[1] Vicomtesse de Noailles, patron and hostess, was involved in a car accident during the war while driving with a German officer.
[2] Poet, minor novelist and wit, Louise de Vilmorin had been able, as the wife of the Hungarian Count Palffy, to travel freely across Germany and was thus regarded with suspicion by the French authorities.

on the tables. Diana, a beautiful tragedy-queen sweeping about in pale blue satin, made no attempt to conceal her sadness. 'Le désespoir de Diana made itself felt,' Nancy remarked. With the Coopers gone, Paris would not be the same.

They were not gone long, however. Ignoring the convention that a departing Ambassador should keep away from his former post for at least a year to give his successor time to establish himself, the Coopers were back within weeks, settling into the pretty Château de Saint-Firmin at Chantilly. Resentful at being turned out of 'her' Embassy, Diana initiated a wonderful new tease called Being Beastly to the Harveys; and, like children in a playground following the bully's lead, 'la bande', with Nancy to the fore, joined in with relish. The Coopers were fashionable, the Harveys were not; it was easy to sneer, and 'we all proudly say we shan't write our names in their book'. What could be more enjoyable than to gloat over Lady Harvey's lumpy English clothes, the fact that her visiting cards were printed (horrors!), not engraved, and that their food was so bad that 'Poor Prince Philip was poisoned . . . & his visit was one long session on the loo.' To Sir Oliver Harvey, a skilled and experienced diplomat, holder of the Grand Cross of the Légion d'Honneur and deeply respected by the leaders of the Fourth Republic, all this mattered not a jot. But to Lady Harvey it was unmitigated pain. True to form, Nancy had only to dine with the new Ambassador and his wife a couple of times for her to turn from hunting with the hounds to running with the hare. Soon she was on the friendliest terms with Maudie Harvey while the peerless Diana began to appear in a less appealing light as her dislike of the French became more and more pronounced. This was the one thing guaranteed to lose Nancy's sympathy. Conversation round the dinner-table at Chantilly, she complained to Evelyn, was like the chorus in *Billy Budd*: 'They all sit round singing *Don't like* the French, the damned Mounseers . . . I get more & more restless in her company owing to her vitriolic hatred & lack of comprehension of the French. I despise people who live here to escape taxes & who hate the French – the Windsors are another case.'

At the end of this year, 1947, Nancy was at last able to rent an apartment of her own. Till then she had had always to be on the move, in and out of hotels of varying degrees of comfort depending on her financial situation; she had rented a flat in the rue Bonaparte, was lent another on the Quai Malaquais, but due to the acute housing shortage had been unable to find a permanent home – one which met the sole criterion on which she insisted, that it should be no more than a few minutes' walk from the Colonel. Number 7, rue Monsieur was a pretty eighteenth-century house standing behind a high wall, between a paved courtyard and a large, leafy garden. Nancy had the ground floor, entered through a small hallway, with a large drawing-room, a dining-room, bedroom and bathroom, and a small room for a maid on the floor above. The maid came with the flat, Marie Renard, a sweet-faced peasant-woman from Normandy. 'I've never liked any house I've lived in as much as this one or ever known such a treasure as Marie . . . She's the servant of one's dreams that's all. I said which is your jour de repos . . . & she said I rather like to go off at about 4 on Sunday afternoon but of course not if you have people for dinner. She gives me Sunday luncheon & prepares my dinner.' Not only that: Marie did all the shopping, all the cooking, all the housework, and washed, ironed and mended Nancy's clothes. Nancy herself was quite helpless in these matters: she could not cook, barely knew how to boil a kettle, and had never learned to thread a needle – when Marie went on holiday, she had to leave several needles ready threaded in case a button fell off in her absence. Marie had the temperament of an angel and hard work was what she enjoyed. She was by nature frugal, knew exactly where to go to save a few centimes on butter or coffee, and was almost incapable of throwing away left-over food. (Nancy once came back from a month's holiday to find in the refrigerator a jug containing a small cannon-ball of solidified milk which Marie had been unable to bring herself to pour down the sink when shutting up the flat four weeks earlier.) Having Marie, and being settled in a home of her own, made all the difference to Nancy. So much so that she was able to tell

Evelyn on December 31, 'My book has begun to go, isn't it wonderful when they do that. Of course it's simply a question of working whatever one may tell oneself.'

It had been worrying Nancy for some time that she was unable to write. She wanted to work, as she explained to Evelyn: 'I'm beginning to feel bored with nothing to do & not fond enough (never have been really) of social life for that to become a whole time job.' More seriously, she needed to earn some money: Linda could not continue much longer to support her expensive Paris life. The trouble was that 'having used up Farve & Fabrice I am utterly done for – all the rations have gone into one cake. Now what?' She tried to make a start during the summer, but it would not come and she began to be afraid she had 'lost the art'. 'The Colonel keeps encouraging me saying I shall never write a good book which isn't about him, & altogether – Still, I must plod on.' But, with her changed circumstances, inspiration returned. The idea for the plot came from a true story, buffed up and embellished and submitted to Evelyn for advice on how to treat it. 'The fact is I've begun to be appalled by the difficulties of technique, a thing which has never worried me at all.' What she wanted to know was whether she could again use the device of first-person narrator. Muv was consulted on social practice ('At a ball one never wore rings outside ones gloves (horrors) but what about bracelets?'); and Jamie Hamilton was asked, 'Are pansies allowed in books? (I know you're very strict but after all think of Proust) . . . No details *of course*.'

But the actual writing of the novel, which had come so easily with *The Pursuit of Love*, this time was a struggle. Nancy was no longer writing her own story which meant that she was having to work much harder on the construction of plot and the development of character. She was further hampered by a constant series of interruptions. Having enjoyed a busy social life among people to whom work was not one of the necessities of existence, it was difficult to cut herself off from these people for the quiet she needed without causing offence. The telephone pealed all day with invitations to dinners and luncheons. 'Counted the telephone calls this morning, 10 before 11 . . . One person went up to 40 rings I always count, that was the best so far.' Then she was a sitting target for the stream of English visitors who from Easter on came over by the boatload expecting to be welcomed with open arms at the rue Monsieur. 'I believe the English think,' Nancy complained to Heywood, 'that Paris is a social desert where nobody knows anybody else & sits waiting for the visitors to cheer them up. Like some little port in the Red Sea.' Then there were members of the family who had to be put up and shown round and taken out to parties. Muv came and was introduced to the Colonel, who 'Rang up this morning & said there was a sort of unnatural quietness about her – I assured him that it is quite usual. "And what did she say about me?" "Nothing" I was obliged to reply.' Next to come were Debo and Andrew, the prospect of whose arrival filled Nancy with alarm, 'rather like the Royal visit to me I must say & almost as alarming since all my friends are so much too old & so much too clever'. In fact it was a success, marred only by an embarrassing moment at dinner with the Windsors when Nancy, from head to foot in tartan, all the rage with the couturiers that year, was met by the Duke dressed in exactly the same: 'It seems I was togged up in royal Stuart tartan,' she wailed, 'how can one tell?' And after they had gone Evelyn arrived and behaved abominably, studiedly rude to the distin-guished cleric Nancy had invited to luncheon at Evelyn's own request, and then, when she took him down to spend the night at Chantilly with the Coopers, deliberately picking a violent quarrel with Duff.

In May Nancy had to break off again to go to England. Muv had been looking after Unity on Inch Kenneth when Bobo had suddenly fallen ill with meningitis. She was taken across to the mainland to hospital in Oban, and here she died. Her body was brought down by train to be buried at Swinbrook. Although never as fond of Bobo as she had been of her brother Tom, to Nancy her death was in some ways much sadder. Tom had had a happy life, whereas Unity's had been so pathetic. 'I have always found that one minds terribly when they are the ones of whom everybody else says far the best,' she wrote to Jim Lees-Milne. 'Lately she had been so very much better & had become quite thin & pretty again, & seemed to enjoy her life again. But her real happiness in life was over – she was a victim of the war as much as anybody wasn't she.'

But more distressing to Nancy than her sister's death was a crisis involving the Colonel. The French edition of *La Poursuite d'Amour* had now come out, and as Gaston had feared the left-wing press immediately jumped on the dedication. Horrified, Nancy wrote to Diana, 'a hateful weekly paper here has come out with enormous headlines "Hitler's mistress's sister dedicates daring book to M. Palewski" . . . He is in a great to do about it . . . You see he is such an ambitious man & you know how the one thing that can't be forgiven is getting in their way politically – Of course it was madness, the dedication, & what I can't tease him with now it was *entirely* his own doing. I said shall I put To the Colonel – G.P. & so on & he absolutely insisted on having his whole name. At the time I suppose he was powerful enough for it not to matter. Now with everything in the balance the Communists have pounced. He says the General will be furious.'

There was no alternative but for Nancy to leave Paris at once and wait till the fuss died down. Fortunately she had been offered some film-work at Ealing Studios[1] which gave her a publicly acceptable excuse to go; after that she could join Peter in Spain where he was putting the finishing touches to his film, '"For Whom the Gate Tolls", he admits himself it is a tollgate to end all TGs, the commentary is delivered by himself!' Nancy hated having to leave Gaston, hated having to go to England – 'one *can* only call it Blighty' – but she would do anything rather than risk the Colonel's displeasure, even at the cost of three months' exile from her cité du bonheur parfait. She went first to London, from where she wrote to Colonel, 'I do miss you so much . . . I see now how dreadful one's life can become at a moment's notice'; from there she moved on to stay with the

---

[1] To revise the script of *Kind Hearts and Coronets*.

Mosleys at their house in Wiltshire ('I miss you'), and to Muv at High Wycombe ('Oh the days do seem long in the country I thought today would never come to an end . . . Je regarde le vieux moulin solitaire et glacé à travers la fenêtre et je suis dans le malheur'), before joining Peter in Madrid: 'Next time that, like the Archangel Gabriel, you chase me away from heavenly Paris, do let it be to somewhere warmer. I'm so cold that, as you see, I can hardly hold a pen. France was white with blossom, the plain round Madrid white with snow. I never want to leave France.' When she finally returned in June Paris was looking more beautiful than ever, the 'dear old military gentleman', to her enormous relief, had got over his panic and was even quite pleased to welcome her back, and she was able to return to work with a free mind.

Love in a Cold Climate, or *Diversion*, as it was first called, was finished in September 1948. As in *The Pursuit of Love* the narrator is Fanny, who during the course of the book marries a don with whom she goes to live in Oxford. Uncle Matthew and the Radletts are still very much in evidence; the plot, however, belongs not to them but to their immensely rich and grand neighbours, Lord and Lady Montdore. The Montdores have one child, a daughter, heir to their enormous wealth and the centre of their lives. Polly is a beauty and her ambitious mother has great plans for her, a duke at least, or even higher – 'an abbey, an altar, an Archbishop, a voice saying "I, Albert Edward Christian George Andrew Patrick David take thee, Leopoldina"'. But Polly, as ruthless in her way as her mother, shatters these hopes by marrying her Uncle Boy – no money, years older, and worst of all Lady Montdore's bosom friend (some say more than a friend) and companion.

In their rage and disappointment the Montdores disinherit Polly, and send for the next in line, an unknown Canadian last heard of living in Nova Scotia, no doubt some kind of half-civilised lumberjack.

The heir, Cedric, eventually tracked down living in Paris, is invited to Hampton. No lumberjack he: 'A glitter of blue and gold crossed the parquet, and a human dragon-fly was kneeling on the

fur rug in front of the Montdores, one long white hand extended
towards each. He was a tall, thin young man, supple as a girl,
dressed in a rather a bright blue suit; his hair was the gold of a
brass bed-knob . . . He was flashing a smile of unearthly perfection.' Cedric, outrageous, flamboyant and unashamedly narcissistic, transforms the lives of his newly discovered relations, in
particular that of Lady Montdore whom he turns from a stout old
woman, impervious to fashion, to a lithe, bird-like creature with
blue curls and a brilliant, flashing smile. 'I make her say "brush"
before she comes into the room,' Cedric explains. 'It fixes at once
this very gay smile on one's face.' So absorbing is this new way of
life – facial massage, punishing diets, up and down to London for
parties – that Polly is forgotten until she and Boy turn up from a
prolonged honeymoon on the Continent, both of them sick to
death of each other. Polly soon abandons her husband for a
neighbouring duke, while Boy, Cedric and Lady Montdore
roll off in the Daimler to France, leaving Lord Montdore in
possession of Hampton and a peaceful old age.

   The book is dominated by two great comic characters, Cedric
and Lady Montdore (both loathed by the greatest comic character of all, Uncle Matthew. 'The hell-hag,' he says of the latter,
'drown her if I were Montdore', while as to Cedric, 'Uncle
Matthew, after one look, found that the word sewer had become
obsolete and inadequate'). Lady Montdore, magnificent in her
rudeness, magnificent in her grandeur ('I think I may say we put
India on the map. Hardly any of one's friends in England had
never even heard of India before we went there, you know'), is
a composite of Helen Dashwood and of Nancy's mother-in-
law Lady Rennell, two ladies well known for a lofty view of themselves and their belief in uncompromising candour. Like Uncle
Matthew, Lady Montdore has a lovable side, a vulnerability and
innocence which make it impossible to regard her as wholly
monstrous. Lord Montdore, with his cardboard qualities, his
wonderful old handsomeness and elaborate courtesy, is Lord
Rennell to the life. Colonel makes a brief appearance as Fabrice
(this is before he has met Linda). Cedric is drawn from Stephen

Tennant, epitomising everything in which Nancy most delighted in her numerous homosexual acquaintance – the frivolity, the theatrical showing-off, the sharp-tongued, very feminine funniness.

And as always there are the private jokes – like the dear old man who comes to lecture on the toll-gates of England and Wales; and Cedric's complaint to Fanny that one has to drive so slowly in England because the roads are full of tweeded colonels going for walks. Don't French colonels go for walks, too, asks Fanny? Certainly not, Cedric replies, '"though I do know a colonel, in Paris, who walks to the antique shops sometimes."

'"How do they take their exercise?" I asked.

'"Quite another way, darling."'

Love in a Cold Climate was published in July 1949 to even greater acclaim than its predecessor. The critics extolled it; it was the first novel ever to be chosen simultaneously as Book of the Month by the Book Society, the *Daily Mail* and the *Evening Standard*; and the catchy title was on everybody's lips. ('The Queen had to act Love in a CC in a charade – she kissed the King & shivered & everybody guessed at once!!') It shot up to the top of the best-seller lists on both sides of the Atlantic, this despite reviews in America that were 'positively insulting', condemning the book for its lack of 'message' and the moral character of Cedric as 'loathesome'. But as Nancy said, 'Either praise or blame from govs [Americans] leaves ONE cold'. Of her friends in England only Evelyn was not entirely congratulatory: having read the book in manuscript, he was disappointed that Nancy had not only ignored many of his suggestions, but had refused point-blank to obey his instruction to rewrite from beginning to end. 'Evelyn said it could have been a work of art – yes but I'm afraid it's here & now & the Colonel I care for.'

The Colonel, more than ever, was the pivot of her existence. The books must be written to earn the money to pay for the life that Nancy wanted: Paris and the Colonel. Her happiness was entirely dependent on him, and how generous a ration of his time and attention he allowed her. During those rare periods of

political inactivity, when he had little to do and welcomed Nancy
running round at all hours to entertain him, she was blissfully
happy; when she could not see him – because he or she was away
from Paris, or because he was simply too busy – her misery was
great. 'I long for you Colonel' was always the refrain when she was
away . . . 'I long for the rue Monsieur & my happy Paris life.'
'Dear darling Colonel how are you?' she wrote to him on one of
her compulsory visits to England. 'I wish I were sitting on your
doorstep like a faithful dog waiting for you to wake up you dear
darling Col . . . Do miss me. Do miss saying "I've got a heavy
political day – LET ME SEE? can you come at 2 minutes to 6?"
. . . Darling colonel good bye NR I know ones not allowed to say it
but I love you.' From the beginning of 1947 the Colonel started
being frantically busy again, with the plans for the General's
return to power and the organisation of the RPF[1], engaged in
what the newspapers described as 'fébrile activité politique'. This
immediately resulted in a sharp swing down on Nancy's emotional barometer. 'You darling colonel my telephone is bust . . . If the
MRP[2] can bear to let you out of their sight for an instant you
might pay a visit to your poor neighbour later in the day . . . I
suppose you are being fébrile . . . Ma petite main est gêlée so I will
stop. What does one do about the telephone – I have paid the bill
& got the receipt, oh Colonel I am so crying. I held it upside down
mais cela n'a rien donné.'

But a far more serious threat to her relationship with the
Colonel was his longing for marriage and for children. She knew
that he would never marry her, his excuse being when it was
discussed between them that it would ruin him politically to
marry a divorcée, and this she had schooled herself to accept: 'I'm
beginning to really wish I could marry the Col,' she confessed to
Diana, 'but for a hundred reasons it isn't possible, so no use
thinking of it.' She had even forced herself to come to terms with
his obsessive womanising. For someone of Nancy's tempera-

[1] Rassemblement du Peuple Française.
[2] Georges Bidault's left-wing party.

ment, romantic and intensely private, this was achieved at pro-
digious cost. Being in love with a man who not only failed to
return that love, but who incessantly and publicly paid court to
other women was a humiliation painfully endured. Many people,
particularly those who saw him only socially, found 'Don Juan'
Palewski a figure of fun, with his rotund figure and slicked-back
hair, to be seen at every party pursuing the pretty women like a
Frenchman in a farce. To his English acquaintance, it was a
ludicrous way for a man of his standing to behave. Regular guests
at the British Embassy used to watch with amusement as Gaston
selected his prey, pressing close to her on one of the huge sofas in
the Salon Jaune, bouncing up and down on the cushions while
urgently hissing in her ear, 'J'ai envie de toi! J'ai envie de toi!' To
Gaston himself their opinions were a matter of indifference; he
wanted to make love to as many women as he could persuade into
bed, and what people thought, or who these women were, was
irrelevant. He tried them all: the wives of friends, the friends of
friends, and Nancy knew that not even her own sisters would be
left unattempted.

The only thing to do was to treat the whole thing as a
tremendous joke and wherever possible affect not to notice. But
Nancy was acutely jealous of Gaston's attentions to other women.
She could not help noticing, and it was too wounding always to be
laughed off. On several occasions when he was publicly laying
siege, she broke down completely and made a scene. This was the
one area where the shop-front could not be kept up. She could
not pretend with Gaston, or play games with him; perhaps it
would have been better if she had. But every time she confronted
him he reassured her, rather impatiently, that whoever it was
meant nothing to him. After a time she came to accept his
compulsive flirtatiousness, his hundreds of little love-affairs, as
a necessary but unimportant part of his life, a life in which she as
his confidante (very much, she told herself, like Madame de
Pompadour with Louis XV) had by far the larger rôle. It was not
always easy to keep faith, particularly when she herself was so
often treated not as the maîtresse en titre, the adored Marquise,

but as one of the many birds of passage hastily to be pushed out of the back door at the first sound of someone approaching. 'When I go round to the Colonel's flat it is like some dreadful spy film,' she told Diana. 'I end by being shut up in a cupboard or hiding on the escalier de service & being found by the concierge – so undignified I nearly die of it – apart from the fact that the whole of the time is taken up by these antics & I get about 5 restless minutes of his company!'

But these humiliations were nothing compared to the very real fear that one day the Colonel might marry and she would lose him altogether and for good. It was always at the back of her mind, and she had had one or two bad frights – there was a Resistance heroine, for instance, who had been in love with Gaston for years whom for a time Nancy was convinced he was planning to marry. But nothing happened and their friendship continued as before. 'Oh the horror of love,' she wrote to Diana. 'The fact is I *couldn't* live through it if he married & what is so dreadful is I know I can stop him – or at least I think so – & that condemns him to the great domestic discomfort in which he lives, to loneliness & having no children.' Unsatisfactory although this was, it was preferable to the alternative, and Nancy lost no opportunity to impress on Gaston the suffering of married life. There was many a spiked reference to the Duke and Duchess of Windsor, ('he a balloon, she like the skeleton of some tiny bird, hopping in her hobble skirt . . . They both look ravaged with misery – she said to the Col "you ought to marry, look at us"'), many a meaningful nod towards the Parc Monceau, that dreary area of Paris loved by nannies with perambulators where couples with young children liked to settle. And in case this left any doubt in the Colonel's mind he was given a glimpse of what the Palewski ménage would be like.

So did you go to the Palewskis last night? Yes, poor people I did feel sorry for them – all ruined by that thunder storm. Gaston had spent the whole afternoon hanging up Japanese lanterns you can't think how sad & sopping they looked. Then we were packed into those downstairs rooms like sardines, you know how hot it was – with the band on the staircase, you couldn't hear your self speak. Goodness she has got a lot of relations hasn't she.

I know – whenever one goes there, all those deadly in laws. Poor Gaston, he is really very patient but you can see what he feels

What happened to all those nice pictures he used to have in the rue Bonaparte?

She doesn't like old things – except of course Antoine Bibesco.

I rather like their glass furniture, you know. Did you see the little girl last night?

Oh yes. Gaston kept telling her to go to bed, but she only said 'oh fa-la' & took no notice.

Whether it was due to Nancy's efforts or not, the Colonel continued in his single state. He talked about marrying, he admitted to a wish for children, but his bachelor existence was extremely agreeable. Eventually, although she remained watchful, Nancy began to relax.

Apart from her periodic anxieties about Gaston, her life now was immensely enjoyable. She was famous, well-off, surrounded by a large circle of friends and living in the centre of the most civilised city on earth. 'How nice it is to be happy in middle age after a wretched youth instead of the other way round,' she remarked contentedly to Diana. There was nothing she regretted in leaving England behind her. Most of her English friends came over to Paris at one time or another, and those who did not she saw on her grudging but regular visits to England. As well as sisters and her parents, there were a number of friends with whom at least once every couple of years she made a point of spending a few days: Gerald Berners at Faringdon, Raymond Mortimer at Crichel, Eddy Sackville-West at Cooleville in Ireland and Gerry Wellington (that 'lovely mixture of pomp & pornography') at Stratfield Saye. Then there were her 'visits to

the major novelists', Leslie Hartley, Evelyn, and Anthony Powell:
'The food of all three about equal (not good). Leslie had the
warmest house & warmest heart. Evelyn by far the coldest house[1]
& Tony Powell the coldest heart but the most fascinating chats &
a pâté de foie gras.' The greatest pleasure of these visits was of
course the return to France, when, with mysterious inevitability,
it was 'Fog in Kent, fog-horns all the way over the Channel, fog
in the Pas de Calais – blazing sunshine here & the chestnuts
out'.

With two best-sellers in the space of four years, Nancy was
much in demand. The *Sunday Times* had commissioned her to
write a weekly letter from Paris, in which she gave an insider's
views of the fashionable and intellectual life of the capital, aired
some of her favourite fantasies about the French, and worked in
discreet references to 'a friend of mine who collects fine furniture', 'a député of my acquaintance'. She had also started to try
her hand at translating, something quite new to her, and after the
hard labour of writing a novel, the kind of work that came easily,
'the pure pleasure of writing without the misery of inventing'.
The Mosleys had recently set up their own publishing house,
Euphorion Books, and the original suggestion was that Nancy
should translate extracts from the *Memoirs of Saint-Simon*, an
idea which she rejected on the grounds that English readers
would never 'be made to accept the fact that a beautiful rich
highly born young woman insists on marrying an old man of 90
qui fit partout dans le lit the 1st night & thinks it all simply perfect
because of the tabouret. Even Debo would hardly believe that!'
Instead she and Diana decided on Mme de la Fayette's novel, *La
Princesse de Clèves*.

The most ambitious of these commissions was the translation
of a comedy by André Roussin, *La Petite Hutte*, which had been
running in Paris for over three years and which the impresario
Binkie Beaumont wanted to bring to London. For those days and

---

[1] 'Nancy came for the weekend and remained seated before the fire for two
days,' Evelyn noted in his diary for December 1945.

for an English audience the plot was a risqué one, involving four castaways on a desert island, a man and his wife, the wife's lover and the ship's black cook, all three men taking it in turns to spend the night with the girl in the Little Hut. 'The reason I was asked to do it,' Nancy told Muv, 'was that I'm supposed to be good at making outrageous situations seem all right,' a sleight of hand involving the transformation of the black cook into a white one, and sprinkling the text with Mitfordisms: 'Do admit' is a favourite expression of the wife, Susan, who confesses that the only thing she misses on the island is the *Tatler*. It was part of the agreement that Nancy should accompany the play on tour and be present for the first night in the West End. They opened at the end of July 1950 in Edinburgh, Nancy of course having left perfect hot summer weather behind her in Paris for bitter freezing cold north of the Border. ('Poor poor poor Marie Stuart I feel for her.') The next stop was Glasgow ('the horror of the town quite indescribable'), then Newcastle and Leeds. While the play was on in Newcastle, Nancy stayed with Farve at Redesdale, only a few miles away. She found him looking frail and old but the days she spent with him were not as restful as she had hoped. 'Farve now lives for cocktail parties – gave one for me – & has sold all his cows because milking time is cocktail time.' Although she complained of the ugliness and the cold, and although she undoubtedly suffered, as always, at being away from the Colonel, the theatrical life was something new, and Nancy could not help but be amused by it. The cast of *The Little Hut* was headed by Robert Morley as the husband, with David Tomlinson playing the lover, and Joan Tetzel the obliging wife. Nancy got on well with Morley – he took her racing and roller-skating, she took him round Castle Howard – and with the director Peter Brook, but the others she thought too idiotic for words. 'The temperament, unbridled by one ray of intelligence, of actors, has come as a revelation to me . . . I never knew such people. Any good line is "*my* good line" or "*my* laugh" & the rest are that's a very flat line of *yours* darling (to me) . . . & the girl talks for 2 hours by the clock about what she calls her "hair do."'

The play, with a pretty, picture-book set by Oliver Messel, opened at the Lyric in London on August 23, and in spite of some rather shocked reactions was an immediate success, playing to full houses for well over a thousand performances. Mark Ogilvie-Grant held a first-night party for the cast at his house in Kew; and Nancy gave a pre-matinée luncheon at the Mayfair Hotel for members of the family and old retainers, including Nanny Dicks, and Mabel who had been with the Mitfords since the early days at Asthall. 'Out of a haze I heard Mabel's voice "then I told her *I* was his Lordship's *head parlourmaid*" as one saying I am Duchess of Malfi still.'

Nancy returned to Paris in September, just in time for the rentrée from the summer holidays and a stream of visitors – Constantia Fenwick, Billa Harrod, 'blissful blissful Pam Berry'[1], two sisters (Pam and Debo), and finally Peter on his way back from a typically Proddish venture on the slopes of Etna in Sicily, where 'he made the peasants dig channels for the lava as a result of which 3 extra villages were destroyed & he was obliged to flee by night'.

It was not until the following month that Nancy was able properly to start on a project which she had been working on intermittently since the beginning of the year. The idea had come from the film-producer Alexander Korda: he had given her a plot with the intention that she should first write the story as a film-script, and then later re-work it as a novel. But Nancy's treatment was not a success and Korda lost interest, leaving Nancy free to do as she liked with the original theme. As working in Paris with all its distractions was impossible, she went to stay with Mrs Hammersley on the Isle of Wight where quiet days punctuated by long healthy walks and bridge in the evenings provided exactly the conditions she needed. Just as *Love in a Cold Climate* had been more of an effort to write than *The Pursuit of*

---

[1] Lady Pamela Berry, daughter of the first Earl of Birkenhead, married to Michael Berry, proprietor of the *Daily Telegraph*.

Love, so the new novel, *The Blessing*, was more difficult than either, as though the further Nancy moved from her own experience, the more laborious the process became. She finished it in March 1951. 'Never again THE LAST,' she wrote to Hamish Hamilton.

The Blessing tells the story of Grace, a beautiful very English Englishwoman married to a very French, French marquis by whom she has a son Sigismond. Grace is dazzled by her Paris life, by the beautiful, chic women, the couture clothes, the brilliant dinner-parties, and falls as deeply in love with her new country as she is with her husband, who, to Grace, was 'the forty kings of France rolled into one, the French race in person walking and breathing'. But part of Charles-Edouard's very Frenchness is his love of women, the absolute necessity of making love to as many pretty women as he can lay his hands on; and this Grace, Anglo-Saxon to the marrow, cannot bring herself to accept. They separate, Grace going back to England, Charles-Edouard remaining in Paris, where they are kept apart by the shameless scheming of eight-year-old Sigi, who finds this life very much to his liking. No longer told to 'run along, darling', by his parents, he is spoilt by both, and flattered and indulged by all the men hoping to marry his rich, beautiful mother, and all the women angling for his rich, handsome papa. In the end, Sigi is caught out, and Grace and Charles-Edouard are reconciled.

If *The Pursuit of Love* was a love-letter to the Colonel, *The Blessing* is a love-letter to the whole of France. Its theme is the rivalry between France and England, le cinq à sept versus nursery tea, and of the superiority on every count of the former to the latter. England is cold, ugly and dark, and it rains all summer long. Grace on her journey home looks out of the train window after leaving the lovely light airiness of northern France, to see 'the little, dark, enclosed Kentish landscape . . . the iron grey sky pressing upon wasteful agriculture, coppices untouched by hand of woodman, tangles of blackberry and gorse, all so familiar to her eyes'. No wonder she is glad at the end to return to warm, luxurious France, back to delicious food, sparkling wit, well-trained, cossetting servants who change the mimosa in her bedroom three times a day[1].

The sub-plot is a guerrilla attack on the one nation on the face of the earth Nancy loathed above all others, America. In the person of the very important and very boring Mr Hector Dexter, in Paris to administer the Marshall Plan, she incorporates everything that in her opinion was wrong with the New World.

'"Now what you need in this little old island," says the unstoppable Mr Dexter, '. . . "is some greater precognition of and practice of (but practice cannot come without knowledge) our American way of living. I should like to see a bottle of Coca-Cola on every table in England, on every table in France, on every –"

'"But isn't it terribly nasty?" said Grace.'

Nancy's anti-Americanism had greatly increased since she had come to live in France. The General's, and thus Gaston's, contempt for their transatlantic allies was loyally parrotted by Nancy, only too ready to sympathise with that feeling of resentment towards America common to many Europeans in the impoverished years immediately after the war. Nancy was essentially European: her great love was for France, and in particular for the France of the eighteenth century, for the grandeur of Versailles, the prettiness of Watteau and Fragonard. To someone of these predilections, the vigorous modernism of the United States was unlikely to appeal, nor was she impressed by the appearance and behaviour of the hordes of American tourists who, with their crammed wallets, loud checks and obese figures, were to be seen making their far from elegant progress round the city's famous monuments. 'Isn't Dulles a wonderful name for an

---

[1] Nancy was clever at putting across the inflection and rhythm of the French language while writing in English – ' "Oh no, but all the same, this is too much . . ."'; and occasionally she makes clever play with verbal 'faux-amis', the errors of literal translation, as when, for instance, in *Love in a Cold Climate* Fabrice's mother, the old Duchesse de Sauveterre, explains that, 'Castle life always annoys Fabrice and makes him nervous!' i.e. 'Country-house life bores Fabrice and makes him restless.'

American?' she would ask provocatively, and John Wilkes Booth was her favourite historical figure because he had killed Lincoln: 'Always rather pleased when there is one American less in the world & I'm sure God will send them to a different place from ONE & Lord Byron.' When confronted with the fact that many of her friends were American, she would answer, 'Yes, but they live in Europe and have *chosen freedom.*'

Colonel/Charles-Edouard, to Nancy's infatuated eye more fascinating than ever, irritated some of her English friends who found him selfish, complacent and insensitive. But to Grace, as to Nancy, he was perfection, except of course for his compulsive promiscuity, but that, it is made very clear, is a trait completely natural for a Frenchman to which only the boorish Anglo-Saxons would object. Nancy's own technique with the Colonel is mirrored in the clever behaviour of Albertine, Charles-Edouard's favourite mistress, who knows exactly how to keep him amused. 'She was certainly quite the reverse of dull, always having something to recount. Not plain slices of life served up on a thick white plate, but wonderful confections embellished with the aromatic and exotic fruits of her own sugary imagination, presented in just such a way as to tempt the appetite of such sophisticated admirers as he. She had endless tales to spin around their mutual friends, could discuss art and objects of art with his own collector's enthusiasm as well as with imaginative knowledge, and, what specially appealed to Charles-Edouard, would talk by the hour, also with imaginative knowledge and with collector's enthusiasm, about himself.'

Nanny Dicks turns up on form as Grace's old nanny who comes with her to France to look after Sigi, remaining uncompromisingly English and thoroughly disapproving – sniff, shrug – of all those nasty foreign ways. Mrs Hammersley has a small part as the cultivated Mrs O'Donovan, described as belonging to 'the category of English person, not rare among the cultivated classes, and not the least respectable of their race, who can find almost literally nothing to criticize where the French are concerned'. And Cyril Connolly puts in an appearance as the Captain, one of

Grace's suitors, owner of an avant-garde theatre run by long-haired girls with dirty feet, closely modelled on the *Horizon* staff, a portrait which, unsurprisingly, gave a great deal of offence to its original.

As before, Evelyn read the manuscript, his main criticism being that Nancy had failed to make Sigi convincing as a little boy of eight and a half. 'How awful about Sigi being 25,' Nancy replied to the charge. 'I had so congratulated myself on his development between a backward 6 & a forward 9. Of course French children are different – somebody once said to me a French boy of 14 has a heavy moustache, 2 mistresses & a hoop!' As before she accepted some of Evelyn's corrections, ignored others, and this time re-wrote the whole thing twice. 'People always think I dash off my books with no real work but it is not so, I very honestly do my best,' she complained. Hamish Hamilton declared himself 'in transports of delight' over the result and, in spite of several less than favourable reviews, *The Blessing* sold 'like the hottest of cakes' on both sides of the Atlantic.

CHAPTER NINE

Rue Monsieur

The nineteen-fifties, the middle years of the century and the years of Nancy's middle age, were in many ways the happiest of her life. She became more settled, was able to develop an annual routine, to make a pattern of life which was in all externals immensely agreeable. At the end of 1951 she was able to arrange a long-term lease on the flat in the rue Monsieur, which gave her not only a greater sense of security but also the opportunity of having round her at last her own furniture. 'I've got Tomford's nice big sofa (think of what IT must have witnessed in its time),' she wrote happily to Mark, '& my Sheraton writing table & Farve's lovely Chinese screens & they all fit in very well . . . Also a great deal (12 pairs) of Muv's linen which is worth its weight in gold now, & my Dresden china clock.' Financially she was well-off and could afford to spend money not only at Dior and Lanvin but also with the expensive antiquaires in and around the rue Jacob to which the Colonel, with his passion for pictures and furniture, had introduced her. Her domestic life ran smoothly and in perfect comfort thanks to the efficiency of the saintly Marie who had become an accomplished cook. Her repertoire was not wide (roast chicken was the speciality), but the food at Nancy's luncheon parties was invariably excellent. When the Colonel was expected there would the day before be an anxious conference between Nancy and Marie, gazing at each other over the kitchen-table searching for inspiration as to what they could give him for pudding: he had a notoriously sweet tooth and Marie's usual fruit compôte he did not consider worthy of his attention – neither sweet enough nor rich enough. (On the day itself Nancy was always restless until Gaston arrived, only half listening to the

conversation, one eye on the window giving out onto the courtyard. As often as not the telephone would ring, and after a minute
Marie would come into the room with, 'Monsieur le Colonel
s'excuse, Madame.') Nancy's social life was brilliant and diver-
sified, and she had a number of rich friends who invited her to
luxurious locations in the South of France where she could 'boil
up', lying on a beach in the hot sun and chatting by the hour.
She stayed with Dolly Radziwill at Montredon, with Tony
Gandarillas at his villa at Hyères, with Daisy Fellowes at Cap
Martin or on her yacht, the *Sister Anne*, cruising round the
Mediterranean.

   But the place that meant more to her than any of these was a
house only a short distance from Paris, Fontaines les Nonnes,
belonging to Countess Costa de Beauregard, an old lady of
distinguished pedigree and deep religious beliefs. Fontaines and
Mme Costa first came into Nancy's life through Violet Hammersley: the two women were half-sisters, Mrs Hammersley
being the illegitimate daughter of Mme Costa's father, Pierre
Jean Aubrey-Vitet. It was from Aubrey-Vitet that Mme Costa had
inherited Fontaines, a beautiful, cream-coloured eighteenth-
century manor-house deep and remote in the flat farmlands of
the Marne. On one side of the house were orange-trees in tubs
and a park, a private chapel and ornamental dovecote, on the
other a working farmyard complete with hens and manure heap.
The way of life that Nancy found there had a timeless quality –
the same ancient servants, the same old friends who had been
going there for years, all now in their eighties, the gossipy
conversations, walks over the stubble, expeditions in search of
Bossuet at Meaux or Rousseau at Ermenonville; and every Friday
at luncheon M. de Rohan-Chabot's unvarying joke as the fish was
brought in, 'Enfin, sole.' Fontaines was almost a second home to
Nancy who, much the youngest, delighted in being treated as 'the
Child', and loved the quiet Chekhovian atmosphere, and the
beauty of the countryside with its tiny stone villages and narrow
poplar avenues stretching across the fields to a wide and distant
horizon. She described Fontaines to Evelyn as a house 'in which

nothing has changed for 100 years. In the drawing room sit 4 old ladies, who have stayed there all of every summer since they were born & M. le Curé aged 87, who has been M. le Curé there since he was 27 . . . One wakes up with the sun shining through pink taffeta curtains & my room, in a tower, has sun all day. Mme Costa spends up to 8 hours a day in the chapel the rest of the time she plays bridge & talks about Dior & déclassées duchesses.'

As Nancy became more deeply ensconced in her French life her ties with the 'Old Land' inevitably became frailer and more chafing. As she had told Muv on first moving to France, all the friends she cared about came regularly to Paris; but in England there were still her parents and sisters; and there was still Peter. Nancy and Peter had not lived together since the beginning of the war, but they remained man and wife. Although Nancy had long accepted that there was no chance of her ever being able to marry the Colonel, and although she knew very well the value of her married status – particularly in the eyes of the French – she had for some time been anxious for a divorce. Her reasons were mainly financial. She was fond of Prodd but she never wanted to live with him again, and with his extravagant habits he had cost her a great deal of money. He was forever turning up on the scrounge at rue Monsieur penniless and in need of a bath, frightening the life out of Marie with his piratical appearance; and worse than that he made it impossible, while he stayed, for Nancy to see the Colonel who, strict to his own moral code, refused to come to the flat while Peter was there.

She complained to Diana, 'I am really fond of Peter you know but the whole thing is complicated, & the person I live for is the Col & if he can't run in & out of my house at all times I know in the end he will feel lonely & his thoughts will turn to marriage. Also I *can't* see what poor Pete gets out of it as I'm not really very nice to him & surely he'd much better marry again & produce an heir to the lands & titles . . . For some reason he is absolutely determined not to have a divorce & I can't make out why, I really can't believe he's so fond of me as I am completely beastly to him all day & trying to be nicer really wears me out, & I have awful remorse &

then begin again. Well you *know*. I honestly do think marriage is the most dreadful trap & that human beings must have been mad to invent such a relationship . . . Nobody except a husband can make one cry with rage, or make me cry at all, & now my hankies are *wet all day*. Oh dear. Still there must be many many worse husbands in the world.'

Whenever she tried to broach the subject of divorce, Peter turned evasive; he agreed that the marriage was over, admitted he was in love with someone else – Peter was always in love with someone else – but somehow could not quite bring himself to end it. The uncertainty drove Nancy frantic. Dealings with Peter were never simple, and the negotiations continued for years. But at last he agreed, and in December 1957 Nancy was summoned to London to appear in court to give evidence that her marriage had broken down. 'The divorce was terribly funny. The judge, & I don't blame him, didn't believe a word of Peter's statement & says he must have Prod in the box to see if he's lying or not. Every time my council [sic] opened his mouth the judge gave a sort of whinney & said Mr *Stable*, you're making everything so difficult for me. However I don't have to go back into court which is the main thing (although I couldn't help rather enjoying it once I was there).'

While in England Nancy took the opportunity to pay what would clearly be her last visit to her father. Farve, living his quiet life up in Redesdale, had for some years been very much of an invalid, frail and deaf, with only occasional flashes of the odd, violent man he once had been. Nancy's feelings towards him were dutifully filial rather than fond, almost as though in writing of him as Uncle Matthew he had ceased to exist for her as Farve. She remembered the rages and the iron rule, the funniness and charm, but the strong emotions they had once provoked had faded. She saw him for the last time that December. He died the following March. Nancy went up to Redesdale for the cremation and then to Swinbrook for the burial. Both services, she told Decca, were 'such tear-jerkers Susan with the old hymns (Holy Holy Holy) & the awful words I was in *fountains each time*. Then the ashes were done up in the sort of parcel *he* used to bring back from London, rich thick brown paper & incredibly neat knots & Woman [Pam] & I & Aunt Iris took it down to Burford & it was buried at Swinbrook. Alas ones life.'

But while her feelings for her father had waned, towards her mother Nancy became increasingly bitter. At Muv's door were laid every ailment and inadequacy of Nancy's adult life: trouble with her teeth was caused by Muv starving her as a baby; her inability to have children was due to Muv's criminal negligence in employing a syphilitic nanny: her difficulty in concentrating while working was because Muv had never allowed her to be properly educated. Reality – that Nancy had been well-fed, her nannies free of venereal disease and her powers of concentration if anything above the ordinary (she was capable of writing for seven or eight hours almost without a break) – had nothing to do with it. Muv's coldness to her in childhood had done the damage, and the disappointments of her life, in so far as they were ever consciously recognised as disappointments, were all blamed on Muv. In 1962 Hamish Hamilton published *The Water Beetle*, a collection of essays based on Nancy's newspaper articles, to which she added an autobiographical memoir of her childhood. In this she described her mother as 'abnormally detached': 'What did my mother do all day? She says now, when cross-examined, that she lived for us. Perhaps she did, but nobody could say that she lived with us.' It is not an unaffectionate portrait, although the abiding impression is one of aloofness and indifference. Understandably Muv was hurt. She wrote an injured letter to Nancy ('It seemed when I read it that everything I had ever done for any of you, had turned out wrong and badly'), who professed to be amazed at her mother's reaction. 'Oh *goodness* I thought it would make you *laugh* . . . Of course the trouble is that I see my childhood (& in fact most of life) as a hilarious joke. But *nobody* could take this seriously . . . all clearly a caricature, what's called Meant to be Funny. If you seem to have been rather frivolous so was everybody at that time; Edwardian women are famous for having been light hearted.' 'FORGIVE', Nancy wrote, and Muv forgave; but the incident did nothing to improve matters between them. Nancy continued to respect her mother, but she never loved her.

Towards the rest of the family, towards her sisters, Nancy's attitude was more complex. Diana was the one she loved most. She was fond of the others but had little in common with them. Pam and Debo were essentially countrywomen: they ran their households, kept horses and dogs, and never opened a book if they could help it. Decca in California was too far away, had been gone too long, and had finished herself in Nancy's eyes by embracing the American way of life and, after Esmond's death, marrying an American husband. But Diana was different: she and Nancy shared much the same taste in books, in friends, and of course in jokes. In most things they thought alike. The exception was politics. Diana knew nothing of Nancy's part in her arrest at the beginning of the war, but she did know that Nancy was completely out of sympathy with Fascism. Diana knew this and accepted it, convinced that, as long as the one dread subject was avoided, she and her sister were more or less as one.

But it was not quite like that on Nancy's side of the fence. Complicating what might otherwise have been a strong but straightforward political disagreement were much more obscure feelings. Nancy envied Diana the mutual love between her and her husband, she envied her her four sons and her demonstrably happy married life. In fact she was jealous of all her married sisters and disliked all her brothers-in-law. Her sisters were her family and she resented anyone encroaching on them. The line was that one way or another her sisters were to be pitied for the awfulness of their lives. Pam (dull country life) got off the lightest as Nancy did not dare tangle with Derek Jackson, a man of brilliant intellect who specialised in a line of cruel teasing with which she, herself a mistress of the art, could not begin to compete; Derek had never forgiven Nancy, either, for her un-kindness to Pam, and there had been in the distant past a rivalry between them for the affections of Hamish. Decca's first husband, Esmond Romilly, had been considered 'loathsome', and her second, Bob Treuhaft, when Nancy finally met him, was instantly perceived to be one of the greatest bores ever to come out of America. And poor Debo, who when Andrew succeeded to the dukedom, became mistress of Chatsworth in Derbyshire, one of the great palaces of Europe, was lumbered for life with a house that with the best will in the world Nancy could only describe as *hideous*, not *one* pretty piece of furniture in it.

But for none of these sisters did her feelings run as deep as they did for Diana: she loved Diana the most and resented Sir Ogre the more. When in 1951 the Mosleys left England to move to Orsay in the Chevreuse valley just outside Paris, Nancy was overjoyed. She had always said that the one ingredient lacking from her perfect Paris life was the presence of Diana; Diana and the Colonel were the two people she loved most in the world. Now she had Diana – but with her came the villainous figure of the Demon King, in Nancy's mythology blood brother to the Devil himself. As the Mosleys settled happily into their new house, sharp-eyed Mrs Rodd saw something sinister in their every move. It was clear to her, if to nobody else, that the Mosleys spent their entire time plotting to incinerate their enemies and take over the world. When on holiday in Morocco it was 'to meet Bormann'; in Spain, to plot with Franco; their friendship with the Windsors was based wholly on a shared nostalgia for the days of the Third Reich ('They [Windsors and Mosleys] want us all to be governed by the kind clever rich Germans & be happy ever after. I wish I knew why they all live in France & not outre-Rhin'. 'I believe their wickedness knows no bounds,' Nancy wrote to Mrs Hammersley. 'D[iana] says Sir O has never been so busy – it makes my flesh creep. No doubt we shall all be in camps very soon. I've ordered a camping suit from Lanvin.'[1] Needless to say the Mosleys themselves never got wind of any of this, and although Sir Oswald found his sister-in-law affected at times and silly, he remained amiably disposed towards her. Nancy and Diana met frequently and talked every day on the telephone.

[1] At the end of her life Nancy apologised to Diana for these dark suspicions and admitted that she now saw they had been groundless.

With three best-selling novels to her credit, Nancy was everywhere in demand; all she touched turned to gold, an effect which had not passed unnoticed by her publisher. At the end of 1951 Hamish Hamilton flew to Paris, and over an expensive lunch at Larue persuaded Nancy to let him reissue her four early novels. As soon as he had flown home again, she knew that she had been wrong to consent. *Wigs on the Green* was now in the worst possible taste, and the others were 'badly written, facetious & *awful*. I can't conceive why he wants it & the fact that he does has shaken my faith in his judgment.' What she failed to take into account was that it was not Hamilton's literary judgment that was in question but a shrewd commercial sense that Nancy's name could sell almost anything. She wrote to him, 'I know it's wrong not right to break one's word but I can't – I'm very very sorry – allow it . . . You must forgive me, I'm too sorry if it disappoints you after coming to Paris & everything but honestly it has poisoned my day reading all that babyish rubbish & I would be too miserable if you reprinted it.' She did, however, make one concession: he could have *Pigeon Pie* on condition that she be allowed to revise it first.

As her fame as a novelist grew, so did her reputation as a journalist. Lord Kemsley, quick to see that someone with such a talent to annoy was a gift to his circulation figures, wrote offering Nancy the freedom of the columns of the *Sunday Times* to write on any subject she chose. This was an irresistible opportunity, an official License to Tease, which she seized with both hands. She teased the Italians after a visit to Rome by comparing the Eternal City to 'a village, with its one post office, one railway station and life centred round the vicarage'; she teased the Irish by laughing at their language; she enraged almost the whole British nation by a derogatory paragraph on that most sacred of institutions, the herbaceous border. ('Every gardener in the country will resent this statement as a calumny of the vilest order,' wrote one furious reader.) The worst row of all was provoked by a piece she wrote about Marie Antoinette, timed to coincide with the opening of an important exhibition at Versailles celebrating the bicentenary of the Queen's birth. To the French one of the most romantic and glamorous figures in their history, Marie Antoinette to Nancy was silly and irritating (and, of course, *not French*). 'She was frivolous without being funny, extravagant without being elegant, her stupidity was monumental . . . In the end, putting class before country, she sent military secrets to the enemy, through her lover Fersen. She certainly deserved a traitor's death.' Not surprisingly this gave enormous offence, and Nancy was flattered to be told by Gaston that, thanks to her, Anglo-French relations had not been so bad since Fashoda[1]. She was quite unrepentant – 'I don't really know what all the fuss is about as I am on *their side* for cutting off the head of an Austrian spy. Why do we dance on 14th July then?' – and went happily off to cook up the next tease, an article inspired by a visit to Greece in June 1955.

For some years Mark Ogilvie-Grant had been living and working in Athens, and it had long been planned between them that Nancy should visit him there. Unfortunately after all the arrangements had been made, Mark at the last moment was called to England; but he alerted his friends and told Nancy what to see and where to go. She arrived full of expectation of romantic ruins and the classical beauty of the unspoiled capital of Ancient Greece. Modern Athens came as a shock. 'I thought of it as very small, rather like Naples or Toulon. I'd no idea it was a sort of New York . . . I thought I was flying away from noise & smell & cocktail parties to small pink islands & Byzantine churches, but these seem so difficult to attain. Nobody will – or can – tell me what to do. Roger Hinks[2] merely closes his eyes & says My dear there's nothing to see.' In the end she enjoyed herself – toured the Peloponnese, went to Delphi and Hosios Loukas, met the King ('Chatting with foreign royalties is always rather easy as for some reason they all seem to have been brought up with the

---

[1] In 1898 a French force hoisted the tricolor at Fashoda, in the Sudan. Kitchener immediately replaced this with the British and Egyptian flags while inviting the French to withdraw – which they eventually did, but only after some days of tense negotiation between London and Paris.
[2] Art-historian and British Council Representative in Athens.

Rodds'), and even had thoughts of returning the following year and taking a house – 'I shall go to Berliz [sic] & learn enough.to say stop throwing stones at that kitten.' But the article she wrote for the *Sunday Times* began with a description of Athens as 'probably the ugliest capital in Europe', and continued with an attack on the barbarity of the American reconstruction, 'in a ghastly graveyard marble', of the Athenian Stoa. The Director of the project, Mr Homer A. Thompson, was deeply hurt, as was Nancy's intention. He protested to Nancy, who replied with all the vigour and rudeness of a defiant child. 'I must tell you that never shall I forget the shock I received when I first saw that *unspeakable* Stoa – which I truly supposed must be a cinema or public swimming bath. The fact is that you & your compatriots are using your enormous power to spoil this world we live in, & are doing so very fast. I am only thankful that I am now old & shall soon be dead – until then, however, I shall protest against all forms of trans Atlantic hideousness in Europe, useless though I know it to be to do so. Yours sincerely Nancy Mitford.'

The *Sunday Times* paid well – up to £500 for one of the longer pieces; the new edition of *Pigeon Pie* was selling briskly; Korda had given £7,000 for the film-rights of *The Blessing*; and *The Little Hut* was still bringing in between £50 and £100 a month. (Nancy had been told by her cousin Bertrand Russell that he went regularly to *The Little Hut*: 'I have always wondered who it is that goes regularly & now we know. Old philosophers.') Nevertheless, conditioned by the financial crises of her childhood, Nancy never stopped worrying about money, always convinced that poverty was just round the corner. In September 1954 she received an offer to go to Hollywood for six months at $6,000 a week, surely a magnificent solution to her financial anxieties. Commonsense told her she must accept; but how could she leave Paris for six whole months? how could she live for six months without the Colonel? what might he not get up to while she was away? Colonel himself advised her to go, and for twenty-four hours she was in an agony of indecision. 'I can't go away for months & leave you alone,' she wrote to him from Hyères. 'Or am I no good to you?

Oh how I wish I could open you like a book & see what is there. Nobody has ever been such a riddle to me. At the same time do I want to go? Do I want more money? Le côté intéressé de tout ça says yes, but when I reflect a moment what do I find? One life, not very long, no heirs – then why do what one doesn't want to, simply for the money. Would I consider it, apart from the money? Of course not. Then I think dollars for France – perhaps its my duty. They say 6000 dollars a week for up to 6 months – 48 million francs, if it were 6 months. 48 million francs, & come back to find the Colonel married to Mme A –. Do you see why I am in a turmoil?'

But the indecision was short-lived. 'I realized that its not a question of whether you need me or not – the point is I can't live without you. I should be too miserable & it can't be right to make oneself miserable for dollars.'

Nancy never wanted to be away from Paris while the Colonel was there. She was obliged to leave 'Mr Street' as she called rue Monsieur for a month every summer to give Marie a holiday, and it was a source of permanent regret that during this month she and the Colonel never could go away together: he would not allow it and that was that. Occasionally if she were staying with people he knew, he would consent to come for a couple of days before disappearing to Paris – or to other parts of the country to stay with unnamed 'relations' in places Nancy knew nothing of. The uncertainty of his arrangements usually ruined any chance she had of enjoying her holiday – will he, won't he, will he, won't he, will he come and stay? Then if he did come there was the worry that he might be bored – he disliked the country (except in the form of 'some large luxurious & worldly house with pretty duchesses playing canasta all around you'), was only really happy in Paris – which would mean that he would be even more reluctant to agree to come the next time. Her letters to him, from the South of France, from Ireland staying with the Devonshires at Lismore or Eddy Sackville-West at Cooleville, sound a single, mournful refrain: 'I always think I can do quite well without you but after a few days it is terrible;' 'I'm so passionately sad & lonely

without you . . . I long for you more than sea & sun & mountains,
much as I love all these;' 'in despair at having left you;' 'lonely &
sad & restless without you;' 'a little love & affection would be very
welcome though quite unexpected . . . I'm torn between hoping
you miss me & hoping you don't even notice I'm not there. A bit of
both I daresay, since an odder man than you has seldom breathed.
Alas, poor Mme Rodd.' Even when, in 1954, she went as far
afield as Moscow to stay with her friends the Hayters[1] at the
British Embassy, a visit she hugely enjoyed and for which she had
prepared with almost childlike excitement, her greatest pleasure
was in looking forward to her return to Paris and to seeing the
Colonel again – 'When I woke up & realized I was back in my own
bed an enormous smile spread over my face.'

But the Colonel continued to be elusive. He was now a very
busy man: as well as his work as a founder member of the RPF, he
was Député for the Seine, Vice-president of the Assemblée
Nationale, and from February 1955 Ministre délégué à la Prési-
dence du Conseil in Faure's government. His day was filled with
official business, his evenings with dinner-parties and with the
pursuit of his innumerable love affairs. Indeed it was this worldly,
frivolous side of his nature that prevented his rise to real power.
The General, a man austere almost to the point of ascetism, had
complete faith in Palewski's loyalty, never doubted his intelligence nor his political acumen, but he could not look with an
approving eye on the much commented on 'entrechats et par-
fums', on 'les succès mondains et féminins' typified by the
procession of ladies of quality and well-known actresses that all
day long made its way up and down the staircase in the rue
Saint-Dominique. As de Gaulle once confided to Palewski's old
protégé Georges Pompidou, 'Rien ne lui nuit plus dans mon
esprit que cette manie de vouloir par vanité se mêler de tout et
être partout.' This apart, the General knew that in Palewski he
had a friend and ally of unswerving loyalty. The only time in his
career that de Gaulle was ever known to ask for a favour, it was for

---

[1] Sir William Hayter was Ambassador in Moscow from 1953 to 1957.

Palewski that he asked: that his old companion in arms should be given the Ambassadorship to Italy.

Nancy was on holiday in Venice when she heard the news of Gaston's appointment. 'O DESESPOIR O RAGE O FELI-CITATIONS' was the wording of the telegram she sent him. The blow was a heavy one; Paris without the Colonel was almost unthinkable. But to the world of course she revealed nothing of what she felt. She wrote casually to Mrs Hammersley, 'The Colonel is off to the Palais Farnèse in the form of Ambassador to Rome. I thought I'd told you. He is very much pleased & I think he'll love it, really made for him. He goes in October after which I shall be as free as air.' These were brave words for Nancy minded desperately. Those who knew her well noticed that her gaiety now had an hysterical edge to it, her relentless raillery was more cruel than funny. Mrs Hammersley complained of it, and so did several of Nancy's Venetian acquaintances, in particular Victor Cunard[1] who, as one of her closest friends there, was goaded past endurance, finally retaliating with a furious outburst which left both of them severely shaken. In a letter to Billa Harrod describing the quarrel, Victor put forward with greater accuracy than he knew his own theory of Nancy's behaviour. It must, he thought, be due to the break-up of her affair with Gaston. 'All her good spirits (or at least most of them) are a bluff and that her almost savage teasing of friends is a sort of safety valve operation. If I am right it is rather pathetic, because if she would only tell one she is unhappy one would do what one could to comfort her.' But that was something Nancy would never do.

Colonel left for Rome in October 1957 and there he remained for five years until recalled by the General in 1962. Nancy missed him painfully and in secret. Although she was not allowed to see much of him in Paris, at least she knew he was there, only a few streets away, with always the possibility of a whirlwind visit between appointments and daily chats on the telephone. In Rome

---

[1] One-time the *Times* correspondent in both Paris and Rome, at this period retired and living in Venice.

he was out of reach, and his letters, due to a 'neurasthénie
épistolaire', were distressingly infrequent. Nancy now saw him
only on the one brief visit he permitted her every year, and on the
rare instances when he was summoned to Paris for a day or two
for a conference. The first of these occasions was during the
Algerian crisis in the summer of 1958. The papers were full of the
army's coup in taking over the government in Algeria, and of the
vociferous demands for the return to power of the General. To
Nancy it was a tormenting exercise in nostalgia as all the memories of the war, and the General, and Colonel in Algiers
overwhelmed her. 'Oh Colonel I seem to be living all those old
years over again today . . . I long for your voice so passionately. I
can't imagine today without you being there – I stayed in all
yesterday expecting you to telephone. Ah Colonel, you see I am in
one of my states. Write a little (lisible) line if you don't come
soon.' Then suddenly he was there, in Paris, for the first time for
nearly a year. 'Colonel arrived on Friday,' Nancy happily informed Mrs Hammersley. 'They telephoned just in time for me
to go to Orly & meet him since when I've hardly seen him as you
may imagine. He is very happy – we cried with happiness – after
so long it seems unbelievable.'

Nancy's visits to Rome had to be undertaken in clandestine
conditions during the height of summer when most of the *gens du
monde* were away. The Colonel was sensitive about his reputation
as France's 'seul ambassadeur célibataire', as *Paris-Match* made a
point of referring to him. He need not have been: within a short
time of his arrival he was known to the Romans as 'l'Embras-
sadeur', and a favourite topic at Roman dinner parties was the
French Ambassador's chasing of pretty women through the vast
salons of the Palazzo Farnese. Nancy's first visit was in August
1958. She left Paris 'in dead secret', telling almost no one. She
found Gaston in excellent spirits, loving the grandeur and pres-
tige, busily involved not only in his diplomatic duties but also in
the social and artistic life of the city. He had brought with him his
own collection of paintings to hang on the walls of the Farnese,
which he proudly told Nancy was now known as 'the pal-exquis'.

She was ecstatically happy to be with him, and they rushed about in the boiling heat doing the sights like a couple of tourists and seeing nobody. But all too soon she was back in (now) dismal Paris. 'I sigh for the land of the cypress & myrtle – I loathe the oak & ash. After 101 degrees in Rome I find it freezing here & pitch dark.'

In the next two years, 1959 and 1960, she stayed at the Farnese for a few days in July; in 1961 she went with Debo in March, and then again on her own for a couple of days four months later. She always felt so well in Rome, she told Debo, huge walks every morning, sun-bathing all afternoon ('what the Colonel calls exposing my limbs to the Spanish embassy'), and the evenings alone with the Colonel in his 'pal-exquis'. She returned to Paris sun-tanned and happy – to be met with news which made her turn cold with horror.

The Colonel had been in love for some years with a married woman, rich and socially prominent, whose husband had always refused to divorce her. The liaison had been conducted in secret but now she had had a child by Palewski, a son, and the story was all round Paris. Appalled and terrified, Nancy wrote to Gaston certain that this would mean their relationship must end: Colonel had the son for whom he had always longed, and no doubt he and his mistress would now marry. Gaston was reassuring: no, there was no question of marriage; he was sorry that she should be so upset but he for his part saw no reason why 'le petit et gentil élément nouveau' should make any difference to their friendship. 'La grand affection que je vous porte n'a en rien diminué et ne diminuerait en rien si des arrangements éventuels me permettaient de m'occuper de mon petit garçon. La chose est si naturelle et serait si évident que l'amour-propre lui-même n'en saurait être atteint.'

So Nancy calmed down – but she was not wholly reassured. She and the Colonel continued to correspond. She went out the following year to visit him as usual. But she remained uneasy. 'I am in a triste état,' she wrote to him. 'I wake up in the night & think of your new situation & I *mind*.' In July 1962 she was in

Venice staying with friends when she read in an English-language newspaper that the French Ambassador to Italy was about to be married. Her worst fears were instantly confirmed. In a mood of resignation and despair she wrote once more to the Colonel. 'Dear Colonel I don't understand your policy. I saw your marriage in the *Daily American* & my whole life seemed to collapse – now I have reconciled myself to it, so reasonable, such a solution to all your problems. But you always said you would tell me – I quite understand *not* telling because almost too difficult . . . All the same I find it odd of you, after a month's silence, to write comme si de rien n'était & ask how I am. I am very sad & also don't know what to do with myself. I can't live in Paris where I miss you more than anywhere, especially it would be too painful with you arranging an hôtel particulier just round the corner so that I would see you from time to time . . . So I feel perplexed I must say. Perhaps I could settle here but then I would miss the French, & what about old Marie? so – you see –' Patiently the Colonel replied: the story in the paper was untrue; he was not about to be married, there was no reason for Nancy to be jealous – the lady in question was the mother of his son and therefore he had a responsibility towards her. Simple as that.

Nancy returned to Paris at the beginning of August 1962, and almost simultaneously the Colonel was recalled. Georges Pompidou, the new Prime Minister, had not forgotten Gaston's early patronage: 'C'est vous,' he used to tell him, 'qui m'avez placé sur le tobogan.' Now he was in a position to return the favour, appointing Palewski Minister of State for Atomic Energy[1]. The Colonel was so excited when he received the telegram that he flew that night to Paris, then had to go straight back to Rome to make his official farewells. Much as he had enjoyed his occupancy of the Palais Farnèse, he had long been pining to return to Paris and his political life. Showing friends round his gorgeous palace he would tell them, 'Je remplacerai tout cela avec la buvette du Palais

---

[1] Ministre d'Etat chargé de la Recherche Scientifique et des Questions Atomiques et Spatiales.

Bourbon.' Now he was back, in tearing spirits, and Nancy was beside herself with happiness: the period of exile was over, the telephone calls and last-minute visits resumed. At the beginning of September she wrote to her sister Decca, 'The marvellous weather goes on I dined last night with the Colonel in his ministry Place de la Concorde & we sat out on the colonade, a new moon over the obelisk, it was really too lovely.'

The Colonel was back in Paris and Nancy was happy, or so she said, but now there was the child, and the mother of the child; and with the Colonel so busy, as Nancy teased him, letting off his bombs, the great emptiness at the centre of her life was impossible completely to disguise. The figure she presented to the world was as elegant and self-possessed as ever: her concern with her appearance in her fifties was as careful as it had always been[1]. The question of the moment was, should she wear more make-up as 'Cecil B [Beaton] Harold A [Acton] & Raymond [Mortimer] all say I don't paint my face enough'. And should she, now that she was turning grey, dye her hair? 'I LOATHE grey hairs worse than death,' she told Debo, but the first attempts at colouring were not a success. 'When I went to Antoines to have it cut Madame Denise said "mais qu'est que ce curieux reflet vert?" Do admit the sadness.' Eventually she found in a chemist in Bakewell, discovered while staying at Chatsworth, a dye that suited her. 'Have my hair dyed boot black,' she triumphantly told Muv, '& look *lovely*.' Every night while she slept she wore a little piece of shaped cardboard, known on the packet as a 'Frownie', which was intended to smooth away the frown lines corrugating her forehead.

Now what she needed was something to do. The obvious answer was to write another novel; but, always a difficulty for Nancy, how to come by a plot? 'Shall Cedric be offered & accept some Ruritanian throne (falling fearfully in love with the Dic-

---

[1] Dressed by Dior, Lanvin or Patou, Nancy was always the epitome of chic, and it was a cause of regret to her that although her clothes were French, she never looked other than unmistakably, one hundred per cent English. 'La bougie anglaise,' 'the English candle', her French friends used to call her.

tator), Fanny & husband at the English embassy, Hector Dexter
as Russian ambassador? I fear it is all too hackneyed or it might be
nice . . . I do think Catholic writers have that advantage,' she told
Evelyn, 'the story is always there to hand, will he won't he will he
won't he will he save his soul? Now don't be cross.' 'I'm fed up &
bored,' she confessed to Hamish Hamilton. 'I must do something
to keep myself amused during the long winter evenings . . . What
about a life of Mme de Pompadour? Shall I have a shot at it, or
does the idea depress you?' Hamilton urged her to start at once.

Creative imagination was never one of Nancy's strong points.
The best of her fiction is closely autobiographical; the nearer she
kept to her own experience, the better the result. With historical
biography the problem of plot was removed; but could an
intensely personal writer such as Nancy achieve sufficient de-
tachment to write history? to write about people long dead, who
had no connection whatsoever with Alconleigh, the Radletts or
Fabrice de Sauveterre? The short answer is, no, she could not:
she did not try. Nancy approached her biography of Madame de
Pompadour exactly as though it were one of her novels, with
herself as the Pompadour and Colonel as Louis XV. 'I do love it
because of the shrieks. They were all exactly like ONE, that's the
truth! . . . Like me, the Marquise preferred objects sculpture &
architecture to paintings, (& pretty things to ugly ones & rich
people to poor people – she liked pink better than brown & ladies
on swings better than women baking bread) C'est comme ça it
takes all sorts to make a world.' The parallels with herself and the
Colonel were impossible to miss. 'Pomp literally worshipped the
King, he was god to her, & never from the age of 9 thought of
anybody else. Very cold, physically, which makes it perhaps
understandable, her great faithfulness, no physical temptations.'
Theirs was a 'delightful relationship of sex mixed up with
laughter . . . After a few years of physical passion on his side it
gradually turned into that ideal friendship which can only exist
between a man and a woman when there has been a long physical
intimacy. There was always love. As in every satisfactory union it
was the man who kept the upper hand.' Versailles itself Nancy

saw as a Utopia, a perpetual romping house-party offering 'a life without worries and without remorse, of a perfectly serene laziness of the spirit, of perpetual youth, of happy days out of doors and happy evenings chatting and gambling in the great wonderful palace, its windows opening wide on the fountains, the forest and the Western sky'. Nancy's Versailles was a fairyland with dear good Louis XV at its head and pretty kind Madame de Pompadour by his side commissioning wonderful works of art and caring about the poor. The blackness of Versailles, the real and terrible power of the King, the ruthless greed of his mistress, Nancy chose to ignore. She read extensively in contemporary memoirs – Voltaire, Saint-Simon, de Luynes – and in the historians of the nineteenth century – Michelet, de Tocqueville and Carlyle – but certain subjects she simply chose not to treat: the brutal religious persecutions of Louis's reign were skated over because 'Catholicism is a closed book to me'; and so was the touchy subject of Free-masonry: 'Nobody whose father was one could take free masons seriously. Waffling off to Oxford with his apron, I can see it now.' The result may not have been history, but it was gay and pretty, full of jokes and personalities, and it brought France and the French court alive for many people who previously had barely heard of Louis XV and Versailles.

Pompadour took Nancy a year to write, part of which she spent in a pension in the town of Versailles itself. As soon as it was finished the manuscript was sent to Raymond Mortimer who, with his wide knowledge of French history and literature, could be relied upon to spot the worst of the howlers. Although (as Evelyn had always been) shocked by her slovenly punctuation and taken aback by the extreme informality of Nancy's style (the Duc de Richelieu was 'perfectly odious', the Dauphine found many French customs 'too common for words'), Raymond was nonetheless captivated by the liveliness of the narrative: 'Your narrative style is so peculiar, so breathless, so remote from what has ever been used for biography,' he wrote to her. 'I feel as if an enchantingly clever woman was pouring out the story to me on the telephone.'

Madame de Pompadour was published in March 1954, with a fanciful jacket by Cecil Beaton and a print-run of 50,000 copies. The consensus among the critics was that it was marvellous entertainment if hardly to be taken seriously as history, an opinion summed up by A. J. P. Taylor in the *Manchester Guardian*: 'All who admired *The Pursuit of Love* will be delighted to hear that its characters have appeared again, this time in fancy dress. They now claim to be leading figures in French history, revolving round Louis XV and his famous mistress, Madame de Pompadour. In reality they still belong to that wonderful never-never land of Miss Mitford's invention, which can be called Versailles as easily as it used to be called Alconleigh . . . This is a book that provides high entertainment – much of it deliberate – from the first page to the last. Certainly no historian could write a novel half as good as Miss Mitford's work of history. Of course he might not try.'

Whether or not orthodox historians approved of the Mitford approach, there was no doubt at all that the *Pompadour* was a success, and one which Nancy was eager to repeat. Within two years she was at work on her next historical subject, the story of the love-affair between Voltaire and the Marquise du Châtelet. It looked promising, she told Colonel: 'Voltaire is so like you. No heart, & all his meals are TAKEN. He collects PICTURES & when exiled asks to go to Sully where he has relations. But we hear no more of the relations – he moves in on the DUKE. So Sauveterre Rides Again.' But in truth the similarities were not profound, as Nancy admitted to Evelyn when she wrote to ask him to suggest a title for the book. 'Colonel Voltaire perhaps – really no they aren't very much alike & even I can't make them. As for Emily heaven preserve ONE from being like her. (It's all right, heaven has.)' Partly because of this inability to identify with her characters, Nancy found Voltaire and Emilie much more difficult to write about than Louis and the exquise Marquise. There was a great corpus of material to be digested, including volumes of published letters and volumes more being prepared for publication by the great Voltaire scholar Theodore Bestermann in Geneva. Nancy did what she could at home, visited Bestermann and the Musée Voltaire in Geneva, and then in order to escape from Paris and the ever-pealing telephone retired for six weeks to write on the island of Torcello in the Venetian lagoon.

It was her old friend Victor Cunard who suggested she stay on Torcello: it was quiet, the hotel comfortable, and it was near enough to Venice for evenings off and dinner with friends. Nancy thought it perfection: 'I suppose all islands are beautiful but there can't be many better than this, anyway in June. The fields have hedges of pink scented roses, poppies in the pale green corn, honeysuckle & vines over everything & huge terracotta sails floating by as there are canals on every side.' The only distraction came from the boatloads of tourists who arrived every day just before lunch, tramped once round the island, inspected the churches and chugged away again in the afternoon, leaving the tiny island once more in peace. 'I mingle with them, hating,' Nancy wrote to Evelyn. The French, of course, were serious and well-behaved; the English smelt of Women's Institute and left an appalling mess – 'Aching feet, come limping off the steamer & gape round & then ache back again, leaving a *litter* behind that makes me die of shame. (Player's Navy Cut wherever you look & flapping Daily Mails)'; and the Americans, interested only in the restaurant, do not go near the churches and move everywhere en masse, 'dangling deaf-aids & asking each other where they live in America what difference can it make? The word duodenal recurs.' The rest of the day, however, was tranquil and Nancy worked well, worried only by her longing for the uncommunicative Colonel ('Dear love do write'), and by a painful condition of her eyes: she was tormented by headaches and after a few hours reading or writing her eyes felt hot and swollen and she was barely able to see. Once a week she gave herself the evening off, went into Venice for dinner with Victor Cunard or Willie Maugham or with George and Elizabeth Chavchavadze.

Nancy adored Venice: if she could not be in Paris, then this was the city where she was happiest, where she could after all lead the nearest approximation to her Paris life. For fifteen years after that first stay on Torcello she returned to Venice every July, putting up at a hotel, once taking a flat, and then for year after year as the guest of Contessa Anna-Maria Cicogna. Anna-Maria was rich, chic, and as a friend 'almost perfect I think – calm, punctual, affectionate, clever & sometimes very funny'. She provided Nancy with exactly the kind of surroundings and society she most appreciated: her house on the Dorsoduro was luxurious and grand, her servants well-trained, her food delicious. Every morning at eleven her motor-boat left for the Lido where her guests would lie baking in the sun, gossiping and dozing until a hot luncheon was served by two footmen in gloves, after which the party returned to the house for a siesta. In the evening, and every evening, there was a dinner-party either at the Gritti or Danieli or in one of the great palazzos, like the Mocenigo where Byron once lived: 'I dined in his flat, quite unchanged, in a lovely stuccoed dining room, by candle light, with a lot of jolly, rather silly Italians, just as he so often did. How I thought of him, longing for Brookses!' The company was always expensively dressed and the backdrop as beautiful as a set at La Scala. Through Victor Cunard and Anna-Maria, Nancy made her Venice friends – the Chavchavadzes, the Graham Sutherlands, Peggy Guggenheim, the Brandolinis, Prince and Princess Clary. These were people she saw every year, highly sophisticated, all of them lovers of art and of Venice, who saw the point of having a good time and were prepared to 'shriek' by the hour. At the end of the month Nancy gave a dinner-party of her own to repay the hospitality she had received. 'Last night I gave my big annual dinner party,' she wrote to Muv on July 27, 1962. '20 people on a platform on the Grand Canal outside the Grand Hotel. It went off very well indeed . . . I had the David Somersets she is Daphne, ex Bath's, daughter & quite lovely & three Italian beauties so the level of looks & clothes was very high indeed & it was a pretty sight with pink table cloths & the dark blue sky & water & the marble palaces.'

Madame de Pompadour was published in 1954, *Voltaire in Love* three years later. After she had finished with 'Pomp' but had not yet started on Voltaire and Emilie, Nancy went through her customary period of worrying about money, 'twiddling my thumbs & waiting for an idea'. At this moment there fell into her lap the subject for an article which, starting off as just another Mitford tease, ended in winning her worldwide notoriety and by giving a new phrase to the language. At luncheon with an American friend Nancy met a Professor Alan Ross, a philologist from Birmingham University who, in answer to a polite enquiry about his work, told her he was writing an article on sociological linguistics for a learned Finnish journal[1] to be entitled 'U and Non-U', denoting Upper-class and Non-Upper-class usage. Nancy was fascinated, so much so that she prevailed on Professor Ross to send her his article in proof where she was thrilled to see *The Pursuit of Love* quoted in a footnote as a source of 'indicators' of English upper-class speech.[2] Scenting in the subject a superlative tease Nancy told Ross he should publish the piece in London under the title of 'Are you a Hon?' 'He blenched.' The following year she tried again, suggesting to Heywood that it was 'a natural for the Xmas market, illustrated by O. Lancaster & entitled Are you U?' But the Professor was not amused ('furious at the idea of his serious pamphlet being frivolously reprinted'), and it was not until it occurred to the editor of *Encounter*, Stephen Spender, to commission Nancy herself to write on the subject that the project got under way. Never had Nancy enjoyed herself so much: 'I lovingly cook away at it all day & think it the best thing I've ever done. It's a sort of anthology of teases – something for everybody.'

Entitled 'The English Aristocracy', Nancy's article was based

[1] Neuphilologische Mitteilungen.

[2] The passage referred to is that disquieting attack of Uncle Matthew's on the vulgarising effects of education on Fanny's vocabulary: '"Education! I was always led to suppose that no educated person ever spoke of notepaper, and yet I hear poor Fanny asking Sadie for notepaper. What is this education? Fanny talks about mirrors and mantelpieces, handbags and perfume, she takes sugar in her coffee, has a tassel on her umbrella, and I have no doubt that, if she is fortunate enough to catch a husband, she will call his father and mother Father and Mother. Will the wonderful education she is getting make up to the unhappy brute for all these endless pinpricks? Fancy hearing one's wife talk about notepaper – the irritation!"'

on Ross's material (although not even he was wholly reliable – 'poor duck speaks of table napkins'), reproducing his examination of class-indicators in speech (U 'bike' versus non-U 'cycle', U 'looking-glass' versus non-U 'mirror') and adding to it an imaginative account of the present way of life of the landed classes with many a glance aside at her own code of practice both in speech and behaviour. We learn, for instance, that the sending of letters by air is common: 'Any sign of undue haste, in fact, is apt to be non-U, and I go so far as preferring, except for business letters, not to use air mail.' So, too, is saying 'Cheers' before drinking, or 'it was so nice seeing you' when taking leave. 'Silence is the only possible U-response,' Nancy wrote. 'In silence, too, one must endure the use of the Christian name by comparative strangers and the horror of being introduced by Christian and surname without any prefix. This unspeakable usage sometimes occurs in letters – Dear XX – which, in silence, are quickly torn up, by me.'

Of course it was all a tremendous joke; but a joke which Nancy herself more than half took seriously. She was not a snob in the sense of looking up to someone solely because he had money or rank; but Nancy was never a member of the public. She saw herself as special and apart; her friends were special and apart; she believed in privilege and tradition, in old-established families in big houses surrounded by acres of land – Uncle Matthew versus Sir Leicester Kroesig. Her tastes were expensive, and she liked to be in the company of people who could afford the sort of things she liked. As she once told Heywood her idea of Utopia 'consists of cottagers, happy in their cottages while I am being happy in the Big House'. In short she believed that everyone should know his place, and in language was to be found one of the most crucial lines of demarcation. Those who speak of 'notepaper', of 'mirrors' and 'mantelpieces' at once give themselves away as belonging on the wrong side of that line. (The fact that Nancy herself, in younger, less self-conscious days, was guilty of such usage was a source now of embarrassment: in younger days the impeccable Miss Mitford had her 'notepaper' stamped at

Harrods[1]; in *Highland Fling* in the Monteaths' flat in Fitzroy Square 'over the mantelpiece hung a Victorian mirror'; and her main object in revising *Pigeon Pie* for the second edition was, she confessed to Evelyn, that it was '*full* of mirrors mantelpieces handbags etc don't tell my public or I'm done for'.)

When that issue of *Encounter* appeared it sold out almost immediately. Nancy had touched a raw nerve. 'I went to WHS here yesterday – manager dashed at me saying all sold out the first day. Heywood who usually sells 20 had sold over 100 last week.' A flood of letters came pouring in – some furious, some amused, some frankly worried; there were newspaper articles and cartoons, endless jokes and sketches, and a coruscating poem in the *New Yorker* by Ogden Nash with the title, 'MS Found Under a Serviette in a Lovely Home.' The following year, 1956, Hamish Hamilton reprinted it in book form under the inspired title, *Noblesse Oblige*, together with Ross's original article, the poem by John Betjeman beginning 'Phone for the fish-knives, Norman', a piece by Peter Fleming ('Strix' of the *Spectator*) on 'Posh Lingo', and an open letter by Evelyn, ponderously waggish in tone, 'To the Honble Mrs Peter Rodd On a Very Serious Subject', in which he is careful to make the point that it was not until Nancy was twelve that her father succeeded to his peerage. 'At that impressionable age an indelible impression was made; Hons were unique and lords were rich.'

By the end of the year nearly 14,000 copies of *Noblesse Oblige* had been sold in Britain; in America 10,000 had gone in the first week. At first Nancy was enormously amused by all the fuss. She had had hundreds of letters, she told Muv, 'Mostly fans, though some abuse "I am circulating it in the monastery – the Prior much impressed by it" "My typist is so angry she refuses to type a letter to you" & so on . . . A friend in London sent me a telegram saying lunch Saturday & the girl on the telephone said "as this is to Miss N M should we not put LUNCHEON?"' She and Hamish

---

[1] 'The last straw is Harrods won't stamp ones notepaper any more.'

Hamilton, both intensely interested in social nuance, corresponded happily for months on the various horrors perpetrated
by those who knew no better. 'Scottish' was one of Nancy's chief
dislikes: 'Both my grandmothers were *Scotch* & would never have
uttered that horrible Scottish', and '*Cook*' she wrote emphatically
all the way from Rocquebrune, '. . . is VERY Non-U one of the
very worst in my opinion.' The jokes went on and on: her
favourite, she told Colonel, was '"I'm dancing with tears in my
eyes 'cos the girl in my arms isn't U"'. But eventually and long
before the topic was exhausted, Nancy grew bored with it. She
and Evelyn started to refer to *Noblesse Oblige* as 'The Book of
Shame' in embarrassed reaction to those among their friends
who found the whole performance distasteful. In a letter to Debo
Diana bewailed the 'horror & vulgarity of the whole notion', an
opinion reiterated in a letter in the *Daily Telegraph*: 'Sir – There
has been a good deal of discussion by your sillier contemporaries
about words and phrases which are "Sub-U and Non-U". I am
sorry to see that this sad little controversy has seeped into your
columns. It is very vulgar . . . I can only beseech you to refrain
from further exposure of decaying tripe. Yours faithfully, Peter
Rodd.'

The writing of *Voltaire in Love* had been a torment to Nancy
because of the debilitating headaches caused by her apparently
failing eyesight. Reading or writing for more than a couple of
hours a day had become too painful to bear, and the prospect of
starting on another book was out of the question. She began to be
seriously worried that she might be going blind and consulted
several specialists in Paris, none of whom came up with an
effective remedy. Then in November 1958 while on a visit to
London she made an appointment to see the distinguished
ophthalmic surgeon, Patrick Trevor-Roper, who 'speaks of a
rheumatic condition of the eyes for which he gives drops but not
very hopefully & he has given me specs which won't be ready for a
week. So we shall see.' But the spectacles worked: 'It is heavenly
to be able to read for a long time on end & now I see how
handicapped I was when doing Voltaire. Now I'll read a lot of

books & then perhaps write a novel.' But she was in no hurry to start; as she told Muv, 'If people knew the boredom & slavery of having to write books they wouldn't put on a silly pretence of envying one!' In January she spent a few days with Madame Costa and the ancient habitués at Fontaines. Then Debo came over to buy clothes: 'She & Diana (my goodness they have become eccentric) rushed about Paris in huge long coats & their heads tied up in white satin like two beauties distracted by tooth-ache. Woolworth bags bulging open & a hundred parcels dangling from their arms. The staring that went on, you can imagine!' After that there was a trip to Brussels to see the Battlefield of Waterloo, staying at the British Embassy with her friends the Labouchères. After this, in July, Nancy went to Venice from where she made a secret sortie to see the Colonel in Rome. Returning to Paris in August, a month she loved for the heat and the emptiness of the streets, she at last started work on her next book, a novel.

Don't Tell Alfred is set in and around the British Embassy in Paris, with the Embassy itself, 'that large, beautiful, honey-coloured house', almost as much a character as the people who inhabit it. Fanny is again the narrator, uprooted from Oxford when her husband Alfred Wincham, the 'Alfred' of the title, is appointed Ambassador in Paris to replace the famously charming, worldly and rich Sir Louis Leone. Dowdy Fanny is understandably terrified, the more so when she arrives at the rue du Faubourg Saint-Honoré to find that Lady Leone has installed herself in an apartment on the Embassy's entresol from which she is entertaining *tout Paris* and spreading disobliging stories about the Winchams. But Fanny, not quite as mousy as she looks, gets rid of her by a clever ruse, and the rest of the novel is devoted to her experiences as Ambassadress. First there is the chaos caused by her niece and social secretary, Northey, a latter-day Zuleika Dobson who, true to her Radlett heritage, is beautiful, amoral and cries at anything sad to do with animals. Then there is the eruption into the dignified diplomatic world of Fanny's two sons, one a brilliant drop-out now running cut-price package-tours to the Costa Brava, the other a bearded weirdie who turns up with wife and baby en route to China and the Zen masters. Through it all, wickedly glinting, runs the theme of the traditional hostilities between England and France, acted out again with relish and in conditions of the greatest comfort and sophistication.

There are several familiar figures from the past: Uncle Matthew is glimpsed at a cocktail party 'standing with his back to the wall, a large glass of water in his hand, glaring furiously into space. The rest of the company was huddled together, rather like a herd of deer with an old lion in the offing.' The Valhuberts, Grace and Charles-Edouard, are here with Sigi, the naughty little boy of *The Blessing*, now being naughty at Eton. And here, too, is Fanny's hypochondriacal Uncle Davey, just out of hospital where he had been choosing 'a few human spare parts, frozen, don't you know, from America'. Lady Leone, the spoilt and beautiful ex-Ambassadress who cannot bear to leave 'her' Embassy, is of course Diana Cooper. Nancy was worried that she might object to the slight element of caricature, but Diana, never averse from a little personal publicity, was reported to be delighted with her rôle as 'the most beautiful woman in the world', although 'cross' that she disappears from the book for good as early as Chapter V.

Of greater cause for concern to Hamish Hamilton when he read the novel was Nancy's instantly recognisable and undeniably libellous portrait of the *Evening Standard*'s Paris correspondent, Sam White, appearing in the book as Amyas Mockbar in mocking reference to his Russian birth[1] and left-wing affiliations. Although wary, Nancy had always rather liked White and been amused by him; the Fiend in Human Form she used to call him, 'a brigand if ever there was one, whom I can't help rather loving'. But then they had fallen out: Nancy was overheard talking about the film version of *The Blessing* in which Maurice Chevalier was cast as Charles-Edouard – absurd miscasting for Chevalier to play an aristocrat, said Nancy, as no one could be more vulgar. White helpfully quoted this in his column, Chevalier read it, was

---

[1] Mockbar is a pun on the Russian spelling of Moscow – Mockba.

furious and threatened to walk off the set. Nancy, rashly denying that she had said anything of the kind, demanded a retraction which the *Standard* refused as she had spoken before witnesses. Nancy was left having to write a couple of grovelling letters to Chevalier[1] and with a determination to get her own back on Sam White.

After the manuscript had been read by Hamilton and his partner Roger Machell, there was an anxious conference in Great Russell Street. Sir John Foster, the eminent QC, was called in to advise and a list of requested alterations was hastily sent off to Nancy in Venice by way of the diplomatic bag:

p. 197 Delete 'saturnine and sardonic'.

p. 230 Delete 'fiendishly clever, deeply annoying to all concerned and only half true'.

p. 264 Delete 'ill-natured, inaccurate'.

But in spite of these amendments Amyas Mockbar remained clearly and unflatteringly Sam White. When the book came out, White, hurt and angry, was stopped from bringing an action only by his proprietor: Lord Beaverbrook argued that as his employee's image was that of hard-bitten journalist, a tough guy with a thick skin, any personal sensitivity about this image would diminish his credibility.

Don't Tell Alfred was published in October 1960 to a tepid reception from the critics and a marked lack of enthusiasm among Nancy's own friends: Mrs Hammersley was reported to be 'bravely struggling', Anna-Maria Cicogna found Fanny 'dreary', and Christopher Sykes violently condemned the beautiful Northey as 'an Arch-Shit'.[2] But in spite of the reviews the book quickly climbed into the best-seller list, with 50,000 copies sold in the first two months. Although, like many writers, she affected to be indifferent to critical opinion, Nancy was

[1] Chevalier replied with aristocratic restraint, 'Ne vous en inquiétez surtout pas. Chaque fois, Madame, qu'il m'arrive quelque chose de ce genre, je me console toujours en pensant qu'il est arrivé bien pire à des gens beaucoup mieux que moi. Et je m'arrange pour survivre.'

[2] But Evelyn Waugh described it as 'her most mature and satisfactory story.'

surprised and hurt by *Alfred's* poor reception. 'Book v. badly received,' she wrote to Evelyn. 'Handy[1] has stabbed me in the back by conjuring up a vision of a Belgian-type mob baying outside the shop for its 15/- I can see the time has come to chuck it & I spend my days & little remaining eyesight counting out my money.'

This was an exaggeration, but Nancy never wrote another novel. It was an unpropitious start to a new decade, one which was to bring a great deal of unhappiness. Although still only in her fifties she was beginning to feel out of tune with the times as her nostalgia for the past grew stronger. She wrote to Debo, 'Oh *Miss* the world! Marie says no *bêtes* any more, nothing but machines – & it is really horrible if one stops to think. Surely one ought to have been able to have washing machines & peers & horses. Well you have sort of managed. (I do admit about washing machines.)' Even the fashions had little to be said for them: 'Bony knees, spindly legs, enormous feet & heads like marmalade cauliflowers all dyed the same brilliant tangerine. Diana & I realise that this is the parting of the ways & we are now old ladies, old fuddy-duddies, comic old things ancient beyond belief.' When she turned sixty in 1964 her line, she told her youngest sister, was to be 'rather wonderful for 60. She's up by 11.30 every morning, rather wonderful & she sometimes spends quite half an hour in the shops & she's so interested in everything, she even watches the television sometimes & do you know she's going to England for Christmas rather *wonderful* for 60.' Nancy had a pen-friend, Sir Hugh Jackson, an old gentleman of wide general knowledge and courteous manners who had first written to her about one of her histories. He and Nancy corresponded regularly and with relish about the horrors of the modern age – hideous buildings, vulgar behaviour, the deleterious effect on civilised life of the Common Market – and the perfection of the Past. Misuse of language was a favourite topic between them: 'Don't you hate "he ordered him

---

[1] Handasyde Buchanan joined the shop in 1945, later becoming a partner. He married Mollie Friese-Greene in 1948.

shot." I continually see that. Also the current use of *this This* I believe instead of I think so, etc. . . . We were strictly brought up not to say very pleased—very interested . . . Oh yes & don't you hate we don't have any instead of we haven't got any. I hear it everywhere. As for pronunciation n'en parlons pas. Even Prince Philip sometimes offends.'

All around her, friends seemed to be dying off at an alarming rate: the forest was getting thin. Victor Cunard was the first to go. When Nancy arrived in Venice for her annual holiday in July 1960, he was already in hospital in Asolo where she went to see him nearly every day. 'It's a great worry & also not much fun panting up there, 3 hours in buses, because he's in such a bad temper. I always thought people on their death beds lay with angelic smiles saying I forgive you – not O.V. who has cooked up every grievance, over a friendship of 25 years, to fling at my head.' He died a few weeks after she left, and when she returned the following year she found she missed him 'too *terribly* . . . I had a long sad talk with our banino, Vittorio, which consisted of him reciting the names of dead people & me crying & saying Oh Vittorio.' She was in Venice when she heard of Eddy Sackville-West's death in 1965. 'Had no idea, on acc of never bothering to look at the paper I suppose. Graham Sutherland said what a pretty shawl you've got on – I said Eddy gave it to me – he said Eddy who's dead? DEAD? I nearly fainted . . . Oh dear, I *mind* Monsewer.'[1] And, three years later, she was in Venice when she

[1] After 'Monsewer' Eddie Gray, a member of The Crazy Gang. The Mitford system of nicknaming could be elaborate. Debo, for instance, was frequently addressed as 'Nine' as that was what her older sister pretended to assume her mental age to be. Alphy Clary was 'Sacred', from the line in Coleridge's poem, *Kubla Khan*, 'Where Alph, the sacred river, ran'. And 'The One without the Parsley' was one of the two French Féray brothers ('Yesterday I was walking past W. H. Smith when I saw the one without the parsley standing like a stork reading that book . . . about the Empress Elizabeth . . . The one without the parsley, by the way, was still deep in the book when I repassed 10 minutes later'). The key to this is that one of the Féray brothers had a moustache, the other did not. In the Eddie Cantor comedy, *Roman Scandals*,

heard the news of Peter's death, dead of an embolism in a hospital in Malta[1]. Diana ran into Nancy walking along the Zattere, 'dressed in *black*. Looking rather *sad* & then needless to say we began laughing again.' She did feel sad, Nancy told her, and remorseful in a way; 'but I couldn't live with him I don't believe a saint could have without going mad.'

Mrs Hammersley died in 1964, the memory of her prophesies of doom and graveyard cerements haunting Fontaines for the two years Nancy continued to go there after her death, until in 1966 Madame Costa died. So did Dolly Radziwill and Roger Hinks (who had been so unencouraging about the sights in Athens): 'Oh yes the Turkish Lady[2] – I MIND. I lunched with him at the Invalides (good restaurant) & there was a great deal of sighing when one oeuf en gêlée was hard – luckily the second one was soft. Had we guessed it would be his last luncheon we could have gone to Maxims! I can never get over the strangeness of death . . . Père Lachaise is full like the Ritz & everything else nowadays. Ay de mi.' In 1969 Mark died of cancer in hospital in London. Nancy wrote to Cecil Beaton, 'I minded passionately about Mark – I suppose he was my oldest intimate friend; he really knew all about

---

the hero has to give the wicked Emperor a chalice of poisoned wine. There are two chalices, one poisoned, one not. To make sure that he gives the right one, he puts a sprig of parsley in the poisoned chalice, saying to himself, 'The one without the parsley is the one without the poison.' Thus, the Féray brother without the moustache . . .

[1] Since the end of the war Peter had found himself at a loose end. His mother had left him a modest income (supplemented from time to time by cheques from Nancy and from his brother Francis) on which he was just able to live without working, first on a boat in the Mediterranean, then, when that broke loose from its moorings and sank, in a small flat in Rome, and finally in an even smaller flat in Malta. He had many love-affairs but never remarried. In the last few years of his life he succeeded in giving up the heavy drinking which had for so long been a habit. A letter from Nancy arrived on the morning of his death, and when he died he was found holding it in his hands.

[2] Roger Hinks used to sit watching the passing scene from the balcony of his house in Athens, looking for all the world, said Nancy, like a Turkish lady of olden times.

me. The reason, so odd, is that he was the only young man my father liked & therefore one could invite him without the risk of his being shaken like a rat.'

Death was very much on Nancy's mind, and in her letters to Evelyn she held several long conversations with him on the subject. 'Darling Evelyn If you're not busy (& if you are, *when* you're not) will you explain something to me? You know *death* – (My brother Tom aged 3 said once Grandfather, you know *adultery* –) Well, one dies, is buried & rises again & is judged. What happens then between death & the end of the world? . . . One or two friends (Catholic) were quite as much puzzled as I am, when I put it to them, & said they wld be glad to know what I find out on the subject.' Evelyn took trouble with his replies ('At the moment of death each individual soul is judged and sent to its appropriate place – the saints straight to heaven, unrepentant sinners to Hell, most (one hopes) to Purgatory where in extreme discomfort but confident hope we shall be prepared for the presence of God. Our bodies remain on earth & decay . . .'); but Nancy, flippant as ever, continued to insist that to her the Last Judgment sounded just like 'finding one's coat after a party I hope the arrangements are efficient . . . I've always felt the great importance of getting into the right set at once on arrival in Heaven. I used to think the Holland House lot would suit me – now I'm not sure. One would get some good belly laughs no doubt, but Sans Souci might provide more nourishment.' Then in 1966 Evelyn himself died, his death depriving Nancy not only of one of her oldest friends but of the source of her most important correspondence. 'Oh Evil when has one been so sad?' she wailed. 'I'm in despair . . . He was such a close friend & I suppose knew more about me than anybody. I think he was v. miserable in the modern world. It killed Théophile Gautier in 1871 (& may well end by killing me).'

In 1963 Muv died. Although deaf and over the past few years shaky from the symptoms of Parkinson's Disease, Muv had continued to live her quiet life, dividing her time between London (padding off to Harrods to change her library-book and going to the cinema with her friend Lady Barnes) and Inch Kenneth, her beloved island off the west coast of Scotland. It was a beautiful place, lying at the mouth of Loch na Keal, surrounded by the craggy slopes of the western Highlands. Here Muv was able to live in perfect peace in a large, comfortable, modern house filled with family photographs and with her favourite French furniture. She kept goats, grew her own vegetables, and walked her little dog José beside the seaweedy rocks of the island's small perimeter.

In April 1963 Nancy came over to London to 'arm' her mother to a family wedding, that of Princess Alexandra to Angus Ogilvy at Westminster Abbey, an occasion which provided some rewarding copy. '*Oh* the get ups I never saw worse . . . Joan Ali Khan next to me in pale green & pale brown paisley satin & blue satin shoes & bedroom hair covered with a net & a bow & she was better than most. Violet [Trefusis] was got up like the Fighting Temerair . . . I'm sure English women are dowdier than when I was young. The hats were nearly all as though made by somebody who had once heard about flowers but never seen one – huge muffs of horror . . . The only one of the foreign royalties who *didn't* look as if she had just been lynched was the Greek Queen – all the others were pathetic – weedy, dowdy & pop-eyed . . . Q of Spain rather splendid – the Queen excellent, though in washy green which I do hate . . . Pss Anne quite lovely . . . Muv, in black velvet, lace & diamonds, was marvellous she looked so pretty.'

Straight after this Muv travelled up to Inch Kenneth while Nancy went over to Ireland to spend a few days with Debo. She was in Ireland when the news reached her that Muv had had a stroke and was dying. All the sisters (except Decca in distant California) gathered at the island – Nancy and Debo from Ireland, Pam from Gloucestershire, Diana from Paris. They took it in turns to sit by Muv's bedside, to keep the fire going and give her little spoonfuls of food or a sip of water. Muv was restless, had to be turned constantly, said again and again how she longed only to die. She asked to be carried to the window to take a last look at the magnificent view up the Loch. 'Two days ago she seemed to be going,' Nancy told Mark '– she said perhaps, who knows, Tom & Bobo & said good bye to everybody & said if there are things in my will you don't like do alter it I said but we should go to prison, & she laughed. (She laughed as she always has). Then she rallied & here she still is – we long for her to go in her sleep quietly.' But for two weeks Muv lived miserably on. Nancy wrote to Decca, 'Here it goes on & poor Muv is getting so fed up. She scolds us now for "dragging her back from the grave – what for?" But all we have done is to give her a little water when she asks which isn't exactly dragging! Three times now we have been gathered round as she seemed to be going & then she has rallied. The fact is she's fearfully *bored* & no wonder . . . Oh dear oh dear *Susan* it's really awful & you're lucky not to be here.'

She died on May 25. A neighbour said prayers over the coffin in the drawing-room, then 'she was taken across on the most perfect evening I ever saw, at high tide (8 pm) Flag on the Puffin at ½ mast – bagpipes wailing – Puffin filled with all of us & about 7 crofters whom she knew, all old friends, who had *done everything* . . . It was very sad but wonderful & one felt how different from dying in the London Clinic, the whole thing seemed natural & REAL.' She was buried at Swinbrook on May 31, laid beside Farve on a day of brilliant sunshine, the Cotswold countryside 'a mass of blossom & cow parsley, brilliant blue sky & flowers for her such as I have never seen . . . I really think I shall never be able to cry again.' Although she had never been close to her, Nancy was deeply shaken by her mother's death. She wrote sadly to the Colonel, 'I have a feeling that nothing really *nice* will ever happen again in my life, things will just go from bad to worse, leading to old age & death.'

CHAPTER TEN

The Last Years

The year following Muv's death, 1964, Nancy began work on a new book, a retelling of the story of Louis XIV and the château of Versailles, 'one of those boring books millionaires give each other for Christmas'. The original suggestion had been a history of the château itself but this Nancy was reluctant to do: she had already covered much of it in 'Pomp', and had no desire to deal with the reign of Louis XVI and the dreaded Marie-Antoinette: 'I loathe M-A, the heroine of the Anglo Saxon race, to such a point that I would find it hard to be fair to her & her wretched husband.' But *The Sun King* would break new ground and, as Heywood shrewdly pointed out, 'Has all the sniff of a seller too, as Hotbrick Hamilton must be twigging'. In order to get started she went in September to stay for six weeks at Fontaines where the dying beauty of the autumnal countryside induced in her a pervasive feeling of melancholy. 'My book has rather come to a standstill,' she wrote to the Colonel. 'After 1700 all the old friends are dead, just like real life. Oh dear, I sometimes feel very sad.' But soon she was under the spell of the high-heeled periwigged tyrant and by January of the following year the book was finished, for once to her complete satisfaction. 'It dazzles me whatever it may do to the public so *somebody* is pleased.'

Hamish Hamilton had intended that *The Sun King* should repeat the conventional format of *Madame de Pompadour*, but while Nancy was still working an her text a new proposition was put forward. George Rainbird, the publisher and inventor of the 'coffee-table book,' had recently had an enormous success with a big, gorgeously illustrated work on Tutankhamun which he now wanted to follow with a similar book on a similar subject – in other words a king who had left behind him great works of art. Louis XIV was an obvious choice. The idea of a co-edition was attractive to Hamish Hamilton as Rainbird's imprimatur guaranteed sales all over the world; Nancy, too, was impressed by the large sums of money mentioned and liked the promise of lavish illustration. Rainbird's chief picture-researcher, Joy Law, came over to Paris to discuss the choice of pictures and the lay-out of the pages. This was a completely new concept in publishing, a book in which the pictures should be not an interruption to, but an integral part of, the text: as you read about Madame de Maintenon or the interior of Louis's magnificent château, so there would be the lady's portrait or a double-page spread in full colour of the Galerie des Glaces.

The result was a book that was as magnificent to look at as it was entertaining to read. From the first sentence – 'Louis XIV fell in love with Versailles and Louise de la Vallière at the same time; Versailles was the love of his life' – one can almost hear the sigh of pleasure and relief with which Nancy returns to the past and her beloved France. *The Sun King*, dedicated to Raymond Mortimer 'in gratitude, I fancy,' he said, 'for my vain attempts to explain to its author the difference between a colon and a semi-colon', was greeted with adulatory reviews, nearly all of them remarking not only the liveliness of Miss Mitford's style but the splendour of the illustrations. There were one or two dissonant voices: Harold Nicolson 'takes exception of the word Sodomite which, he says, reminds him of Mr Odoni & the Bishop of Sodor & Man. I asked what I ought to call the adherents of that cult & he says metallists. All right – so long as one knows'; and, as with *Madame de Pompadour*, some critics objected to the pure gold light in which Nancy bathed her far from pure gold subject. Lucy Norton, the learned translator of the *Memoirs of Saint-Simon*, was one, but Nancy's rose-coloured vision was not to be tainted by reality. 'Of course I suppose there was that black side but I'm sure people like La Montespan, Mme la duchesse or all the little chatterers round the Dsse de Bourgogne never noticed it & I don't believe I would have. Mme de Maintenon did but then she was a life-hater. You speak of the Inquisition but the worst we hear of is ghastly Mme Guyon's eight comfortable years in the Bastille – and she asked for it . . . I feel one would have said who is tired of Versailles is tired of life. I did try to put a little shade by going on about those tiresome peasants & galley slaves. But there you are – it's all a matter of temperament isn't it.' What meant more to Nancy than any of the 'rave' reviews, more even than the phenomenal sales[1] was the news that General de Gaulle had read *The Sun King*, praised it, and been heard to say that every member of his Cabinet should buy it. 'MISS!' Nancy exclaimed to Debo. 'I nearly fainted with excitement.' It was on the strength of this that the Colonel approached de Gaulle with a request that Madame Rodd should be awarded the Légion d'Honneur, on the grounds that '[Ses] romans . . . montrent tous la France sous un aspect attirant et sympathetique . . . Elle est devenue une sorte d'incarnation de la francophilie britannique . . .' But on this occasion the answer from the General was a characteristic 'Non'.

With *The Sun King* out of the way Nancy awarded herself a long holiday, going first to Ireland, then to Chatsworth for the ball to celebrate the coming of age of her nephew Peregrine, then to Venice as usual in July. 'Enjoyed it in patches,' she told Debo, but there were too many sewers about, the most objectionable of whom were Brigitte Bardot and a crowd of film people staying with the Agnellis. 'Audrey Hepburn looks charming (& makes idiotic observations but at least her looks are nice) But Yul Brner [sic] looks utterly revolting & has got a showing-off American wife & as for A.H.'s bearded American husband all I can say is DON'T. They are all quite without grey matter. *Actors*, & when you've said that you've said everything.' After Venice she went on to Florence to stay with Harold Acton at La Pietra – 'complete perfection . . . One wakes up in a room larger than the Chatsworth drawing room with sun streaming onto the bed so that one has a comfortable sun bath. Then the art, both in the house & the

---

[1] A quarter of a million copies within two years, earning over £350,000.

galleries knocked me silly. We lunched & dined out in wonderful villas with such gardens. Oh Italy, there's nothing like it.'

These letters were written on paper Nancy recently had had made especially for taking away with her: no address on the top, but a little mole (the Mitford crest) embossed in gold in the left-hand corner. It was very pretty. Aunt Iris wrote appreciatively on receiving a sample, 'I have fallen deeply in love with your charming little golden cunt (Glostershire of my young days for moles, few people now know what it means).' '*She's* not in the Tynan set, obviously,' Nancy observed.

By the autumn of 1966, when *The Sun King* came out, Nancy was back in rue Monsieur and feeling fretful. Paris was no longer what it had been: for one thing, 'There are so few agreeable English people here now . . . they are all true horrors & loathe the French as common English always have. One long beef about plumbers doesn't make for interesting conversations!'; then there was the noise and the traffic and the shrill voices of the children playing outside her window. ('When I see fillette dans le coma depuis 4 jours I do so wish it could be all the children in this courtyard'.) Never mentioned but ever present was the torment-ing truth that she was seeing less and less of the Colonel: there was somebody else in his life – there had to be, to account for that evasive look on his face, the infrequency, now, of his telephone calls.

So it was that Nancy left Paris and moved to Versailles. It was what she had always wanted, her friends were told; she had always wanted to live in the suburbs. Number 4, rue d'Artois was a small, two-storey, eighteenth-century house, flat-faced and painted white, standing inconspicuously in a narrow side-street away from the centre of town, with a few shops and a solid grey parish church just round the corner. It was an undistinguished little house, but it had half an acre of walled garden and Nancy thought it complete perfection. By the time she was ready to move in January 1967, she had cut her ties with Paris and could hardly wait to leave. Versailles was superior in nearly every respect, and the Versaillais, it was quickly noted, were much easier to get on

with than the cross Parisians. A few days before Christmas she
went to the house to see how work was progressing: 'I went
yesterday & made a huge bonfire in the garden (oh how enjoyable) &, in spite of it being Sat afternoon the sweet deaf & dumb
painter was there & of course joined in. Nobody ever can resist,
can they? Marvellous sunset & rooks flying home & a moon
coming up – goodness, I *long* to move. The old servant of the next
door chemist was shutting the shutters, I never saw such a dear
old face, like olden times.'

In spite of her urban way of life and the sophistication of her
appearance, Nancy always retained a strong streak of the coun-
trywoman. Rue Monsieur had presented small opportunity either
for gardening or for keeping animals – although for some years
Nancy and Marie had kept a quarrelsome old cat, Minet, brought
over from England by Diana; and there was a hen Marie pur-
chased in the market and which, as neither of them could bear to
have it killed, was allowed to live out its natural span in the
kitchen, going comfortably to bed every night in the oven. Now
Nancy's half-acre of garden became a passionate and absorbing
interest. Debo, herself an experienced gardener, was the main
recipient of Nancy's horticultural confidences. What she wanted
at rue d'Artois, Nancy told her, was a wild garden, a 'champ
fleuri'. 'I want a lot of weed seeds – poppies, valerian, irises,
orchids, buttercups, marsh marrow, daisies & *hare bells* . . . A dear
little boy comes every Thursday & hacks down vile things like
budlea copper beech maple japonica & various nameless brutes.
There is a thing I recognise as having hideous pink flowers like in
London parks. The neighbours beg me with tears to leave it what
am I to do. I loathe it. I am going to dot the grass with rose bushes
& sow many a weed. I will *not* mow. I loathe lawns (London
parks).'

The arrival of spring ('*Oh the spring* how could I have lived in
Paris all these years!') brought many an exciting new discovery. 'I
see that this is a most thwarting hobby. For instance, I noted
jasmin in a catalogue & ordered it (much of it) Well I thought
jasmin was a lovely exotic bloom, like for a Monastery Garden or

In a Persian Market, of which scent was made. Well when it came it turned out to be that dismal little yellow flower on a sort of stick insect plant redolent of London parks. My grass is rather tufty so I pretend to be a cow & pluck it with a grazing motion, to a chorus of offers to lend mowing machines.' With the spring, too, a whole animal world came to life before Nancy's fascinated gaze. A tortoise crawled out of hibernation: 'Tortie is sheer therapy. Col, not finding me the other day, said to Marie oh there she is, watching the tortoise;' so did a pair of hedgehogs, with whose domestic saga Debo was kept well up to date: 'Hot news here the hedgehogs have had a baby. I saw it last night, drinking the milk we put for them. *Oh* the sweetness.' Then there were the bees and the birds, with a different but equally absorbing set of problems. 'The water I put out for my precious birds is now taken over by bees who sit closely packed round the rim, drinking (or I'm told filling bags to take back to the hive) All right, but there is one horrid bee whose function it is to chase away the birds in which it is only too successful – even the vainglorious black bird flees & all my friends have departed.' What she longed for, she told Debo, was a pet: a dog was out of the question ('I crave one dreadfully but its the loo trouble my garden isn't big enough'); so what about a rabbit? But then 'I suppose if I had a large white rabbit with pink ears it would entail cleaning out?' By the summer the garden was in full and glorious flower; to the eyes of her friends it looked a jungle, but to the happy owner it was a ravishing wilderness – 'My garden looks as if 1000 Edwardian hats had fallen into it (roses).'

Nancy was now a rich woman[1], thanks to the continuing enormous sales of *The Sun King. Madame de Pompadour* was to be reissued in a new illustrated edition as companion to Louis; and Hamish Hamilton was agitating for another big best-seller. For some time Nancy had been toying with the idea of a life of the Prussian king Frederick the Great, at first glance a bizarre choice of subject for someone on whose personal hate-list the Germans

---

[1] Her income in 1968 was £22,000.

came second only to the unspeakable Americans. The attraction
was that Frederick, although German, was an honorary Frenchman: he spoke French (considered the German language fit only
for horses), he wrote in French, his culture was entirely French,
and he was the friend and patron of Voltaire. Like Voltaire he was
an arch-tease. No wonder Nancy found him irresistible. 'Goodness F must have been funny – that's why I love him so much.
The jokes are perfect.' Hamish Hamilton, however, was distinctly
dubious, while George Rainbird 'groans at the prospect &
longs for Catherine the Great ... I'm dreadfully afraid the
English only like books about Mary Q of S & Marie Antoinette &
that new ground won't go down – specially German ground.'
Worse than that from a publisher's point of view was the problem
of Frederick's love-life: there wasn't any. 'I don't think he *loved*
anybody & that whether or not he fondled pretty young officers
after breakfast is really immaterial . . . It's not that I don't want to
say that Fred: had affairs – I long to (& my publisher turned white
to the lips when I said I couldn't find a scrap of real evidence for
any love affair) but the truth is what is interesting about people.'

However, both Hamilton and Rainbird knew better than to
stand in Nancy's way: she was the goose that laid the golden eggs
and the last thing either of them wanted was to stop the laying. It
was in her favour, too, that Frederick was a good subject for
Rainbird's format: lots of colour pictures of his collection of
paintings and furniture, of his great palaces and his soldiers'
pretty uniforms. The services of the indispensable Joy Law were,
at Nancy's insistence, once again engaged, and in August 1968
she was ready to begin.

The plan was that Nancy, accompanied by Pam who spoke the
language, should go to East Germany to look at what remained of
Frederick's realm; but then the Russians invaded Czechoslovakia
which put paid to that. In November she went alone to Prague,
staying with the British Ambassador. 'Nobody in the least bit
interested in any historical figures exc: Kafka. I never got to the
battlefield of Kollin but you can be sure if Kafka had fought there
I wld have been taken the first day!' Nonetheless she came back

excited by what she had seen, her head full of ideas about Frederick. 'I can never tell you the fascination of the story of Fred,' she wrote to Professor Robert Halsband, '& if I write a rotten book I can't blame the material. The mystery to me is how other writers have managed to cast such an aura of boredom over it!' The other mystery remained Frederick's sex-life: 'I think perhaps I fail to understand the nature of homosexuality – I am excessively normal myself & have never had the slightest leaning in that direction even as a child. My own feeling about F is that he was almost or quite sexless . . . The interest of a love affair lies in the changing nature of the relationship & if there is no evidence available how can one describe it? Allez-oop with young officers is really very dull.'

At the end of that year, 1968, Nancy began to be aware of a distracting pain in her left leg – rheumatism, perhaps, or sciatica. 'As I am unused to pain it gets me down', she told Debo. 'Nothing to be done for it I fear so I don't bother to try. Besides I'm too busy.' But the weeks passed and the pain would not be ignored. Her doctor thought it might be a slipped disc, or even something wrong with her kidneys ('Cancer, I expect,' Nancy joked), and that she should go into hospital for tests. Meanwhile he advised her to stay at home flat on her back for a fortnight to see if complete rest would effect the cure.

This was at the end of March 1969. During that fortnight when Nancy was lying supine in her bedroom in the rue d'Artois, a small announcement appeared one morning in the *Figaro*: 'Nous sommes heureux d'annoncer,' it began, 'le mariage de M. Gaston PALEWSKI avec Violette de TALLEYRAND-PERIGORD duchesse de SAGAN.' The marriage, the announcement continued, 'a été célébré dans la plus stricte intimité, le 20 mars'. The event that Nancy had been dreading for nearly thirty years had finally taken place: Colonel was married. For him it was the greatest good fortune: his wife was rich and the owner of one of the most beautiful châteaux in France, Le Marais, only forty kilometres outside Paris. He had been in love with her for years but the affair had had to be discreetly conducted as only recently had her husband consented to a divorce. She had a son, too, of whom Colonel was particularly fond, thus providing him with the sense of family for which he had always felt the need.

But good fortune for the Colonel heralded the end for Nancy. It was almost literally a death-blow, the bitterness of it exacerbated by the fact that Gaston's wife was a divorced woman: for years Nancy had accepted the face-saving excuse that he could never marry her because he dare not risk his political career by marrying a divorcée. Now retired from politics, he could marry where he chose, and his choice was not Nancy. She admitted her misery to no one. Those of her friends who enquired about it were told in a manner studiedly casual – all too silly, a marriage for those of mature years, no nonsense about living together, Violette a sort of non-person: 'I think we'll see the old boy as per & I don't think anything will change for better or worse – he's to go on living in the rue Bonaparte . . . Nothing changed whatever in other words.'

In the beginning of April Nancy finally went into hospital, her long rest in bed having done nothing at all to alleviate the pain. She was operated on and a lump the size of a grapefruit removed from her liver. The surgeon told Diana and Debo that the tumour was malignant and that the patient was unlikely to live for more than another four months. It was decided, after much agonising on the part of the sisters, that Nancy should not be told, that she would not be able to accept the nearness of death. She came out of hospital weak and tired but relieved that the pain had gone, and happy beyond measure to be back in her little house. On warm days she sat out under the apple-tree in the garden, feeling so much better than she was even able to think of starting again on her book.

Then the pain came back, worse than before. It was now not only in her leg but in the small of her back. Strong pain-killers, including morphine, were prescribed, which made her feel stupid, but if she did not take them the pain was unbearable and she was left 'literally bellowing in anguish . . . the doctors look at me sadly, because there is nothing wrong with my back whatever, it is pristine. They seem in a sea of total ignorance in fact & fall back on that meaningless word rheumatism.'

The next four years, the long four years it took Nancy to die, were characterised by weeks of appalling pain interspersed with brief periods of remission, during which she would be convinced that she was cured. It was almost as though the pain were an expression of thirty years of suppressed jealousy, misery and rage over the disappointment of her love for the Colonel, periodically palliated by her own high spirits and enthusiasm for life. Nancy was a difficult patient to treat as she had inherited to the full her mother's distrust of medicine and of the entire medical profession. She distrusted her doctors, thought them ignorant and avaricious. She believed she had an unusually high resistance to pain-killers, which was not in fact true: the pain itself was so terrible that there was almost nothing that would bring it under control. The cause of the pain was a mystery: contrary to the surgeon's prediction the operation to cut out the tumour from her liver had been completely successful and the growth did not recur. But the pain continued. In these four years, during which Nancy saw thirty-seven different doctors, she went into hospital for operations both in Paris and London, submitted to tests, X-rays and a blood transfusion, underwent massage and manipulation, and adhered to any number of theories (from a twisted muscle to a too-tight waistband on a pair of trousers) as the cause of the pain. Not until the end was the correct diagnosis made, that Nancy was suffering from a rare form of Hodgkin's Disease, a malignant enlargement of the lymph glands, in her case rooted, which is rare, in the spine. The pain is known to be one of the two most severe a human being can suffer.

But this, in the summer of 1969, was still in the future. Nancy was in pain, but for the moment it was not unendurable. Decca came over from California for a visit, and was relieved to note that her sister was as sharp-tongued as ever. In June the saintly Marie, now in her seventies and no longer able to toil up and down stairs with laden trays several times a day, left to return to her family in Normandy. Nancy missed her 'more terribly than words can say

. . . The spiritual nourishment I got from old Marie can't ever be replaced & everything is much duller – viz I never look at the télé now, it bores me.' Marie's replacement, a Mlle Delcourt, was efficient but a bore; she was, however, an excellent cook, '& she is very very well disposed & anxious to please. The kitchen is so tidy it looks like a kitchen in a play.' Even more marvellous, 'the new lady, (new Marie) seeing me writhing about in true agony said I could cure you. Me, rather bored, looking out of the window . . . I doubt it. N.L. May I try? Me Oh all right – no no no you mustn't *touch* my back. N.L. touches it, terrifies me, grip of iron. Cured. Period. Can you beat it? She says I had a twisted muscle which she has straightened up.' It seemed too good to be true, the first time Nancy had been free of pain for seven months. Now she was out of bed ('no more bed at all in fact it is *made*, with its cover'); she had walked to the hairdresser, and she told Diana, 'I am so cured I can't remember being ill.' Now she was impatient to get on with her book.

This posed a new problem: if Nancy were to follow the schedule she had planned for herself the probability was that she would not live to finish it. Diana wrote to Debo, 'N says she has got on so well with the book that there is absolutely no hurry . . . This kills one with guilt, in case finally she reproaches & says I *could* have gone quicker & finished if I'd known. So I have got a plot to ask the man they all like at Rainbird to ask her as a great favour to let them have it a bit sooner – telling him why.' Nancy swallowed the ploy, writing to Joy Law that she was having to hurry on with 'Fred' as 'it seems Hamilton has got a poor list for '71'.

She was so much encouraged by the apparent improvement in her health and the interest shown in her book that she now felt able to undertake the long-postponed expedition to see Frederick's Prussian palaces and battlefields before finishing the book. In October 1969 Nancy and Pam with Joy Law and her husband flew to East Germany as guests of the government. They were provided with two chauffeur-driven limousines and an English-speaking guide who escorted them round Potsdam,

Dresden and East Berlin. It was Pam who kept Nancy going, getting her up every morning at eight and seeing that she had a chair to sit on in museums. When they got back Nancy reported on the trip to Alvilde Lees-Milne[1]: 'The journey was simply amazing & I'm thankful I went . . . I had a lot of pain but no worse than when I'm here & they were so kind about bringing chairs & bringing the car to forbidden places & so on. The only thing was no baths only showers & I depend greatly on lying in a hot bath so that was rather a blow. Food *delicious* because they haven't got round to broilers & so on & the taste was what one has forgotten but of course if you say so they are deeply offended & say by next year all the farms will be factories. Like in all commy countries nothing works & the first evening I was stuck in a mad lift which whirled up & down for 35 minutes. I thought I was for it & Woman thought I'd been kidnapped . . . I thought East B *vastly* preferable to West which is like a huge Oxford Street. The people so much nicer wherever you look . . . I've seldom enjoyed myself more. I've finished the book which is now being typed & my health has taken a *distinct* turn for the better, so everything seems rosy again.'

The turn for the better was short-lived. Immediately after Christmas Nancy succumbed to a bad attack of influenza, so did Mlle Delcourt, and so did Mme Guimant, the nice charwoman who lived in the same street and came in every day to clean. Pam was appealed to for rescue, but she, too, was ill. Diana at Orsay was looking after Sir Oswald just out of hospital after an operation. For three days nobody at all came to the little house in the rue d'Artois. For three days Nancy, unable to go downstairs, had nothing to eat. Never had she felt so wretched. She lay on her unmade bed all day crying and hungry and longing for Marie. Her loneliness appalled her sisters: as Diana said, 'The awful thing is, she doesn't come *first* with anybody.'

After this period of darkness the efficient Mlle Delcourt left to be replaced by a young, smiling, curly-haired Moroccan boy.

---

[1] Alvilde Chaplin had married Jim Lees-Milne in 1951.

Nancy liked Hassan from the beginning. He was willing, cheerful, and 'a real cook, absolutely the top – I'm so thrilled. Then so *smart* & nice, & kind he found one of my hedgehogs & brought it in & so on – you know, the sort of person one can do with'. His single disadvantage was that every Saturday at midday he took off for Paris, not to reappear until breakfast on Monday. 'On Sunday which is Hassan's day off the gracious living of rue d'Artois collapses. The butter stays in silver paper for fear of dirtying a plate – I had cheese & brioche for lunch & was to make porridge for dinner shown by Woo ['Woman', a nickname for Pam]. But I bought some milk in a sort of celluloid container *which I couldn't open* so I drove a nail into it upon which two great jets of milk burst forth like Moses smiting the rock was it Moses? one into my eye the other on the floor neither in the jug . . . Oh I *loathe* it all so terribly.'

In April 1970 Nancy went into the Hôpital Rothschild in Paris for a series of tests. There were no private rooms and the experience was one which left her deeply shaken. 'On this étage all the patients have got skin diseases & one queues up for the loo with people like that picture of Napoleon at Aleppo – male & female – who have not been trained in use of same by English nannies.' At first she shared a room with an old Roumanian peasant woman 'with such an agonizing skin disease that she shrieked & not with laughter for 20 hours a day. For 4 hours she slept & her snores were louder than her shrieks. She allowed no window open you know what that means to me!' Then for the last week 'I was cast on my back, no pillow, unable to write & almost unable to read, with, as fellow, the wife of a vigneron from Champagne, & I don't mean Odette Pol-Roger! . . . She not only allowed no window but it had to be covered with linoleum & she peed all night into an open pot between our beds.'

The tests, on the bone-marrow, were painful and made her weak and giddy. But once she was home she felt better, well enough to accept Anna-Maria Cicogna's invitation to Venice in July in the hope that the strong Italian sun would cure her. Diana saw her off in her wheelchair at Orly, and she arrived in good spirits, staying up till 10.30 on her first evening for dinner with the Clarys. Every morning she was carried like a parcel to the beach, and all afternoon she rested in a pretty bedroom 'which looks over the Zattere & I see the big ships, bigger than churches, being pulled in & out'. Then there was a frightening relapse. 'Went out to dine at Harry['s Bar] & was in too much pain to describe – after, to my horror, we were to go to the Gritti for a boat. After a few yards I began to cry & said to Francis Watson its no good I can't So he propped me against the wall & dashed off & got the boat faithful soul.' Anna-Maria called a doctor and not for the first time the result was miraculous. 'I think I'm cured,' she told Diana. 'Dined on the Wrightsmans' yacht never a twinge & this morning nothing at all . . . I believe he has done the trick. *Imagine* if he has!' Now she was able to enjoy her holiday and take an interest in the people around her. Serge Lifar was one of the new arrivals ('a most friendly soul, tho like all stage people he has but the one topic'), Cecil Beaton was another: 'He is fearfully worried about a tiny wrinkle on his cheek. People gaze in the glass & don't realise that the *general effect* is 100. I saw the old soul from my balcony – didn't know he was coming & wondered who the *old* gentle was until I heard the voice. Nothing to do with the tiny wrinkle.' But then, bite bite, back came the pain. She was unable to sleep and suffered agonies from constipation. 'Really doctors how right Muv was one thought her cranky but you see.' Just before she left for Paris she wrote a despairing letter to the Colonel: 'Oh dear je suis dans un triste état. . . Cette douleur qui me ronge m'enlève le goût de la vie je dois dire . . . Je ne sais pas pourquoi je vous écrire en mauvais français tout à coup ça doit faire partie de l'abrutissement général Do come Love N.'

Once home the search continued for a treatment that would work. She was prescribed Cortisone, but it frightened her and after the first dose she refused to have more. Alphy Clary told her of a doctor in London who had 'cured' him of exactly what Nancy was suffering from now. 'He is English but one hasn't heard of him actually killing anybody unlike most English drs. The horror of going to London & seeing Knightsbridge barracks which I had hoped for ever to avoid might be compensated for if I could be cured of this grinding pain. I'd really go to Hell – anywhere exc: New York in fact.' Alphy's treatment was disagreeable and did nothing to alleviate the pain. While she was in London *Frederick the Great* came out to reviews that were more respectful than enthusiastic, but Nancy was in no condition to care very much what anybody said. Occasionally when the pain subsided her natural high spirits, that innate love of life that never quite deserted her, rose to the surface. She had ordered for the visit to London a new dress from Saint-Laurent: 'I love it so much I practically go to bed in it Its a sack coloured sack, to the ankles, hideous & smart beyond belief.' And in London, the Colonel was told, 'I bought, in waves of pain, a long black (sham) sealskin coat like Proust's it is very funny but also very pretty . . . Ma chère etc I am etc Connaught Hotel Very low.'

Nancy returned to France at the end of the year. The pain was as bad as ever and she was driven to boosting the analgesics with brandy. 'When I'm drunk I'm all right but I've got a very strong head, it takes a huge amount & the effect doesn't last very long & then I feel of course liverish as well. Oh bugger it all.' In January 1971 she went again to London where she underwent an investigative operation at the Nuffield Hospital in Bryanston Square, which left her feeling iller than before. She now weighed less than seven stone and found it almost impossible to eat. Debo and Pam visited her every day as did faithful friends such as Helen Dashwood, Joy Law and Nancy's cousin, Clementine Beit. Even Colonel flew over from Paris for 'une petite heure'. In April she was home and in a state of deepest depression, writing to Alvilde, 'I can't work & can't see what is to become of me for the first time in my life I am wallowing in gloom & self pity. Those bull doctors diagnosed what I've got as intractable pain. I can tell you there is nothing worse on earth.'

But there were periods of remission and there were still aspects of her life in which Nancy was able to take pleasure. She was fascinated by the bird-life in her garden, what she could see of it from her bed. There was a family of tits that she fed from her window-sill. 'The old ones have been coming for ages now there are 3 intensely disagreeable children. My old chums look so tired & battered & the children so fat & pretty it is unfair. They are all in a perpetual rage like an English family on holiday & I'm sure the old 'uns must wish they had never bothered to breed no gratitude, just like humans.' There was a hen-blackbird with a torn wing which Hassan rescued from a cat, and which Nancy nursed for two days in the bathroom: 'I'm getting a water pistol for H would gladly give him a real gun,' she told Alvilde. And to Debo, the wild-life expert, 'The blackbird we so dote on has made its nest in the lilac by the drawing room window & there are now three hunting cats never out of the garden – does the team think we could keep them out of the tree which even I could climb with barbed wire? . . . If it were not for the cats *the pleasure* of a nest almost in one's room is great, the beady eye fixed on one in total confidence. I know how they make the nest & every detail of their private lives.'

Nancy read insatiably, kept supplied by the faithful shop with proof copies of new books which were then discussed at length with Raymond. 'My consolation these awful days has been Goethe's Italian journey in a marvellous translation (Penguin) Written in 1786 it describes Italy as you & I have known it. Oh dear that earnest, noble young German *how* different from Voltaire & the Great King & how much one prefers really those two old sinners! . . . Then what's so funny, he keeps describing his own works & makes them sound *utterly* unreadable . . . Carrington fascinated & horrified me & oh how I disliked her[1]. A strong smell of death throughout. Then somebody sent me a dreadfully brilliant book by Simon Raven then I read Mr Norris which is even more pourri – just as Carrington beats the present day lot for vice, she must, it would be impossible to be more vicious I suppose. The mixture of vice & dowdiness is so unattractive & so is all that sentiment. What a nasty book.'

---

[1] Raymond had loved Carrington and therefore Nancy knew this would tease and could not resist it.

The more helpless Nancy became, the more dependent she was on her sisters. Diana, her main support, drove over nearly every day from Orsay; Debo came when she could and kept in close touch by telephone; Pam, unshakably loyal, repaying hand over fist with kindness all Nancy's cruelty when they were children, came again and again, acting as matron and house-keeper combined. Women friends, such as Billa Harrod, Alvilde and Cynthia Gladwyn made themselves available to take a turn in looking after the invalid. Friends in England, appalled by Nancy's agonised letters, besieged her with remedies, everything from 'green pills' to acupuncture, holy medals and even a poultice soaked in Lourdes water for her leg. Tom Driberg had prayers said for her, but 'It's very sad for me,' Nancy wrote. 'I used to believe so unshakeably in God but I can't any more;' somebody else sent a faith-healer, 'a sort of poor man's Liz Taylor . . . instead of hymns she fell upon my ill nerve & teased it just as Alphy's London quack did, so that I've had three days of martyrdom, no drug the very slightest use . . . I know I ought to retire, like Capt Oates, but the mechanics are so difficult.' During the worst days the only people Nancy would see were her sisters and of course the Colonel who, with his little spaniel Léa, dropped in several times a week on his way from the rue Bonaparte to the Marais. Sometimes she felt better, hopeful that a cure was just round the corner, that after all life was worth living; then she would be overwhelmed by pain, convinced that nobody cared, the doctors (to whom she was often childishly rude)[1] were only after her money, and the sooner she could die the better. On days when the pain was under control she allowed Hassan to carry her into the garden where she lay in the sun on a straw mattress. From time to time she even felt well enough to see friends for luncheon. Hamish came – 'so nice quite like old times I was awfully pleased to see him' – and so did Cyril Connolly. 'Cyril did that thing I call *rude* of, as though one's entrée were

[1] To one of her English specialists she sent a picture-postcard of a graveyard, and written on the back, 'No wonder these places are full up, with people like you about.'

sure to be uneatable, bringing plovers eggs from Hédiard. THEY WERE RAW. So the first ones went over everybodies clothes & the second lot were hot. Col in a hurry was annoyed by all the delays. Then I had opened a bottle of Rothschild Lafitte 1952 & Cyril in a temper because of his old eggs pretended not to like it (it was nectar) so I was put out. Then the pain came down & blacked out everything & I had to creep to the sofa & that was that. By the time they came to the drawing room & Col had gone Cyril had become amiable again I had taken a Palfium which is a good but not lasting drug & I very much enjoyed an hour of chat with the old boy who was suddenly very mellow praised my house & so on.'

In the spring of 1972 Nancy was at last awarded the Légion d'Honneur, the only honour she had ever wanted. Colonel came down to Versailles to give it to her. Half-carried by Diana, she managed very slowly to come downstairs and stand just long enough for Colonel to pin it to her dress. Afterwards she cried with happiness. Almost at once, as if in counter-attack, came the news from the other side of the Channel (*strictly* confidential) that she was to be nominated for the CBE. At first affecting indifference, Nancy pretended she had never heard of the English honour, that English honours meant nothing to her. But when a letter arrived warning her that by talking about it she was in danger of losing it (Diana Cooper, who under oath of secrecy had been told, was busily spreading the news round London), 'then of course I conceived a wild desire for the medal & mum became the word'. She was pleased to discover that 'it enables me to sit above a knight's widow so you must find me one to take everywhere with me. (I do, anyway, without wishing to boast, as a peer's daughter . . .)'

Soon after this a pain came like the end of the world, and Nancy was reduced to stuffing her pillow into her mouth to stop herself from screaming aloud. She was given an injection to kill the nerve in her leg, but it had no effect whatsoever. In desperation she agreed to go yet again to London, back to the Nuffield. Cynthia Gladwyn came over to fetch her, bringing a nurse to accompany them in the aeroplane. This time, finally, Hodgkin's Disease was diagnosed. 'They hope to cure me,' Nancy wrote to her friend and translator Jacques Brousse. 'If not they promise to let me go without the horrors to which American & I believe French doctors submit one. After 4 such years as I have had one looks at death in a very different way.'

She came back to France in the New Year of 1973, the last year of her life. She now weighed less than six stone, suffering agonies and longing only to die. Her leg was swollen, 'like Louis XVIII's & hurts . . . I'm in worse tortures than I've ever had. The pills no good any more & there is no let up day or night . . . Does one struggle on? I am so fond of life but not this sort . . . The trouble is I feel no hope.'

At Easter, and much against Nancy's will, a nurse was brought in to live in the house: she could no longer sit unsupported, nor eat nor wash herself. Swallowing pain-killers by the handful[1], she was also having daily injections of morphine; but the effect was short-lived, and the injections themselves were a torture: she was so thin it was difficult to find a place in which to insert the needle, and even the gentlest pressure hurt her. The only people she would see were her sisters and Colonel, although through all the agony and horror she continued to write letters, now in a tiny, cramped hand at times barely legible. Her letters were her life-line. To Cynthia Gladwyn she described the nurse, Old Gamp she called her. 'If you ask her to brush your hair she gives you two sharp blows with the brushes – the bed pan is an all-in wrestling match at which I am, screaming with pain, the loser & as for washing, one is the kitchen floor . . . Oh I can't go on, so sorry this pain is nag nag nag.' Every part of her body was now agonisingly sensitive and she could hardly bear to be touched; the vibration of a heavy van going down the street would hurt her, and the effort of turning her head to look out of the window was

---

[1] French law prohibited doctors from prescribing unlimited quantities of the pain-killing drug Nancy needed, so secret supplies had to be smuggled over by friends coming from London.

almost too great to make. She so longed 'to see the blackbird in the Montana & the tits in that yellow stuff on the wall'. The water bloating her legs had now reached her chest which, she said, felt as though it were full of heavy stones, and her liver was painfully enlarged. She was eating almost nothing, one or two tiny biscuits topped with a prawn and a spot of cream cheese.

On June 8 she wrote to the Colonel, 'Dearest I'm truly very ill . . . Je souffre comme je n'avais pas imaginée la morphine fait très peu d'effet . . . Je pense et j'espère mourir, mais le docteur ne croit pas ou pas encore – s'en trop la torture vous ne savez pas . . .' It was her last letter.

Decca arrived from California on the 13th, making herself useful as an interpreter between the French doctor and the two new nurses, a couple of cheerful Australian girls brought in to replace 'old Beastie'. 'Je veux me dépêcher,' Decca heard Nancy murmur in the doctor's ear. After a week Decca left to go back to America knowing she would never see her sister again. On the evening of June 24 Diana and Sir Oswald came in to visit Nancy on their way to a dinner-party in Paris. She felt miserable, she whispered, but was no longer in pain. 'Anne (the nurse) thinks it might go on like this for ages,' Diana wrote to Debo, 'but I somehow felt last night it couldn't be much longer.'

On the morning of June 30, as the Colonel was driving through the outskirts of Versailles on his way in to Paris from Le Marais, he was overcome by a strong presentiment that he should go at once to see Nancy. Arriving at the rue d'Artois he went straight upstairs, his little dog running ahead of him as she always did. He found Nancy apparently unconscious; but she smiled as he took her hand.

A few hours later she died. Her body was cremated at Père Lachaise, after which her ashes were flown to England. She was buried next to her sister Unity in the churchyard at Swinbrook, on a cloudless summer day when the green Cotswold countryside was looking its most beautiful.

Books by Nancy Mitford

Highland Fling   1931
Christmas Pudding   1932
Wigs on the Green   1935
Pigeon Pie   1940
The Pursuit of Love   1945
Love in a Cold Climate   1949
The Blessing   1951
Madame de Pompadour   1954
Voltaire in Love   1957
Don't Tell Alfred   1960
The Water Beetle   1962
The Sun King   1966
Frederick the Great   1970

Edited by Nancy Mitford:

The Ladies of Alderley   1938
The Stanleys of Alderley   1939

Translations:

The Princesse de Clèves   1950
The Little Hut   1951

Contributed to:

Noblesse Oblige   1956

Select Bibliography

Harold Acton *Memoirs of an Aesthete*
Harold Acton *More Memoirs of an Aesthete*
Harold Acton *Nancy Mitford: a Memoir*
Susan Mary Alsop *To Marietta from Paris, 1945–1960*
Mark Amory (ed.) *The Letters of Evelyn Waugh*
Patrick Balfour *Society Racket*
Andrew Barrow *Gossip, 1920–1970*
Cecil Beaton *Diaries (6 vols)*
Gerald Berners *First Childhood*
C. M. Bowra *Memories, 1898–1939*
Kenneth Young (ed.) *The Diaries of Sir Robert Bruce Lockhart*
Robert Rhodes James (ed.) *Chips: the Diaries of Sir Henry Channon*
Stanley Clark *The Man Who Is France*
Richard Collier *1940: the World in Flames*
Michael Davie (ed.) *The Diaries of Evelyn Waugh*
Jennifer Ellis (ed.) *Thatched with Gold: the Memoirs of Mabell, Countess of Airlie*
Jacques Dumaine *Quai d'Orsay*
Beatrix Dunning (ed.) *Graham Street Memories*
Constantine Fitzgibbon *The Blitz*
Charles de Gaulle *Mémoires de la Guerre*
Cynthia Gladwyn *The Paris Embassy*
Lord Gladwyn *Memories*
Robert Graves and Alan Hodge *The Long Weekend*
Martin Green *Children of the Sun*
Jonathan Guinness with Catherine Guinness *The House of Mitford*
Kay Halle *Randolph Churchill: the Young Unpretender*
Marie-Jacqueline Lancaster (ed.) *Brian Howard: Portrait of a Failure*
James Lees-Milne *Another Self, Ancestral Voices, Prophesying War, Caves of Ice*
Philippe Jullian and John Phillips *Violet Trefusis*
Stella Margetson *The Long Party*
Brian Masters *Great Hostesses*
Jessica Mitford *Hons and Rebels*
Jessica Mitford *A Fine Old Conflict*
Diana Mosley *A Life of Contrasts*
Diana Mosley *Loved Ones*
Nicholas Mosley *The Rules of the Game*

Nicholas Mosley *Beyond the Pale*
Sir Oswald Mosley *My Life*
Gaston Palewski *Hier et Aujourd'Hui*
Georges Pompidou *Pour Rétablir une Verité*
David Pryce-Jones *Cyril Connolly*
David Pryce-Jones *Unity Mitford*
David Pryce-Jones (ed.) *Evelyn Waugh and His World*
Peter Quennell *The Marble Foot*
Peter Quennell *The Sign of the Fish*
Lord Redesdale *Memories (2 vols)*
Giles & Esmond Romilly *Out of Bounds*
Charles Ritchie *The Siren Years*
Lord Rosslyn *My Gamble with Life*
Henrietta Sharpe *A Solitary Woman: a Life of Violet Trefusis*
Robert Skidelsky *Oswald Mosley*
Edward Stanley *Sea Peace*
Violet Stuart Wortley *Life without Theory*
Christopher Sykes *Evelyn Waugh*
Christopher Sykes *Four Studies in Loyalty*
Hugh Thomas *The Spanish Civil War*
Philip Toynbee *Friends Apart*
Sam White *Sam White's Paris*
Evelyn Waugh *A Little Learning*
Philip Ziegler *Diana Cooper*

Index